The Corporate Sabotage of America's Future

And What We Can Do about It

Robert Weissman
and Joan Claybrook

Foreword by Joseph W. Cotchett

Published and distributed in the United States by Public Citizen and
Essential Books, Washington, DC.

ISBN 978-1-893520-09-7

This book was set in the typefaces Adobe Garamond, Visby CF,
and Manifold DSA.

Printed in the United States of America.

Composition and design by Daylight Communications, Inc.

TABLE OF CONTENTS

PART IV: Big Tech

PART V: Solutions

APPENDIX: Talking Points to Take on Corporate Power

FOREWORD

by Joseph W. Cotchett

A few years ago, I wrote a book called *The People vs. Greed* about the stealing of America by large corporations. Since then, things have gotten even worse across our country. Economic inequality is rising, health care is more expensive and less available, racial disparities remain sky-high despite protest movements, the cost of drugs are through the roof—and our government is more captured by corporations than ever.

Americans, irrespective of partisan preference, know that things have gone off track in this country. The strong majority believe that our democracy is under threat. As noted by Nate Cohn in *The New York Times* in October 2022 about a recent *Times* poll on democracy, "When respondents were asked to volunteer one or two words to summarize the current threat to democracy, 'government corruption' was brought up most often."

Cohn added: "Many respondents volunteered exactly that kind of language. One said, 'I don't think they are honestly thinking about the people.' Another said politicians 'forget about normal people.' Greed, power and money were familiar themes."

These are issues that Americans of all political stripes think about based on their experience. It is the story laid out so brilliantly in this book, *The Corporate Sabotage of America's Future.*

Corporate corruption empowers giant corporations to steal from the public—to win giant tax subsidies, inflated contracts, discounted oil drilling rights and more—costing the people hundreds of billions of dollars every year. Corporate corruption stops government from doing its job—to protect us from poisons in the air, rip-offs at the gas pump, discrimination on the job, incursions on our privacy, unsafe drugs and more.

Driven by boundless greed and unshackled from regulatory restraint, Big Business keeps pushing the boundaries and inventing new ways to make more money at the public's expense:

- The global price for oil is soaring while drilling costs remain constant and consumers are made to pay more to generate record profits.
- People need their life-saving medicines, and they will pay whatever it takes until they can't, up to the point of bankruptcy.

- Tech forces consumers to accept contract terms—including online "click" acceptance of contracts that no one reads—stripping consumers of the right to retain their personal rights.
- Big Tech knows more about individual consumers than has ever been possible, vacuums up personal information for sale to advertisers and totally overrides concerns for people's privacy.
- Most horrific: The scientific community agrees that we must move away from burning fossil fuels to prevent or mitigate a climate catastrophe. But that would hurt the profits of Big Oil and the fossil fuel giants, so they have suppressed and denied the science and delayed action—even though it will impose trillions of dollars in costs on the public.
- The whole new world of artificial intelligence, AI, under the control of Big Tech companies, could disrupt and change our entire educational system and perhaps our entire society—if it hasn't already begun to do so.

Corporate America has long looked at the government, not as an enemy, but as a source of profit. That's more true now than ever before, as corporate welfare expenditures grow larger and public money is being given to corporations tax free.

Consider the case of Medicare drug purchasing. In 2003, Congress created the Medicare Part D program to provide drug coverage for Medicare recipients. Big Pharma originally opposed it but then supported the idea. Why? Because they were worried that Medicare would demand reasonable pricing of the drugs it covered. Then Big Pharma finagled what may be the most corrupt arrangement in modern political history. Medicare would be authorized to pay for drugs for seniors—but the government wouldn't be permitted to negotiate prices. So what became the world's largest drug purchaser, our government, was prohibited from using its buying power to cut a fair deal for people—mostly seniors.

Big Pharma has been very happy to get rich making this deal to take advantage of those who need the medicines to help them live. Finally, in 2022, Congress overcame Big Pharma opposition and empowered Medicare to negotiate prices for just a few drugs. Even that small change will save taxpayers and consumers about $100 billion.

Meanwhile, Big Tech's goal is addicting users to maximize profits. Last year, Facebook's ad revenue hit $113.6 billion. YouTube generated over $29 billion from advertising, TikTok over $11 billion, and Snapchat generated $4.6 billion. That is billions of dollars with a "B."

Social media addiction is among the most critical emerging problems in our country. The new iGen generation of children (those who were born into smartphone use) are suffering deep and lasting trauma due to social media addiction specifically with the use of designed algorithms. Rates of suicide, depression, body dysmorphic disorder, and cyberbullying are sharply rising, and the rise is correlated to social media use and the profit from advertising. Social media is also leading the way to extraordinary gun use and violence among teenagers.

Want more evidence of how corporations are undermining the public interest? Look at how corporations evade paying taxes. Congress did almost no legislating to control corporate greed during the Trump administration. In fact, the CEOs and lobbyists staffing Trump at the beginning of his administration had one overriding objective: cut taxes on corporations and the rich.

Tax cuts exploded. The corporate tax rate was slashed from 35 to 21 percent—a lower tax rate for giant corporations than middle-income taxpayers. But many of the largest corporations pay ZERO in federal tax—over 50 in 2020 alone. After Trump, it was a hard-fought victory in 2022 when Congress passed tax reform legislation under President Biden that required all profitable corporations to pay at least 15 percent in taxes.

A great deal of what corporations get away with is legal. This conduct shouldn't be legal—like tax trickery, or price-gouging for drugs, or making windfall profits on gasoline or emitting dangerous pollutants into the air—but it is. But it's also true that a great deal of what corporations get away with isn't legal.

When corporations break the law, it's generally the case that they get away with it. That's because they have used their political power and influence to impose a two-tier system of justice. Of course, corporations have way more resources than street criminal defendants—but the problem goes far beyond that.

Corporations routinely break the law without getting caught. Often, they are able to hide evidence of their wrongdoing—like internal documents showing that they knew they were putting a dangerous pesticide on the market. Much of the time, the government just doesn't have the resources to inspect corporate operations to find wrongdoing—like hazardous conditions on the job.

Even when they are caught red-handed, corporations are typically able to maneuver to avoid serious penalties. For one thing, corporations can't be jailed. Fines are typically way too small compared to the profits a corporation has made by its unlawful conduct. Frequently, federal prosecutors will cut leniency deals with corporations, declining to prosecute in exchange for a promise the corporation won't break the law in the future. CEOs and executives almost never go to jail. For years, the Securities and Exchange Commission (SEC) was useless in controlling security fraud in the markets.

None of this is by accident—it is a direct result of Big Business political power. Corporate lobbyists make sure the penalties are light for suppressing evidence of harm, and they work to gut the government prosecutors' budgets allocated to prosecuting corporate crime and wrongdoing.

It's no exaggeration to say the rich bullies are out of control in Washington, D.C., and in our state capitals. They were given superpowers by the U.S. Supreme Court in an outrageous 5-4 decision called *Citizens United* in 2010, which basically allows corporations and multi-millionaires unfettered control of the elections of public officials, by allowing them to spend unlimited sums on elections.

Big Money infecting government is the root of the problem—lobbyists, hidden dollars and people who think they can buy (or bury) the truth have taken the reins.

All this corporate abuse has a devastating effect on real people:

- The family that went bankrupt paying for cancer care for a young father—even though they had insurance.
- The family that lost a daughter in a Boeing jet crash that could have been avoided if the company had not permitted dangerous planes to fly.
- The indigenous Alaskan communities forced to abandon their traditional lands because of climate chaos-induced flooding.
- The workers underpaid and then deprived of overtime pay by unscrupulous employers.
- The farmers indentured to chemical companies who provide seed, pesticides, fertilizer—and who are sued if genetically modified seed blows from one property to another's land and starts growing.
- The family whose son died because they could not afford his overpriced insulin.
- The family who must watch their daughter suffer from asthma worsened by pollution from nearby oil and chemical plants.
- Residents sickened or displaced by railroad crashes that could have been avoided with proper safety operations.
- The farmworkers who must toil in the sun without adequate water, breaks, shade, adequate housing, and basic wages.
- Parents who have to bury their babies killed by military-like assault rifles sold every day by gun manufacturers.

When you put names and faces to these stories, as I have been able to do through 50 years of law practice, it's heartbreaking, because a great deal of this suffering is avoidable. But when you put names and faces to these issues, it's also infuriating—and activating.

When you know how much all these issues matter, you understand the impact on real people, and you know things could be different. When you read or see the gun violence on our streets and in our schools due to the greed of gun manufacturers and the National Rifle Association, who wave the American flag—you realize the trouble we are in.

Only those who cherish America's greatest values—fairness, equality, liberty, and opportunity for all—can save our nation. This isn't a movie and no hero is coming to save us. Those who abuse wealth and power, as they toss fellow Americans on the street, will get away with the hijacking of our nation if we ignore the crisis and do nothing.

For the sake of our country and future generations, we can't let that happen. Everyone must get involved with the future of our great country. Not just those who wear or have worn a uniform for our country—but every citizen who cares about tomorrow—and the future of democracy.

This book is a tribute to Robert Weissman, Joan Claybrook, and all the people who contributed to its research and content. It should be required reading for our students and people who are the future of our country.

CHAPTER 1

The Pervasive Problem of Corporate Power

It is now conventional wisdom that America is a divided country, with bitter partisan splits over just about everything.

It's undoubtedly true that Americans have divergent views on many important topics.

But the narrative of a Divided America obscures an equally important and rarely acknowledged truth: Americans agree on a great deal.

Americans of all political stripes believe that big corporations have too much power and are weakening the nation.

- Corporations regularly rip us off with illegitimate fees, monopolistic pricing and windfall profiteering. Americans agree: This is wrong and the government should end corporate ripoffs.
- Corporations poison the air we breathe and the water we drink, spreading asthma and other diseases. Americans agree: This is wrong and the government should protect our health and the environment from corporate polluters.
- Corporations crashed the economy in 2008, costing us trillions of dollars and throwing millions out of work, and forcing millions of families out of their homes. Americans agreed: This was wrong and the executives responsible should be held accountable, and the Big Banks most responsible should be broken up.
- Corporations gorge at the public trough, gouging taxpayers by extracting a vast array of ill-advised subsidies, giveaways, guarantees and other corporate welfare programs. Americans agree: This is wrong and the government should manage our public assets in the interests of the public.
- Corporations pay workers too little, oppose raising the minimum wage, undermine union organizing and expose workers to dangers. Americans agree: This is wrong and the government should guarantee workers' rights.

This book is about this central fact upon which Americans agree—the need to confront corporate power—and how we can do that.

Americans Agree: Corporate Power is Out of Control

It's not an exaggeration to say Americans are united around the idea of controlling corporate power.

For just a moment, let's dive into some of the details.

By overwhelming margins, Americans favor steps to crack down on corporate abuses and protect regular people. For example:

- Roughly 90 percent of Americans want Medicare to negotiate drug prices.[1]
- More than 80 percent of Americans want to end Dark Money—secret spending—in elections.[2]
- In fact, there's virtual unanimity among the public about the need to transform the campaign funding system. The only debate is between those who favor "fundamental changes" and those who think it should be "completely rebuilt."[3]
- Seven in 10 Americans favor transitioning the U.S. economy from fossil fuels to 100 percent clean energy by 2050.[4]
- Three-quarters of Americans want stricter limits on smog.[5] Even given the false choice between environmental protection and economic growth, voters overwhelmingly favor environmental protection.[6]
- More than 4 in 5 favor banning single-use plastics.[7]
- By a greater than 2-1 margin, voters support empowering Americans to sue corporations directly when they violate federal regulations.[8]
- More than 3 in 4 Americans believe CEOs should be held accountable for the crimes their companies commit, including being sent to jail, because there should be real consequences to corporate wrongdoing.[9]
- Eight in 10 Americans think the minimum wage is too low, and a strong majority favor raising it to $15 an hour (more than double the current federal minimum).[10]
- Four in 5 Americans support a requirement for paid family and medical leave.[11]
- Three quarters of Americans want the government to do more to protect online privacy.[12]
- Over two-thirds of Americans favor increased taxes on corporations and the wealthy.[13]
- With near unanimity, voters believe there should be increased enforcement of laws and regulations in the U.S. against corporations.[14]

The list goes on and on and on. Americans believe corporations are causing major problems and they want action.

This is not the profile of a divided nation!

(To appreciate just how astounding all these findings are, consider that only three in four people correctly believe the earth revolves around the sun.[15])

OK, so Americans agree on an agenda to limit corporate abuse across a broad range of policies, from protecting the environment to taxation, campaign finance to drug pricing and more.

Why don't we get what we want?

The simple answer to that question is: Too much corporate power.

As Americans almost uniformly understand, excessive corporate power rigs the political system. Corporations and the super-rich slather politicians with money—or intimidate them with Dark Money attack ads—and they expect, and receive, consideration in return.

But as important as campaign money is, it's not just funding that rigs the political system. Corporations hire legions of lobbyists to influence Congress and regulatory agencies. A very substantial portion of these lobbyists worked in Congress or the very agencies they are paid to influence. They are able to draw not only on their insider knowledge of how things work, but on their personal connections with members of Congress, congressional staff and key officials in regulatory agencies.

Corporations understand very well that public opinion matters in policy debates. So along with playing the inside political game, they spend hundreds of millions every year to commission studies, support think tanks and academics, hold conferences, and pay for issue advertisements to try to muddle public opinion.

Corporations aim to do more than influence public opinion with all that spending. The reports and papers from academics and think tanks lend a veneer of legitimacy when corporations make their arguments to policymakers. And the advertising is aimed to intimidate lawmakers—this money could easily be spent against you—into conforming with corporate demands.

Corporations also bring a superpower to political fights: The ability to argue that almost any measure that might reduce their profitability will threaten jobs and the overall well-being of the American economy. "Make us pay higher wages and we'll have to lay people off." "Require us to reduce greenhouse gas emissions and we'll lose out to overseas competitors." "Make us pay our fair share in taxes and we'll lose our incentive to invest." "Require us to pay a fair return to the government on the public resources we use and prices will go up for consumers."

We hear these arguments endlessly. They have great force, and not just because people need jobs and don't want to pay more for things they need. They have such force because corporations have a tight grip on the economy and people and politicians fear their power. This is true even though we've seen time and again that when we make corporations behave fairly, they do just fine. In fact, many of the things forced on corporations—from the minimum wage to safety belts and airbags in cars, from safe drug regulation to anti-monopoly rules—have *strengthened* the economy and provided new profitable opportunities for business.

Dissecting Corporate Power: The Plan of this Book

This book examines the problems posed by excessive corporate power. It highlights two cross-cutting issues—corporate dominance of our politics and corporate welfare—and it looks at three industry sectors: Big Pharma, Big Oil and Big Tech. These are among the most profitable and impactful industries in the world, each heavily dependent on the federal government and each exerting enormous influence over that same government.

Part I looks broadly at the two cross-cutting issues. It reveals how corporations corrupt the policy making process and how the Supreme Court's 2010 *Citizens United* decision empowered a very tiny class of individuals and corporations to dominate our elections and helped usher in a New Gilded Age. And it examines how corporations leverage their political power to obtain tens of billions annually in corporate welfare. In so doing, they siphon public funds at the expense of the priority needs of the nation and sabotage the government's ability to operate of, by and for the people.

Part II focuses on Big Pharma. It details the harms that Big Pharma has inflicted on the nation—from sky-high prices that force rationing, selling dangerous drugs, pushing opioids and more. It documents Big Pharma's political influence as the largest lobby in Washington, D.C. And it shows how Big Pharma benefits from corporate welfare, including via one of the most corrupt schemes in modern American history.

Part III homes in on Big Oil. It shows the oil giants are profiteering at our expense, polluting the air we breathe and endangering low-income, indigenous and people of color communities that live near pipelines, refineries and petrochemical plants. It recounts Big Oil's decades-long campaign of deceit to deny the reality of climate change and block measures to transition us to a clean energy future. In so doing, the industry is imperiling humanity's very existence. Part III closes by showing how the industry scores tens of billions in tax and other subsidies.

Part IV spotlights the most powerful rising industry sector, Big Tech. It examines the many ways in which Big Tech is surveilling us, undermining our privacy, degrading our culture and endangering a decent and democratic society. It shows how Big Tech has converted its money power into political power, forestalling popular anti-monopoly legislation. And it exposes how Big Tech companies use the complexity of the federal tax code as well as raw political power to escape billions and billions of federal, state and local taxes.

Part V concludes by identifying some cross-cutting solutions to the problem of excessive corporate power. It reminds us that We the People have, throughout our history, imposed controls on corporations—and thereby made the nation safer, healthier, fairer, more sustainable and more just.

It's the central thesis of this book that corporations have far, far too much power.

But at the end of the day, We the People have more—if we choose to organize, mobilize and demand the transformative changes that we support by overwhelming majorities.

PART I

Raw Power— Political Influence and Government Subsidies

CHAPTER 2

Rigging the System

An ambulance rushed a bleeding Andrew Heymann to the hospital in 2014. Helping a friend move, a glass table had shattered and gashed open Heymann's ankle. The ambulance rushed him to a nearby hospital, which he knew was included in his health insurer's network. A plastic surgeon closed his wound.

But that wasn't the end of the story for Heymann. He was hit with a bill for $6,000—even though the hospital was in-network for his insurer. It turned out that while the hospital was in-network, the plastic surgeon was not.[16]

Heymann's was one of millions of "surprise billing" stories that rolled across the country in the latter half of the 2010s.

Ashley, a young mother in Missouri, told a similar story. She was rushed to the emergency room because of a life-threatening problem with her pregnancy. "We went to the ER at our local in-network hospital (where I had been having prenatal visits), were sent to the obstetrics department, and then were transported to a larger in-network hospital, where [our daughter] was born and stayed in the NICU for 18 days. I stayed for 2 days following her delivery."

"The bills started pouring in after we came home—separate bills from the ER, my OBGYN, obstetrics doctors who delivered our baby, neonatal doctors, anesthesiologists, the ambulance company, and the hospitals themselves... approximately over $12,000."[17]

When stories like Andrew Heymann's and Ashley's first started popping up, they were hard to believe. Surely there was a mistake or misunderstanding? It *had* to be that these situations would get sorted out. Sure, we all know how frustrating it is to deal with insurance and hospital bureaucracies, but eventually the mix-ups would be resolved, right?

Well, wrong.

These early stories weren't outliers, they were harbingers. By the latter half of the 2010s, nearly one-in-five emergency bills resulted in a surprise bill, and surprise billing was spiking for scheduled, in-patient care as well.[18]

Short of fundamental and needed restructuring of our health care system, patient and consumer advocates demanded the obvious and only solution to the surprise billing shakedown: legislation to end the practice. But the predatory companies that invented and benefited from this rip-off were prepared for political pushback. They spent tens or hundreds of millions of dollars to delay action; and when legislation was inevitable, they pivoted and succeeded in watering it down.

Surprise billing was an outgrowth of hospitals' decision to rely on third-party physician staffing companies to cover their emergency rooms, and provide anesthesiology, radiology, pathology and other services. The promise for hospitals is that third parties can do the work more "efficiently"—though there's every reason to think that what the third-party staffing companies really provide is lower quality and rushed care.[19]

In this new model of third-party staffing, a set of predatory investors saw an opportunity. "Private equity" companies—for-profit investor groups that buy up businesses and squeeze as much profit out of them as possible—recognized a chance to squeeze more money out of the health system than anyone thought possible. Not only could they cut costs by slashing care, they could circumvent insurers' cost-containment rules by socking patients directly with outrageous bills.

Surprise billing was the perfect scheme, at least for utterly unscrupulous predatory private equity corporations.

Think about it: When you go to an in-network hospital, you of course assume your insurance is going to cover your care. It's in-network, after all! If, for some reason, you wanted to know the cost of your care, there's almost nothing you can do in advance—it's not like going to a gas station, where the price is posted as you drive up. Compounding the problem, you typically don't know what care you need or are going to receive when you go the hospital. Moreover, hospital bills are famously inscrutable, extremely difficult to decipher even when you receive them after care has been delivered.

But here's the most important thing, at least about emergency care: When you're going in, it's an emergency! There's no time to compare prices. In the best case, you feel terrible. In the worst case, you're facing serious and possibly even life-threatening conditions. You're in no position to do comparison shopping, negotiate over charges or decline care you're told you need.

As surprise billing became more pervasive and as patients started sharing their outrageous stories, state legislators started acting. A number did what they could: require insurers to hold patients harmless for out-of-network costs from surprise bills and to pay providers the average rate for services provided. But because of the complexity of our health care system, state law is not able to regulate many large employer plans. And, although some states took aggressive action, most did not.[20]

So the action turned to Congress, which has the power to provide protections for all patients. Following what the most aggressive states had done, it was plain how to solve the problem of surprise billing: require all insurers to cover outsourced care for their in-network hospitals and providers and establish that insurers would pay the third-party service providers—the outfits providing emergency room staffing, anesthesiologists, radiologists and so on—the average rate they would pay in-network. That solution would prevent patients being socked with giant bills and it would ensure third-party providers get paid a reasonable rate, but no more.

That solution was fair to all the parties. But the predatory private equity companies weren't looking for fair. They were looking to perpetuate their price gouging.

By summer 2019, public ire about surprise billing had broken through. Leaders in both parties had negotiated the outlines of a good deal to end surprise billing.

Then came a nationwide flurry of TV ads aired by a mysterious group calling itself "Doctor Patient Unity."

Showing paramedics arriving with a patient on a gurney at an empty emergency room, one ad from the group warned, "Imagine if the care we needed wasn't there when we needed it the most." It warned about the dangers of "government rate-setting," saying it "could mean closed hospitals."

Direct mail from the group screamed that "Big Insurance Companies have a scheme to profit from patients' pain through rate setting." Doctor Patient Unity pushed similarly hysterical messages through online advertising.

For weeks, the ads and propaganda blanketed the nation. By September 2019, Doctor Patient Unity had spent more than $28 million on TV ads—more than was spent in support of Supreme Court Justice nominee Brett Kavanagh. Finally, in September, *The New York Times* cracked the code and identified the backers of Doctor Patient Unity: TeamHealth, owned by the Blackstone Group, among the largest private-equity corporations, and Envision Healthcare, owned by another major private-equity outfit, KKR.[21]

The ad blitz was only one part of the predatory private equity strategy. The firms deployed their lobbyists—many dozens working for Blackstone, KKR, and a company called Welsh, Carson, Anderson and Stowe (WCAS), with a heavy health care presence—to monkey up the process. Most of these lobbyists had previously worked for members of Congress or in the Department of Health and Human Services or other government agencies, so they knew where the weak points were. They knew who would listen to and be sympathetic to their arguments, and they knew who had the power to slow legislative momentum.

Because our health care system is so complicated and fragmented, many Congressional committees claim jurisdiction over health care legislation. Even though the bipartisan leaders of the House and Senate health committees were making progress on a bill to curtail surprise billing, the lobbyists knew they had a chance to muck things up at the powerful House of Representatives Ways and Means Committee.

The companies started lavishing political contributions on the Republican and Democratic leaders of the committee, a Public Citizen investigation found.[22]

Employees of WCAS and Blackstone and their subsidiaries threw $335,400 at the Republican House Ways and Means leader Kevin Brady and contributed another $55,800 to Democratic Committee Chair Richard Neal. Both Brady and Neal had served in Congress for decades, but through 2020, WCAS and Blackstone channeled 95 percent of their contributions to the two Committee leaders after 2015.

Neal had received less than $10,000 from Blackstone employees in the course of his three-decade career. Then, in September 2019, Blackstone donors showered him with $30,800.

Less than two months later, House and Senate negotiators closed in on a deal, supported by the Trump administration. Then Neal and Brady announced that they had arrived at their own compromise, with the vague outline of a plan favored by private equity firms. According to those involved in negotiating the House-Senate deal, Neal and Brady's outline ended all hope of the deal's passage in 2019.[23]

Eventually, a deal was reached and included in a major government spending bill passed at the end of 2020. The No Surprises Act, which went into effect in 2022, aims to prevent patients from getting hit with surprise bills ever again. But it was weaker than what consumer advocates had urged, enabling third-party providers—those outsourcing companies—to seek higher rates than they should be entitled to.

This was a tale of a very small number of predatory corporations that identified a way to exploit the irrationalities in our health care system to carry off one of the most egregious consumer rip-offs in recent memory. It was systemic and widespread, affecting millions of people from all backgrounds, with no remotely plausible economic or policy justification.

The predatory private equity companies found a regulatory gap. And then they invested comparatively small amounts in the political system—in advertising, public relations, lobbying and campaign contributions—to defend the unjustifiable. For a period of time, they fended off any limits on surprise billing whatsoever. When the political momentum to quash the surprise billing scam was too great, they maneuvered to water down the unstoppable reforms and to prop up their bottom lines.

In that way, the surprise billing story was no aberration. Rather, it is a representation of how powerful corporate interests couple their dominance over the economy and society with dominance over the political system. So too is it representative in illustrating the twin foundations of corporate political influence: lobbying and campaign contributions.

Lobbyists: Channeling Big Business Power in the Halls of Power

Every major industry and virtually every major corporation—and plenty of not-so-major corporations—has a team of lobbyists working for them in Washington, D.C. Some of these lobbyists are on a company's payroll. Others are employed by lobby firms and are available for hire.

Lobbying is itself Big Business. More than $4 *billion* goes to federal lobbyists annually[24]—and this is a major undercount. It reflects only the amount spent on officially registered lobbyists, not the swarms of lawyers, PR flacks, think tanks and others that work to influence policy. There are more than 12,000 officially registered lobbyists.

The *overwhelming* portion of lobbying in D.C. is done by or on behalf of corporations. The top 20 lobbying spenders are all corporations or corporate trade associations, with the single exception of AARP, which usually ranks around 12th.[25] Big Business spending on lobbying exceeds labor spending by a ratio of 68-1. Sixty-eight to one! Big Business spends 18 times more on lobbying than all advocacy groups put together—everyone from the National Rifle Association to the Sierra Club, Planned Parenthood to the Heritage Foundation.[26]

This staggering imbalance in lobbyists is, just by itself, a threat to democracy. It means that Big Business is far more represented on Capitol Hill and at executive agencies than are regular people. Basically, there's *always* a business lobbyist whispering to and cajoling members of Congress, congressional staff and other government officials; public interest representatives are far, far more scarce. Business lobbyists are always present to explain things from their clients' point of view; most often, the public is not even part of the debate.

The lobbyist imbalance also creates massive information asymmetry: the work of government is so vast and often so complicated that you can't really know what's going on unless you are specialized and in constant contact with decision makers, legislative staff, agency officials and bureaucrats. Corporate lobbyists can specialize in arcane issues of interest to particular industries—a few lines in the tax code, a specific regulation—and carefully monitor what's going on. Public interest representatives and the public may not even know anything is happening at all.

But the problem is a lot worse than just unequal access to information and decision makers.

The defining feature of modern-day lobbying in Washington, D.C., is the "revolving door"—with people leaving an official position in government for the riches of lobbying. A secondary feature is the "reverse revolving door"—when people leave work as lobbyists or for corporations to enter government. More than a few people cycle back and forth.

The majority of Big Business lobbyists have spun through the revolving door—more than 70 percent of those hustling for Wall Street, three quarters on the payroll of Big Tech, two thirds of lobbyists working for Big Oil.[27]

The revolving door is pervasive and normalized. In 2019, Public Citizen looked at the employment status of members of Congress who had left office at the start of the year. Within five months, the analysis found, nearly two-thirds of recently retired or defeated U.S. lawmakers working outside politics had landed jobs with lobbying shops, consulting firms, trade groups or business associations aiming to influence federal policy.[28]

It's quite understandable why lobby shops want former government officials or staff to come work for them. Those people are issue experts. They know best how to influence the people who have taken their jobs. And they maintain relationships and friendships in their old workplaces that provide easy access and casual sway.

The revolving door phenomenon makes the problem of the imbalance in lobby power exponentially worse. It's the richest lobby shops and the biggest corporations that can hire former Members of Congress, cabinet secretaries, chiefs of staff and other top officials who carry the strongest relationships with current decision makers.

Not infrequently, these corporate lobbyists can translate their relationships and expertise into directly shaping the position of members of Congress or government agencies, including in some cases by directly drafting bills. In one example that is unique only in that *The New York Times* reporters were able to access an email exchange revealing what happened, Citigroup lobbyists in 2013 were essentially able to draft legislation on complicated financial derivatives that passed the House of Representatives and eventually led to a watering down of regulatory agency proposals. "In a sign of Wall Street's resurgent influence in Washington," just a few years after the Wall Street financial collapse and bailout, the *Times* reported, "Citigroup's recommendations were reflected in more than 70 lines of the House committee's 85-line bill. Two crucial paragraphs, prepared by Citigroup in conjunction with other Wall Street banks, were copied nearly word for word. (Lawmakers changed two words to make them plural.)"[29]

When asked for comment, Wall Street lobbyists were unabashed about what happened. "Industry officials acknowledged that they played a role in drafting the legislation, but argued that the practice was common in Washington."[30]

Well, you have to appreciate the honesty.

Those officials were right. This case wasn't unusual. And it's even more frequent in state houses, where legislators are thinly staffed and especially reliant on corporate lobbyists for ideas and help. An investigation by *USA Today*, the *Arizona Republic* and the Center for Public Integrity found more than 4,000 bills introduced by state legislators that were copies of model bills drafted by corporate interests. Between 2010 and 2018, more than 1,000 of these corporate-drafted bills became law.[31] And this is only the model laws—not the bills drafted by corporate lobbyists for individual states or state legislators.

The problem goes well beyond Congress or state legislatures. It's ubiquitous at regulatory agencies: the people in charge of regulating corporations routinely leave government and take jobs working for those very same corporations, either directly or as lobbyists and consultants. This creates the same problem we saw with legislatures: Corporations are not only able to monopolize the best talent, they are able to capitalize on the relationships that former regulators have with those currently staffing their old positions. Who better to urge Justice Department lawyers to go soft on a corporate wrongdoer than an old Justice Department prosecutor?[32] Who better to coax a bloated military contract than a former general or Defense Department contracting officer?[33] Who better to encourage the U.S. Department of Agriculture to set policy to favor Big Agribusiness over family farmers than former USDA officials?[34]

But the corrupting influence of the revolving door is not just the undue influence that former officials can exert on behalf of corporations. The reality of the revolving door impacts what regulators do *while they are still in government.*

More than three quarters of former top officials at the Federal Trade Commission (FTC, a key consumer protection agency) have either left the agency to serve corporate interests confronting FTC issues, joined the agency after serving corporate interests on these issues, or both. More than 60 percent of the top officials have worked on behalf of the technology sector.[35] There has been a dramatic shift in personnel and policy at the FTC during the Biden administration, but during previous years, the agency famously treated Big Tech with kid gloves—permitting mergers it should have blocked, failing to rein in data privacy abuses, standing by as social media enabled scams, and more. The revolving door makes it easier to understand why this happened. It's awfully hard for top FTC officials to be tough on tech company wrongdoing if they know their next jobs are likely to be working for the companies they are overseeing. In that scenario, being "too tough" just may endanger your future employment prospects. It doesn't matter whether regulators are conscious or not of this corrupting influence; it's unavoidable.

Consider how this plays out at the Pentagon. There are literally thousands of former generals, admirals, contracting officers and Pentagon acquisition officials working for military contractors.[36] Yes, thousands. The military itself has long recognized that the revolving door entrenches a culture of waste and deference to contractors. "If a colonel or a general stands up and makes a fuss about high cost and poor quality no nice man will come to see him when he retires," reads a 1983 internal U.S. Air Force memo, referencing post-retirement work with military contractors.[37] Now, the Project on Government Oversight reports, the revolving door is institutionalized through industry programs like "From Battlefield to Board Room," which connects soon-to-be retired military officers with corporations, including private contractors, with executive job openings.[38]

On top of all this, there's the problem of the reverse revolving door—lobbyists taking positions in government. Here, the conflicts are most extreme. Sure, a lobbyist now in government is no longer being paid by their old clients. But have they really abandoned all loyalty to them—especially given the high likelihood that they will return to working for them in the future? Under a series of executive orders issued first by President Obama, lobbyists and corporate officials are not supposed to work for a period of time (generally two years) on matters affecting their old employers.[39] When enforced reasonably, this has helped things a bit. But enforcement can be uneven—and was almost non-existent under the Trump administration.

And that brings us to the illustrative, if extreme, case of David Bernhardt, Secretary of the Interior in the Trump administration. Bernhardt spent several years advancing through several jobs at the Interior Department under President George W. Bush, ending the Bush administration as the Interior Department's solicitor. After President Barack Obama's election, Bernhardt returned to his corporate law and lobbying practice. Over the course of his lobbying career, oil and gas companies have paid Bernhardt more than $2 million; mining corporations paid him more than $1 million.[40] Bernhardt rejoined the Interior Department in 2017 as deputy secretary, becoming secretary in 2019. Bernhardt came to the department with a list of conflicts so extensive that he had to carry around an index card to remember them.[41]

Bernhardt's former legal and lobbying clients included onshore and offshore oil and gas firms, water pipeline projects, tribal interests, agribusiness and mining firms, among others. With their man heading the

Department of Interior, these corporations doubled down on their lobbying investments, spending $30 million on lobbying during the first three years of the Trump administration.[42]

Carrying around that card certainly didn't stop Bernhardt from delivering for his former clients. (Public Citizen and others filed complaints alleging ethical improprieties, but whether Bernhardt adhered to the formal ethics requirements or not is beside the point.) Among other things, Bernhardt: pushed to allow oil drilling in the formerly off-limits Arctic National Wildlife Refuge, weakened Endangered Species Act enforcement, rolled back numerous rules and polices protecting clean air, water and wildlife to allow more drilling and mining on public lands, opening land in California to fracking and easing offshore oil drilling safety rules.[43]

As all these examples make clear, relationships are central to how corporations lobby effectively.

But let's get real: The relationships are greased by money.

Jimmy Williams is a former congressional staffer turned corporate lobbyist—who quit the job in disgust after six years. "Most lobbyists are engaged in a system of bribery," he explains, "but it's the *legal* kind, the kind that runs rampant in the corridors of Washington."[44]

Lobbyists make political contributions. Lots and lots of political contributions.

Those contributions make sure they get the meetings they want and the responses they want—whether it's asking a question at a hearing, sending a letter or sponsoring a bill.

"Unlimited expense accounts, nights out on the town, expensive bottles of wine, elaborate meals with sitting senators and Congress members—that was my life," Williams explained. "I attended fundraising breakfasts that led to committee hearings with the same Congress members or senators—a meeting that cost me or my political action committee a hefty $2,500 voting on the very legislation we'd talked about over bacon and eggs that morning. Then there'd be a lunch fundraiser with a different Congress member, paid for by another $2,500 check to discuss the issues my clients cared about. Then they'd go and vote on those issues. It was an endless cycle of money trading hands for votes."[45]

The Corrupting Influence of Campaign Finance, Super Charged by *Citizens United*

As Williams explained from his perspective as a lobbyist, Big Money dominance of campaign finance is the bedrock problem of political corruption in the United States. Unfortunately, the problem has worsened since Williams left the lobbying racket in 2010.

That year, the Supreme Court issued its notorious *Citizens United* decision. *Citizens United* struck down as unconstitutional a federal law that had prohibited corporations and unions from spending money to influence federal elections. Predictably, it has empowered a very tiny class of individuals and corporations to dominate our elections.

Citizens United has helped give rise to growing social discontent and a dangerous degree of political alienation. As more and more people perceive the system to be rigged and fundamentally corrupt—as polling shows to be the case—our government's democratic legitimacy is now at stake. Without that legitimacy, we face frightening prospects: oligarchic rule over an alienated and apathetic population, and/or demagogic appeals from an authoritarian leader who can redirect people's anger toward the weak and vulnerable among us.

The problem is not just people's sense of alienation. Big Money dominance of our elections is concentrating political power among the political class and blocking policy changes that the American people want and need.[46] The Big Money dominance that *Citizens United* supercharged lies behind the explosion of abuses documented in this book.

Make no mistake: American democracy was suffering before *Citizens United* was decided. But the decision transformed the electoral landscape—worsening dangerous trends already underway and introducing new encroachments on democratic self-governance. *Citizens United* exerts an outsized and undemocratic effect on who runs for office, how candidates campaign, what policies are debated, who wins, and what is considered the boundaries of legitimate policy debate. Appreciating the totality of the damage requires considering its impact on multiple dimensions of modern politics.

A Tidal Wave of Spending by Unaccountable Outside Groups

The defining feature of the post-*Citizens United* campaign finance system is the sharp rise in election spending by unaccountable and often secretive outside organizations, especially super PACs. (Super PACs are independent political committees—supposedly not connected to candidates—that can accept unlimited donations from corporations or super-rich individuals.) These outside groups—overwhelmingly funded by a small number of super-rich people—frequently spend more on election races than the candidates' official campaigns.

In 2010, the first mid-term election year following *Citizens United,* outside spending fueled by the super-rich rose by a factor of four. Outside spending in the 2022 midterm election smashed the record set in previous non-presidential years, totaling just shy of $2 billion—almost double the total from 2018 and a 2,700 percent increase from where it had been in 2006.[47]

Figure 1. Outside Spending in Presidential Election Years

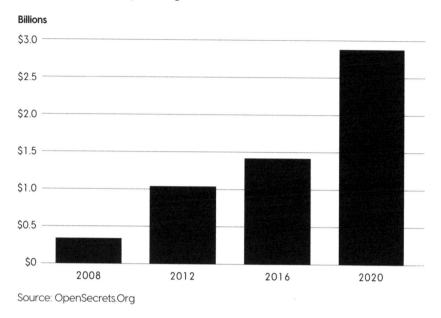

Source: OpenSecrets.Org

Figure 2. Outside Spending in Mid-Term Elections

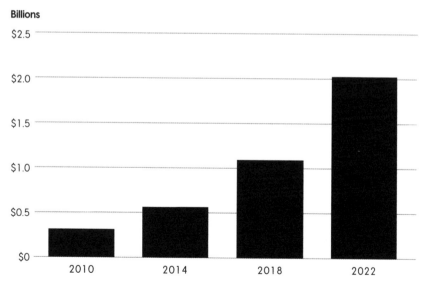

Source: OpenSecrets.Org

The Center for Responsive Politics calculates that together, non-party outside groups spent nearly $4.6 billion influencing elections in the decade following *Citizens United*. That was *six times the previous two decades combined*.[48]

Outside spending, in short, has jumped from a relatively tiny portion of overall campaign spending—5 percent or less—to become a raging river of money, a defining feature of the current political environment. In recent elections, outside spending has constituted roughly a fifth of overall campaign spending.[49]

Our democracy could perhaps somehow stomach this torrent of outsized spending if it were funded by small donations from a cross-section of voters. But as described below, the opposite is the case. The funds come overwhelmingly from a very small, non-representative group of extremely wealthy individuals.

An American Oligarchy

An extraordinarily small number of people is responsible for the bulk of outside spending. Given the centrality of this money in deciding elections in the post-*Citizens United* era, this extreme donor concentration is a very real drift toward oligarchy and away from democracy.

A Public Citizen study found that just 25 ultra-wealthy donors made up nearly half (47 percent) of all individual contributions to super PACs between 2010 and 2018. Again: *Just 25 people are responsible for almost half of all super PAC spending since* Citizens United *was handed down!*[50]

Figure 3. Breakdown of Individual Super PAC Contributions, 2010-2020

Top 5	$838,441,506
Top 10	$1,093,043,431
Top 100	$1,787,942,315
Top 500	$2,289,806,530
All	$2,965,935,814

Source: Public Citizen analysis of Federal Election Commission data

Unsurprisingly, given the extreme wealth and inequality of our era, Wall Street and financial sector moguls are the biggest contributors to super PACs, by far.[51]

This concentration of donors is intolerable on its face. What kind of democracy can we have with such a small number of individuals super-empowered to influence elections just by sheer willingness to spend gargantuan sums?

The situation becomes only marginally better if the scope of analysis is expanded beyond super PACs to all federal election spending. The top .01 percent of the population is responsible for roughly 40 percent of all campaign contributions.[52]

Big Money donors don't just make contributions because of their political philosophy (which turns out to be hostile to protecting vulnerable people compared to the views of the general public[53])—and corporations almost never do. The super-rich and corporations' business interests are entangled with government policy. As we'll see throughout this book, when Big Money interests deploy their campaign contributions, lobby power and PR campaigns, they expect something in return for their investment.

Super-Rich Power Heightens Racial Disparities

Reflecting the enormous racial wealth gap in the United States, a political giving system that rewards and empowers the super-rich inevitably exhibits extreme racial disparities.

Even before the rise of super PACs and unlimited donations, low-income, majority-minority districts were greatly under-represented among campaign contributions. For example, in the 2004 election cycle, the top contributing zip code to presidential campaigns was 10021, on Manhattan's exclusive Upper East Side. Contributors in that one zip code provided more presidential campaign money than all the 377 zip codes with the largest proportion of African-Americans and the 365 zip codes with the largest proportion of Latino or Hispanic Americans.[54]

Citizens United has supercharged this problem. Public Citizen's analysis of super PAC donors in the 2017-2018 election cycle found that 97 out of the 100 largest individual donors to outside spending groups were white.[55]

Overall, the vast majority of contributions to candidates and super PACs comes from majority-white zip codes. Majority-white zip codes give about 20 times more to political campaigns than majority-minority zip codes, and 25 times more to super PACs.[56]

It's rarely said in Washington, D.C., because it is simply taken for granted, but this enormous racial disparity in giving translates directly into a severe racial disparity in political power.

A Massive Increase in Secret Political Spending

In the decade following *Citizens United*, spending by Dark Money groups, which are not required to disclose their donors, totaled just shy of $1 billion—an increase of about 675 percent from the previous decade.[57]

Dark Money spending—where the donors remain secret—is the most unaccountable of all the outside spending enabled by *Citizens United*. It means that victims of attacks from Dark Money groups are helpless even to defend themselves by identifying and criticizing their attackers.

Such spending is utterly incompatible with a functioning democracy. But most of it is legal, at least under misguided Internal Revenue Service interpretations. Those permit advocacy nonprofits and trade associations to direct up to half of their expenditures to election-related advertising and activities.

Corporate Spending Unshackled

The bulk of money flowing into super PACs and outside spending entities since *Citizens United* has come from super-rich individuals, but corporations also have made enormous contributions, much of it obscured

Figure 4. Donations from Top 10 Zip Codes for Campaign Contributions, by Majority Race/Ethnicity, 2010-2018

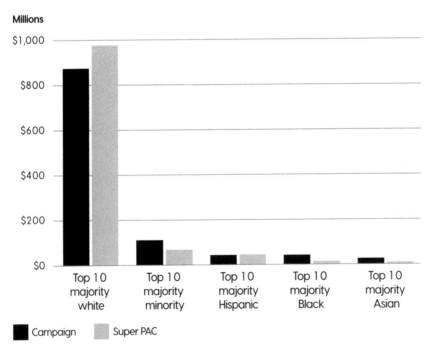

Source: Public Citizen analysis of data from Maplight (campaign contributions over $200) Federal Election Commission (Super PAC contributions)

by their reliance on Dark Money conduits. In the decade after *Citizens United,* corporations spent more than half a billion dollars to influence elections. More than 2,200 corporations reported $310 million on election-related spending, primarily contributions to super PACs. Additionally, 30 corporate trade groups, which do not disclose their donors, have spent $226 million for the purpose of influencing elections. That totals to more than $536 million in political spending. This is only the money that can be tracked down. It is surely a massive undercount, because it does not count corporate contributions to Dark Money organizations.[58]

As with individual contributions, a small number of corporate contributors are responsible for a disproportionate amount of total spending. The top 20 corporate donors through 2020 account for $118 million, more than a third of all corporate donations reported to the FEC, and those funds went exclusively to super PACs that back Republicans. Only four of these top corporate donors are publicly traded. Three are energy corporations—Chevron, NextEra Energy and Pinnacle West Capital—and the fourth is a subsidiary of British American Tobacco. Twenty of the top corporate donors have executives, chairpersons or other top figures who also have donated generously to political campaigns.

The U.S. Chamber of Commerce is by far the most consequential of the non-disclosing corporate trade groups. From 2010 to 2020, it spent $143 million, nearly two-thirds of the total election-related spending by corporate trade associations.

Going Negative—Attack Ads Saturation

Negative campaigning traces back to the nation's earliest days, but *Citizens United* has supercharged negative campaigning in the modern period. Since *Citizens United,* real debate has been displaced by misleading personal attacks, with the overwhelming share of super PAC and outside money devoted to attack ads. Eighty-five percent of unregulated independent expenditures made by the top 12 non-party outside groups in the 2018 election cycle financed negative messages, a Public Citizen analysis found. This proportion of negative campaigning has remained roughly consistent since *Citizens United.*

Outside groups spend money on attack ads because they work. Although the ads may seem over-the-top and so apocalyptic in tone as to be self-discrediting, people in fact do *not* tune them out.[59] The stark messaging and frightening emotional appeals draw in viewers and activate heightened attention levels.[60] Sufficiently repeated and shared on social media, the ads work to shift voter perception of targeted candidates, and evidence suggests they have influence even on sophisticated voters and on those both trustful and distrustful of government.[61]

While the academic research on negative advertising is not uniform, practitioners share a near-absolute consensus: "Those of us who make our livelihoods doing this [political consultants] know that it can be the best strategy for getting to the magic number that means victory," writes political consultant Andrew Ricci.[62]

While candidates may be reluctant to run attack ads because voters may hold them accountable for the tone of their campaign, outside groups are not so deterred.[63] Outside groups' only accountability is to their donors, who have every reason to favor attack ads due to their efficacy. Similarly, outside groups have greater freedom to exaggerate, mischaracterize and mislead. And Dark Money donors have no reason whatsoever to hold back.

Negative campaigning can have an appropriate role in drawing distinctions and providing information about political rivals. At the same time, it would be hard to find a voter who believes American politics have an appropriate balance of negative and positive advertising messages, and it is basic common sense that the deluge of negative ads spurs political cynicism and diminishes democratic legitimacy.

That these ads are powered by outside groups that air them in such proportions precisely because they are not accountable strongly suggests something has gone seriously awry. "Super PACs are the drone missiles of the political scene," said Robert Zimmerman, a major Democratic donor who will not contribute to them. "Their mission is a destructive one, by definition."[64]

The Boundaries of "Serious" Policy Debate

As shocking, depressing and anti-democratic as these snapshots of the world *Citizens United* created can be, they still understate the scale of the problem. Big Money donors have an inordinate, undemocratic influence on which individuals win and lose elections, and that is important but secondary. In very real terms, the world *Citizens United* made is, for the corporate class, a case of "Heads I win, tails you lose."

The corporate donor class is now superpowered to frame political debates. Outside groups define the tone of the campaigns, often establish the terms of debate, and affect the entire national race in ways not easily quantified—for example, by forcing opponents to spend limited resources on races that otherwise would be safe. The need for candidates to raise extraordinary sums forces them to spend lots of time with the ultra-wealthy and less time with regular people. It also makes them more accountable to donors and less to everyone else. Thus does Big Money have an outsized impact, whether it backs winners or losers.

Big Money exerts a permanent chilling effect on candidates and elected officials, limiting the boundaries of what are considered "serious" policy proposals. Candidates backed by corporations and the wealthy are of course likely to carry water for their backers. Even more important is this: candidates who won despite running against Big Business know that the same entities will try again to defeat them next time. They know they cannot afford to sidestep, much less challenge, corporate interests when it could mean being targeted by those with infinitely deep pockets.

As a result, no matter who wins, Big Money spenders obtain massively enhanced power to set the national policy agenda. That includes taking popular measures off the table. As one House of Representatives staffer asked during a congressional briefing shortly after *Citizens United* was handed down, "How do I say 'no' to a deep-pocketed corporate lobbyist who now has all the resources necessary to defeat my boss in the next election?"

Former Senator Bob Kerrey spoke clearly about the chilling effect of Big Money, post-*Citizens United*. The issue wasn't explicit threats, he emphasized, because "you're already threatened." He explained: "If I vote to raise the minimum wage, I know the Chamber [of Commerce] is coming in here. I know. I don't have to be told. They don't have to threaten me." The overall effect, Kerrey explained, is a kind of self-censorship that goes far deeper than what Big Money donors could do directly: "I'm afraid to do what I think is right. Or I persuaded myself: I'm already doing what I think is right, and they're just supporting me because of it. Either way, now it might be a situation where you actually believe that, and therefore, they're supporting you for it."[65]

Our democracy can't survive this.

CHAPTER 3

Looting America: The Corporate Welfare State

A significant percentage of the business of Washington, D.C., revolves around corporate welfare, as lobbyists, trade associations and business executives press legislators and regulators to obtain or protect special, favorable treatment from the federal government.

These special benefits include giveaways of publicly funded assets, below-market sales of government-owned resources, access to government-funded research and development, bailouts for failing companies, tax breaks, escapes and loopholes, loans and loan guarantees, overseas marketing assistance, grants and direct subsidies, sweetheart contracts, privatization, immunities from liability and more.

"Corporate welfare" is not a precise term. It refers to programs and policies that confer special monetary preferences on corporations—by direct payments, tax escapes, government giveaways and much more—*but not to society in general.*

So, for example, government investment created the internet, which became a platform that has made possible the existence, and extraordinary profitability, of Big Tech companies. But the internet is available to everyone, so its creation was not a form of corporate welfare. By contrast, when Amazon exploits tax loopholes to avoid paying more than $5 billion in taxes,[66] we can tally that as $5 billion in corporate welfare.

Corporate welfare recipients spend great sums on think tanks, academics, PR firms and advertising to justify and rationalize the programs from which they profit. They frequently spin tales about the purported efficiency of the corporate sector or the special needs of particular companies. They may claim to advance national security or create jobs.

Very often, and with no evident self-consciousness, shame or embarrassment, they claim corporate giveaways serve the interests of the "free market!"

Corporate welfare should make us angry.

While there can be corporate subsidies that are good policy, most often nothing is at stake other than corporate greed: Are corporations able to strip public assets and use them for private profit? Or will the government demand public resources be shared equitably and corporations pay their fair share of taxes?

But more is at stake here than the injustice of corporations scheming to get richer, as outrageous as that is. Looting the public treasury makes it appear we do not have the resources to address priority needs, from education to health care to preventing climate chaos and more. Corporate welfare means the government ends up serving the rich and powerful at the direct expense of most Americans and especially those most in need of stronger public programs: communities of color, low-income kids, seniors with unmet health needs and more.

There's nothing theoretical about this. President Biden's Build Back Better plan aimed to provide universal child care and pre-K school, expand Medicare to provide hearing coverage and make the largest investment ever in affordable housing. Those proposed transformative investments—and they truly would have transformed the nation to be kinder, more decent and more just—were dropped from the legislation that eventually became the Inflation Reduction Act, largely on the grounds that "we can't afford it."

But we *could* have afforded it, and we still can—simply by shutting down corporate welfare waste and using public money to meet real public priorities.

Let's zoom in now and explore some of the most egregious examples of corporate welfare, after which we'll zoom back out and consider the phenomenon of corporate welfare more broadly.

Corporate Tax Breaks, Escapes and Evasions

A discussion of corporate welfare has to begin with corporate tax policy, because rigging and exploiting the tax system is such a big part of what corporations do in Washington—and because the amounts involved are so staggeringly large.

Let's start with this simple truth: Big Business has turned the Internal Revenue Code into the Corporate Welfare Code.

Industry lobbyists—commonly former congressional staff—work the halls of Congress to lower corporate tax rates, win tax breaks for particular industries or companies, or sneak lines into the tax code to create loopholes that may save companies billions in tax obligations. The amazing complexity of the tax code works to the benefit of large corporations; their lobbyists and lawyers can help write the rules and then manipulate them in ways that are effectively invisible to regular people.

Corporate tax breaks owe their existence and persistence to Republican and Democratic legislators alike—especially those who serve on the tax-writing committees. But Republicans stand apart in making lower tax rates for corporations and the wealthy the singularly unifying feature

Figure 5. Profitable Corporations that Paid Zero or Negative Income Taxes from 2018-2020

Advanced Micro Devices	DTE Energy	Salesforce.com
Agilent Technologies	Duke Energy	Sanmina-SCI
Alliant Energy	Edison International	SpartanNash
Ally Financial	Evergy	Sealed Air
Ameren	FedEx	Telephone & Data
American Electric Power	FirstEnergy	Systems
Archer Daniels Midland	Juniper Networks	Textron
Atmos Energy	Kinder Morgan	T-Mobile US
Ball	Mohawk Industries	UGI
Booz Allen Hamilton	NRG Energy	Unum Group
Cabot Oil & Gas	Oneok	Westlake Chemical
Celanese	Penske Automotive	Williams
CMS Energy	Group	Xcel Energy
Dish Network	PPL	
Dominion Resources	Principal Financial	

Source: Institute for Tax and Economic Policy.

of their policy agenda. The Trump tax cuts of 2017 (The Tax Cuts and Jobs Act) slashed the corporate tax rate from 35 to 21 percent. The cost to taxpayers is estimated at $750 billion over 10 years.[67]

Manipulation of the tax code is enabling dozens of major corporations to pay ZERO in taxes. The Institute for Tax and Economic Policy (ITEP) found that from 2018 to 2020—the first three years of the Trump tax cut—39 profitable major corporations paid no taxes at all. Collectively, the 39 companies reported $122 billion in profits during the three-year period.[68]

Look, tax policy can be complicated and it's easy to give up or grow bored with the details. (In fact, the corporate lawyers and lobbyists count on the public not paying attention to their shenanigans.)

But there's nothing complicated about this, so let's forget about the tricks these companies used to escape paying their fair share and just focus on the bottom line: 39 corporations made $122 billion over a three-year period and paid nothing in taxes. NOTHING.

We look in more detail at specific corporate tax rip-offs in subsequent chapters.

Wall Street's Bailout Bonanza

In 2008, the U.S. and world financial systems seized up and the United States plunged into the Great Recession. This was a world-historic economic calamity brought on by Big Banks and Wall Street recklessness.

They fueled a housing bubble, deployed dubious and illegal accounting tricks, pursued reckless financial practices—and eventually crashed the national and worldwide economies.

The costs of the Great Recession were staggering, the worst since the Great Depression. The Government Accountability Office (GAO, a congressional research agency) reported that cumulative loss was expected to total around $13 trillion and that homeowners would lose about $9 trillion in home equity.[69] The recession threw millions out of their homes and left millions more jobless or underemployed.

Remarkably, given the scale of corporate wrongdoing and the devastation it wreaked, the perpetrators of the Great Recession escaped any criminal prosecution. There was no criminal prosecution of the big banks, and none for their executives.

Instead, the big banks were bailed out. To prevent the collapse of the financial system, the federal government provided incomprehensibly huge financial supports. It started with $700 billion in the Troubled Assets Relief Program (TARP), which ultimately allocated around $475 billion to banks and other firms.[70] But that was just the tip of the iceberg.[71] Through aggressive interventions by the Federal Reserve and other maneuvers, the federal government provided as much as $23 trillion in supports to the financial system, according to the best governmental estimates.[72]

Bank regulators and Congress alike were scrambling in 2008, making rapid-fire decisions in fear of what would happen to the stock market and the broader economy if they did not act urgently. But even with the rush, it was notable even at the time that they did not condition the bailouts on commitments for changed behavior from the firms they saved from ruin, other than trivial and temporary restraints on executive compensation.

Completely absent were two structural reforms that could have both softened the economic crisis and de-concentrated the economy. First, the government could have required banks to write down mortgage loans that were underwater. (A mortgage is "underwater" if a person owes more on the loan than their ownership stake in the house. This can happen when a person has put a relatively small down payment on their home and the value of the home declines.) If loans had been written down, it would have been possible for many of the people who lost their homes to keep them. In fact, Congress, led by Senator Richard Durbin, D-Illinois, did try to force banks to accept such a "cramdown," at least for people in bankruptcy. But the banks defeated the proposal. "The banks—hard to believe in a time when we're facing a banking crisis that many of the banks created—are still the most powerful lobby on Capitol Hill," Durbin said. "And they frankly own the place."[73]

The banks could also have been required to permit former owners to stay in their homes as renters.[74] But neither Congress nor regulators pursued this option, even though it would not have imposed costs on the banks.

The second condition that might have been attached to the bailouts was a requirement that the Big Banks be broken up. It was widely recognized that the bailout was needed because the banks were "too big to fail." So how about making them smaller so that the situation wouldn't repeat itself?[75] Congress not only failed to take this step, but the Big Banks managed to emerge with a far *greater* market share after the housing bubble burst and the market crashed.[76]

Though they were used to having their way in Washington, even the giant banks must have been amazed by what happened. Having caused the worst economic crisis in 70 years, they were not only rescued by Uncle Sam but allowed to grow even bigger and more powerful.

The outcome was no source of amazement for the American people. The banks got their bailout, but millions of Americans lost their homes and jobs and received no bailout whatsoever.

Medicare Disadvantage: Cherry-Picking, Upcoding and Other Insurance Tricks

Medicare accounts for more than one-in-five dollars spent on health care in the United States—more than $800 billion annually and fast growing. Medicare is a public insurance program, to which workers contribute from their paychecks. But with so much money at stake, private insurers have weaseled in and found a way to grab a growing share of that gigantic spending.

As a result, half of all seniors enrolled in Medicare are now members of private plans paid for in large part with Medicare funds. This partial privatization of Medicare is delivering inferior care to patients, fattening insurance corporation bottom lines and costing taxpayers hundreds of billions of dollars.

Yes, hundreds of billions of dollars.

Some private plans have been associated with Medicare since its inception, but their role was limited in the early decades of the program. In the 1980s, with the rise of HMOs (health maintenance organizations), a substantial portion of Medicare recipients migrated to private plans, hitting around 14 percent in 1997.

The passage of the Medicare Modernization Act in 2003 launched the current era of "Medicare Advantage" plans.[77] Private insurance companies and their lobbyists told a story that they would be able to give consumers better choices and lower prices than Medicare. The reality—as critics predicted at the time—has proven very different.

Private, profit-driven insurance companies aggressively market their Medicare Advantage plans as an alternative to traditional Medicare Part A and Part B coverage (covering hospitals and doctor visits), blanketing the airwaves during annual enrollment periods. Television ads for Medicare Advantage plans often tout a variety of benefits not provided by Medicare Part B, such as dental, vision and hearing coverage.

Many seniors who enroll in Medicare Advantage plans are unaware of these plans' significant disadvantages. For example, most such plans limit choice by requiring enrollees to use only health care providers who participate in the plan's network, whereas patients enrolled in traditional Medicare can choose to go to just about any doctor or hospital, as the vast majority accept Medicare patients.[78] Perhaps the most troubling aspect of Medicare Advantage plans is their use of a payment model that provides an incentive for companies to deny beneficiaries access to medical care, even if it is supposed to be covered.

Over the past two decades, enrollment in Medicare Advantage plans has steadily increased from about six million Medicare beneficiaries in 2002 to 30 million in 2023. That amounts to 50 percent of Medicare beneficiaries. In 2022, Medicare Advantage plans claimed $427 billion (55 percent) of total federal Medicare spending.[79]

The history and structure of these deceptively named "Advantage" plans prove that their purported benefits of saving money and providing improved care are a lie. In fact, they do the opposite. They have a long record of receiving overpayments and disadvantaging Medicare. One study estimated that Medicare overpayments to private plans cost the federal government more than $280 billion from 1985-2012.[80] The Affordable Care Act aimed to cut back on overpayments to Medicare Advantage, but a federal court invalidated the Act's Overpayment Rule in September 2018, removing the enforcement mechanism. The rule had sought to ensure that Medicare Advantage care providers are not paid more for any particular treatment than Medicare would spend on the same treatment.

The problem of overpayments to Medicare Advantage continues and is worsening. At the core of the overpayment problem is "upcoding"— through a variety of tricks, Medicare Advantage plans characterize the people they insure as sicker than they are. With more diagnoses, patients appear to be riskier than they are, and Medicare pays the insurers more.[81] By way of illustration, Medicare Advantage plans "received an estimated $9.2 billion in payments in 2017 for beneficiary diagnoses reported solely on chart reviews or health risk assessments, with no other records of services for those diagnoses in the encounter data," according to Erin Bliss of the inspector general's office for the Department of Health and Human Services.[82]

The stakes are shockingly large. Richard Kronick, a former federal health policy researcher and a professor at the University of California San Diego, estimates that Medicare overpaid Medicare Advantage by more than $106 billion from 2010 through 2019 because of the way the private plans charge for sicker patients. The problem is getting worse, in part because Medicare Advantage's market share is growing. Kronick found that $34 billion of that excess payment came in just 2018 and 2019, the most recent years for which data was available.[83]

Insurance corporation gaming of Medicare Advantage—and ripping off taxpayers—is a defining trait of the system. Government regulators are completely unable to maintain pace with the unscrupulous innovations of the industry, all of which end up imposing additional, wasteful costs on Medicare.

One of many examples: "crosswalking," where Medicare Advantage insurers carve up and merge plans in order to maintain high ratings from Medicare, ratings which translate into substantial bonus payments.[84] A *Wall Street Journal* analysis found that UnitedHealth, the biggest Medicare Advantage insurer, in 2016 merged plans covering 162,088 members, across more than 15 states including Indiana, Texas and Georgia, into a contract that had included just 1,729 members in Rhode Island and Massachusetts. By doing so, UnitedHealth was able to use the high rating for the small plans and apply it to the big plan, earning a nice $63 million bonus in the process. Analysts from JPMorgan Chase concluded that Humana generated an extra $600 million from employing the tactic, according to the *Journal*.[85]

Along with the Medicare Advantage overpayments problem is a more structural issue: cherry picking. Private insurers often limit their coverage pool to lower-risk parties—which, in the case of health insurance, means insuring primarily healthier people. This problem is pervasive in the seniors' health insurance markets and is practically unavoidable: Medicare Advantage insurers can attract those healthier people by offering lower premiums for plans with less access to the more expensive treatments and services that less healthy people need. The result is to leave traditional Medicare with a pool of less healthy people, raising its per patient cost. Various reforms have sought to address this problem, but the structural incentives for cherry picking consistently lead insurers to find ways around regulatory controls.

Sicker seniors are more likely to switch from Medicare Advantage to traditional Medicare. A GAO analysis concluded that roughly one third of the Medicare Advantage plans with high disenrollment rates were biased against sick people, presumably prompting sick people to leave the plan when they become ill.[86] Similarly, seniors in the final year of life—when health care costs are disproportionately high—shift from Medicare

Advantage and to traditional Medicare at more than twice the rate of other Medicare Advantage beneficiaries.[87]

Not all of the Medicare Advantage corporate manipulations are legal. In fact, illegality seems baked into the business model, with most Medicare Advantage insurers submitting improper bills or engaging in fraud.[88]

Alongside the massive subsidy to private insurance corporations through Medicare Advantage, there is a severe quality-of-care issue. With profit incentives to deny care, Medicare Advantage plans regularly refuse to authorize or reimburse care that patients need.[89]

A study by the Department of Health and Human Services inspector general found that 13 percent of the Medicare Advantage denials for prior authorization were for services that met Medicare coverage rules, "likely preventing or delaying medically necessary care for Medicare Advantage beneficiaries." The inspector general emphasized that "these denials may be particularly harmful for beneficiaries who cannot afford to pay for services directly and for critically ill beneficiaries who may suffer negative health consequences from delayed or denied care."

To summarize: Private insurers used their political influence to corrupt the nation's most important public insurance program. Through partial privatization, they have undermined the quality and consistency of Medicare, systematically overbilled, committed widespread fraud—and burglarized hundreds of billions of dollars from the American people.

The Pentagon Boondoggle

Can it be that there are other corporate rip-offs of the public on the scale of Medicare Advantage, costing taxpayers tens of billions every year?

Yes, it can. Let's talk about the military-industrial complex.

In spring 2022, President Biden proposed a Pentagon budget for fiscal year 2023 of $813 billion, an increase of $30 billion from the previous year and $60 billion more than the final Trump Pentagon budget. Congress raised that funding level by $45 billion. In two years, the Pentagon budget grew more than $100 billion from the final year of the Trump administration.

No national security threats exist that justify such an increase.[90] U.S. Secretary of Defense Lloyd Austin testified in April 2022 that $813 billion is sufficient to meet the Pentagon's needs, and no defensible reason was put forward by those who argued that even this gigantic sum needed to be boosted.[91] "This is a robust budget, and I think it allows us to get the capabilities that we need to support our operational concepts," Austin said. In fact, the United States spends more on defense than the next nine largest military spenders combined.[92]

The case for cutting the Pentagon budget—or, at minimum, not continuing to raise it—is powerful and overwhelming:

- The Pentagon has so much money that it literally can't keep track of it. Since being required to undergo an audit, the Pentagon has failed to pass on four successive occasions.[93] It hopes finally to pass an audit by the end of the decade!
- The Pentagon budget is replete with waste and fraud and spending on needless weapons. The Pentagon itself has identified more than $100 billion *of waste* in its own budget.[94]
- Funding for the Pentagon comes at the expense of other priorities. The United States is under-investing in measures to address non-military national security threats, notably climate chaos and future pandemics. And core human needs are going unmet, from housing to health care and beyond. Among many examples: Congress failed to continue funding a $3 billion per year program of free school lunches to prevent 10 million kids from going hungry.

There is one overriding reason why the Pentagon budget continues to skyrocket, despite no valid security rationale and massive waste and fraud: the political power and influence of military contractors. As Pentagon budget analyst William Hartung explained about Pentagon spending that Congress added to Biden's request, "The vast bulk of the added funds will go to pad the bottom lines of contractors like Boeing, Lockheed Martin and General Dynamics. Of the $37 billion in add-ons to the Pentagon's proposal, over two thirds—or $25 billion—will go to weapons procurement and research and development, categories of funding that mostly go to contractors. By contrast, the increase for military personnel and health was just $1 billion, an indication that corporate profits continue to come before the needs of the troops."[95] Overall, nearly half the current Pentagon budget goes to private contractors.[96]

The Pentagon budget exists in a unique sphere of the federal budgeting process. Funding is tight for every other part of the U.S. government's discretionary budget. Agencies are underfunded in trying to enforce food safety standards and issue new rules to protect worker health. Programs to reduce child poverty, expand dental coverage for Medicare recipients or mitigate catastrophic climate change are abandoned for lack of funds. But there's always more money for the Pentagon and its contractors.

The constant upward pressure for more Pentagon spending is directly tied to the political power of Pentagon contractors. One way they deploy this power is through campaign donations, especially to members of the House and Senate Armed Services Committees. These are the people who determine funding for the Pentagon when they consider, amend and vote on the annual Pentagon policy bill, the National Defense Authorization

Act. So defense contractors pour money into these members' reelection campaigns, creating a self-fulfilling feedback loop that many call the "military-industrial-congressional complex."

In the 2022 election cycle, the military-industrial complex gave $10.2 million in campaign contributions to members of the House and Senate Armed Services Committees prior to their votes to increase overall defense spending for the 2023 fiscal year. Notably, the average campaign contribution from these corporations to the committee members who voted "yes" on that increase was more than triple the average gift the complex gave to those who voted "no"—$151,722 for the yes-men and women, $42,967 for the naysayers.

It was money well spent. When the dust settled and Congress raised the Pentagon budget $45 billion above Biden's request, Pentagon contractors clinched a return of nearly 450,000 percent on their $10 million investment.

These extraordinary spending levels are not about taking care of the troops, many of whom live in poverty and in shockingly poor housing. It is about taking care of contractors. Indeed, Pentagon contractors may constitute the most extreme form of "corporate socialism," since many live largely or entirely on public funding.

The U.S. military has long relied on contractors, who have long ripped off taxpayers,[97] but that dependence has soared in the last two decades. By 2011, reports Brown University's Cost of War Project, "there were more private contract employees involved in the wars in Iraq and Afghanistan than uniformed military personnel. By 2019, the ratio of contractors to troops had grown to 1.5:1, or 50 percent more contractors than troops in the U.S. Central Command region that includes Iraq and Afghanistan.[98]

"More than half of the annual Department of Defense budget is now spent on military contractors, and payments to contractors have risen more than 164 percent since 2001, from about $140 billion in 2001 to about $370 billion in 2019. A large portion of these contracts have gone to just five major corporations: Lockheed Martin, Boeing, General Dynamics, Raytheon and Northrop Grumman."[99]

A very significant portion of the government funding flowing to military contractors is for super-expensive weapons and systems that are widely regarded as unnecessary or of dubious value, or both. For example, the F-35 jet is the department's costliest weapon system program and is expected to cost $1.7 trillion, even though the aircraft does not yet operate correctly, the program is rife with delays and cost overruns, and a substantial number of the aircraft will be procured before they are proved to have reached "an acceptable level of performance and reliability."[100]

Can you imagine buying fighter jets before they have reached "an acceptable level of performance and reliability?"

Well, Congress can. The House amendments to the Biden budget added three additional F-35s to projected spending for fiscal year 2023.

Lockheed Martin's F-35 is extraordinary in its unfathomable cost, but it is not unusual for contractors to receive enormous contracts for weapons and equipment that do not work. Even when the Pentagon itself wants to cancel programs, contractors are often able to leverage their political power to keep the programs—and their corporate welfare subsidies—alive. The U.S. Navy's Littoral Combat Ship, for example, cannot protect itself from submarine threats, so the Navy proposed in the FY23 budget to retire nine of them.[101]

Chief of Naval Operations (CNO) Admiral Michael Gilday testified to the House that "after about a year and a half study, I refuse to put an additional dollar against a system that wouldn't be able to track a high-end submarine in today's environment."[102]

But the House Armed Services Committee didn't care. It passed an amendment to the defense authorization bill to keep five of the nine ships in the water. And in July the full House defeated an amendment that would have retired the ships.[103]

In short, there is bipartisan support for the massively wasteful contractor bonanza of Pentagon spending, the biggest of Big Government's corporate welfare programs. That spending has nothing to do with national security and everything to do with taking care of donors.

The Corporate Welfare Big Picture

So far, we've looked at a diverse set of large-scale corporate welfare programs: the Trump corporate tax cuts, the Wall Street bailout, partial privatization of Medicare and inflated and wasteful Pentagon contracting. Later chapters in this book will explore corporate welfare programs benefiting Big Pharma, Big Oil and Big Tech.

There are so many examples of corporate welfare, it's virtually impossible to track them all. Grouping them into categories can help us get a sense of the big picture.

Giveaways of publicly owned assets. Accepting free gifts from the government is a good deal for corporations if they can do it. It happens! One example is the giveaway of hard-rock minerals on federal lands. Under the 1872 Mining Act, any person or corporation can stake a claim to hard-rock mining rights on 350 million acres of federal land, mostly in the West and Alaska. To stake a claim, you put down $250 and must pay $5 per acre. Yes, you read it right—not $5 million, but five dollars. You pay zero royalties on the metals you extract—it's a total giveaway.

In the 150 years of the Mining Act, miners have extracted an estimated $300 billion in gold, silver, platinum and other minerals—and paid virtually nothing. They have, however, left huge environmental problems behind, including a vast array of abandoned, toxic mines. The estimated cost of cleaning up abandoned mines in the United States is on the order of $50 billion.[104]

Below-market sales of government-owned resources. In contrast to hard-rock minerals, the federal government does impose royalties for oil and gas drilled on public land. But the rate was long stuck at a low 12.5 percent. The Inflation Reduction Act, which passed in 2022, will tick up the royalty rate to 16.67 percent for new drilling, still below a fair return. Over the past decade, these discount sales have cost taxpayers more than $13 billion. We discuss these discount sales in more detail in the chapter on Big Oil corporate welfare.

Unconditioned access to government-funded research and development. The federal government devotes tens of billions of dollars every year to research and development, through the National Institutes of Health, the National Science Foundation, the Defense Department and other agencies. What happens to the fruits of that investment? A lot of the results are basic research, which goes into the public domain, building the knowledge base of humanity. But some of the research leads to specific inventions with commercial applications. What then?

In biomedical research—medicines, vaccines, genetic tools, etc.—the government will generally license the invention for use only by a single corporation. Often, the licensing is done by a university that invented a product using government funding. The licensee will generally pay compensation, typically a royalty on sales of the product. But that license normally comes with few if any protections for patients—who often are forced to pay extravagant amounts for drugs invented with taxpayer dollars. We explore this issue in detail in the chapter on Big Pharma corporate welfare.

Bailouts. If a restaurant or small business can't make a go of things, it normally shuts down. A larger company will likely go into bankruptcy—if it has a viable business but was just facing hard times, it can reorganize, pay what it can to creditors and keep going. If it's not a viable business, it has to unwind. But if a company is really large and facing collapse, it often will ask the government for a bailout—direct loans or even outright payments to keep afloat. Bailouts happen more often than you might think. Many recent bailout payments went to assist companies, including airlines, cope with economic dislocations caused by the Covid-19 pandemic. By and large, these were good policy choices, although too often the payments came with too few conditions. More troubling was the Wall Street bailout that followed the 2008 financial crash. As we have seen, government help kept the giant Wall Street firms afloat with few conditions, letting them emerge bigger and as reckless as ever.

Corporate tax breaks, escapes and loopholes. Tax breaks are probably the most consequential form of corporate welfare. As we will see throughout this book, they are omnipresent at the federal, state and local level; corporations are masters at lobbying for tiny changes in tax policy that make a huge difference to their bottom line—and at blackmailing governments with threats to move facilities and jobs if they don't get those breaks.

Loans and loan guarantees. What's a corporation to do if it needs to borrow lots of money to invest in a facility, but banks and lenders don't trust the company's ability to pay back the loan? If you're a big corporation with the right connections, you turn to the federal government—either for a direct loan or a guarantee to pay back your loans if you can't. Loan guarantees have helped keep the nuclear power industry going, just barely, even though the technology has proved both unsafe and far more expensive than alternatives. The Vogtle Electric Generating Plant in eastern Georgia, for example, is a nuclear power facility jointly owned by Georgia Power and other utilities. Its construction is years behind schedule and on course to cost more than $30 billion—twice the original estimate.[105] You can see why private lenders might be reluctant to lend to such an operation! But Georgia Power and its co-owners have managed to keep the money flow going with billions of loan guarantees from the federal government.[106]

Grants and direct subsidies. Sometimes the government simply gives money directly to companies. Not surprisingly, this is usually the product of a determined lobbying effort. Case in point: government subsidies for biodiesel, a fuel substitute made from soy and other vegetable oils. Under a long-running program, the government provides a biodiesel tax credit—a direct $1 tax offset for each gallon of biodiesel used. The subsidy now costs taxpayers $3 billion a year.[107] Its proponents say that biodiesel offsets greenhouse gas emissions, but it turns out that using biodiesel actually *increases* emissions,[108] and the conversion of cropland to produce soy and other biodiesel crops is driving up global grain and food prices.

Sweetheart contracts and corporate pork. Government contracts that overpay corporate suppliers and purchase unneeded items are a major form of corporate welfare. And, as we have seen, no government agency specializes more in sweetheart contracts and corporate pork than the Pentagon. More than half the gargantuan Pentagon budget—fast approaching $1 trillion annually—goes to military contractors. Fraud, waste and cost overruns are routine among Pentagon contractors, a result not just of Pentagon profligacy but the very structure of Pentagon contracting. These contracts often commit the Pentagon to pay for services before determining what will be procured or holding a competitive bidding process. They commit the

Pentagon to purchase major, expensive weapons before they have proved to work. And they commit the Pentagon to pay contractors on a "cost-plus" basis, which incentivizes them to spend more.

Privatization. One good trick for corporations to loot the taxpayer is privatization—sometimes selling off government assets to corporations, more often contracting with corporations to perform services that the government previously provided. Privatizers regularly claim that corporations will bring more efficiency to service provision and save money. Much more often, they provide lower quality service at a higher price. When there are savings, they commonly are achieved by paying workers less, not from any managerial efficiency. Just as bad as this taxpayer rip-off is the way public services carried out with a public-minded mission are converted into corporate services with a commercial mission. The very nature of the service is often altered in the process.

The partial privatization of Medicare discussed earlier in this chapter is a good example. Another odious example is the federal and state reliance on private prisons. Private prisons claim to deliver cost savings, but in fact cost the same or more than public prisons.[109] Yet private prisons pay their staff far less, have far more turnover, and report much more violence against inmates. Private prison corporations need a constant inflow of inmates to make money, so they become lobbyists for harsher sentencing and contributors to politicians who pledge to build more prisons and put more people behind bars.[110]

Government-provided insurance. Businesses need insurance in order to pay for the damage from extreme and non-routine events. Private insurers offer insurance to businesses based on the likelihood of an event and an expectation of likely damages. If insurers think the risk or likely cost is too great, they won't offer insurance. If a business can't obtain insurance, that's a warning sign about its business model. So there's reason to take notice when the government steps in to provide insurance that private companies won't.

Nuclear insurance and liability protection. There is such a convoluted system of subsidies for the nuclear power industry that it deserves special mention. The Price-Anderson Indemnity Act limits the liability of the nuclear industry (plant operators, their suppliers and vendors) in the event of a major nuclear accident. Under Price-Anderson, each utility is required to maintain $300 million in liability insurance per reactor. If claims following an accident exceed that amount, all other nuclear operators are required to pay up to around $100 million for each reactor they operate. Under the terms of Price-Anderson, neither the owner of a unit that has a major accident nor the entire utility can be held liable for more than these sums. This system caps insurance coverage for any accident at just shy of $14 billion.

In 1982, the most detailed government study estimated the potential property damage from a serious nuclear accident at $300 billion.[111] That is more than $900 billion in 2023 dollars—which means the nuclear industry's liability is capped at 1/60th of the potential costs of a single accident. And that excludes potential health impacts. Price-Anderson has been around since the inception of the nuclear industry—it was originally justified as needed to help a nascent industry—and over time has grown into an extraordinary subsidy, permitting the industry to spend vastly less on insurance than its operations and potential liability would otherwise require.[112] In 1990, three decades ago, Professors Jeffrey Dubin and Geoffrey Rothwell estimated the cumulative Price-Anderson subsidy to the nuclear industry through 1988 to be $111 billion in 1985 dollars.[113]

This is by no means an exhaustive list of corporate welfare programs. Other tools of corporate power include government-provided export assistance, insurance for overseas investments, overseas marketing assistance, special insurance programs, liability limits, protected monopolies and more.

We should note that not every corporate subsidy is bad policy. Corporate welfare programs need to be judged on their individual merits, and sometimes corporate subsidies make good sense. Yet even where such programs are meritorious, there remains a question about whether beneficiaries are subject to reciprocal obligations. If a corporation gets bailed out, is it reasonable to impose limits on what it can pay its CEO? If a corporation licenses technology from the U.S. government, should it be required to set reasonable prices for the products it makes with that publicly funded technology? If a manufacturer is receiving tax credits and incentives, is it required to invest in factories in the United States? And so on.

Trillions in Corporate Welfare

One thing is for sure: All these subsidies for big corporations add up! It's not possible to precisely calculate the dollar cost to taxpayers, but we can get a sense of its magnitude by looking at some of the biggest components.

Over a decade, just four corporate welfare programs—corporate tax breaks, partial Medicare privatization, the prohibition on Medicare drug price negotiation (see Chapter 5) and Pentagon pork—confer more than $1.75 *trillion* in benefits on large corporations, over a 10-year period. That is a government-forced transfer of wealth from the public to corporations on an epic scale.

As we close this discussion, it's important to contrast corporate welfare with social programs.

Poor children don't have the lobbying clout of Boeing, Pfizer or Amazon—and they don't fare nearly as well in Congress, despite being far more deserving. Instead, a program like the expanded Child Tax Credit—which reduced child poverty by a third—is criticized for including middle-class children and canceled on the grounds that it is too expensive. Yet there's no means testing for corporate welfare, and the budgetary effects are routinely ignored. Proposals to cancel student debt—which would disproportionately assist less well-off people and people of color—are criticized as improper "bailouts," while permanent subsidies for Big Business persist. Ordinary people pay what they owe in taxes—typically through automatic withholdings. Dozens of giant corporations manipulate the tax system to pay nothing at all in income tax.

These contrasts show the price we pay for out-of-control corporate welfare spending. It's not just a looting of the taxpayer and an upward transfer of wealth. It's the corporate exploitation of political power that degrades our democracy and breeds cynicism. It's the draining of public funds at the expense of the priority needs of the nation—everything from health care to addressing climate change to investing in housing to child care, and much, much more. It's the perversion of the government's mission and the sabotage of its ability—and the nation's belief in its ability—to operate of, by and for the people.

PART II

Big Pharma

CHAPTER 4

Dying for—and from—Drugs

Big Pharma regularly ranks as the most hated industry in America (though after the price spikes following the Russian invasion of Ukraine, Big Oil gave it a run for its money).[114] It's quite a feat for an industry that delivers treatments that save lives and alleviate suffering for millions of Americans.

But the antipathy is well deserved. Big Pharma's sky-high prices deprive people of life-saving and critical medicines, or force people into debt to pay for prescriptions. Time and again, Big Pharma has rushed dangerous drugs onto the market, often hiding information about serious side effects, with terrible consequences for patients. And Big Pharma's marketing mania turned opioids with a legitimate if limited purpose into the source of a lethal abuse epidemic now taking 100,000 lives annually.

Rationing in America

"I got a call that no parent wants to get," says Nicole Smith-Holt.

"My son Alec had just turned 26 when he died from rationing insulin in 2017. After his birthday, he was no longer eligible to be covered by my

Figure 6. Big Pharma Profits and CEO Compensation, 2018-2022

Corporation Name	Profits, 2018-2022	CEO Compensation, 2018-2022
Abbvie	$41.6 billion	$117.1 million
AstraZeneca	$9.8 billion	*(inadequate data)*
Bristol Myers Squibb	$12.7 billion	$98.1 million
GSK	$36.7 billion	$49.8 million
Johnson & Johnson	$83.9 billion	$88 million
Merck	$50.6 billion	$103 million
Novartis	$63.4 billion	$54 million
Pfizer	$89.9 billion	$106.2 million
Roche	$76.7 billion	*(inadequate data)*
Sanofi	$44.1 billion	*(inadequate data)*

Source: Public Citizen compilation based on Top 10 Pharma companies' Securities and Exchange Commission filings.

health insurance. The pharmacist told him he would have to pay $1,300 a month for his supplies.

"Alec worked full time as a restaurant manager, but his workplace did not offer insurance. His $35,000 annual salary put him above the income limit for Medicaid in Minnesota, but he was still not able to afford the sky-high premiums and deductibles. We looked into different health insurance options under the Affordable Care Act, but the options were so expensive that he would end up paying for his insulin out of pocket."[115]

Alec didn't tell Nicole, and he wasn't able to afford the out-of-pocket costs. So he started rationing his insulin. He died alone in his apartment after falling into a coma.[116]

Nicole now works with T1 International (led by people with Type-1 diabetes) to advocate for lower insulin and drug prices. Thanks to her efforts, Minnesota in 2020 passed the Alec Smith Insulin Affordability Act, enabling eligible people to get a monthly supply of insulin for $35.[117]

But there's an awful lot more work to do. Sadly and disgracefully in the United States of America, Alec's story is not unique.

Critical medicines—the kind that people need to treat serious health conditions and to alleviate suffering or cure illnesses—aren't like regular goods, for at least two important reasons. First, as a consumer, you have no choice *not* to use the product. If you're carnivorous and think the price of steak is too high, you don't have to buy steak. But if you've been prescribed a life-saving cancer medication, you'll pay any price. Second, when it comes to patent-protected drugs, you generally can't choose an alternative product, or you have very limited choices among other patent-protected drugs. This is different from the vast majority of consumer products, which do not enjoy government-granted monopoly protection. If you think one make of car is too expensive, you can choose another, for example.

What this means, in short, is that Big Pharma has enormous pricing power. Big Pharma companies can charge whatever they want—what will make them the most money—and they do. They try to rationalize their prices by citing their investments in research and development (R&D), but their prices have nothing to do with R&D spending. Industry R&D spending is actually pretty modest relative to sales. In fact, the industry is spending more on stock buybacks—basically what a corporation does when it has too much money on its hands—than it does on R&D. From 2016 to 2020, the 14 leading drug companies spent $577 billion on stock buybacks and dividends—$56 billion more than they spent on R&D over the same period.[118] (A "stock buyback" is when a corporation buys back its own stock. This reduces the number of shares remaining and thereby increases their value.)

When Big Pharma companies price drugs to maximize profits, they are necessarily setting prices out of reach for many people, especially those with no insurance, limited insurance or insurance with high co-pays. The median launch price of a new drug in the United States jumped from $2,115 in 2008 to $180,007 in 2021, a 20 percent annual inflation rate, according to researchers at Brigham and Women's Hospital in Boston.[119]

As a result of these soaring prices, non-adherence to drug regimens due to price—the cost of drugs, co-pays and deductibles—is at epidemic levels. Thirty percent of Americans report that they have skipped drug treatments or otherwise haven't taken medicines as prescribed because of cost.[120]

Let's pause for just a moment and absorb that startling and profoundly disturbing fact: *Roughly one in three Americans don't take medicines as prescribed because they can't afford them.*

Insulin was discovered as a treatment for diabetes 100 years ago. As a discovery of a naturally occurring substance, it was not patentable. But starting in the 1980s, Big Pharma companies began synthesizing insulin that mimicked human-made insulin,[121] and those products were patentable. Over time, the companies found ways to extend patent and other monopolies on their insulin products by making some minor improvements, combining insulin with devices (such as injector pens) and other means.[122]

The House Oversight and Government Reform Committee found that the top three insulin companies "have engaged in strategies to maintain monopoly pricing and defend against competition from biosimilars

Figure 7. U.S. Pharmaceutical Spending vs. Other Countries

Country	Spending
Sweden	$351
Norway	$401
Netherlands	$417
Australia	$427
United Kingdom	$497
France	$553
Canada	$669
Germany	$686
Switzerland	$783
United States	$1,011

Spending amount per capita. Source: Commonwealth Fund.

[generics]. These strategies include manipulating the patent system and the marketing exclusivities granted by the Food and Drug Administration (FDA), pursuing tactics to switch patients to new formulations of their products before losing exclusivity, and engaging in 'shadow pricing'—raising prices in lockstep with competitors—which keeps prices high."[123]

Since 1996, pharmaceutical corporations began exploiting their patent monopolies much more aggressively, increasing the price of a vial of insulin by more than 1,200 percent—from $21 to more than $275.[124] Confronted with industry price-gouging, more than a third of U.S. patients who rely on insulin to survive have reported rationing it.[125] Since 2017, at least 12 people in the United States have died from rationing insulin.[126]

There's only one reason insulin makers charge so much in the United States: because they can. Other countries impose various forms of price controls and don't permit individuals or their health system to be exploited. A Rand study found the average price per insulin unit in the United States to be $98.70. In Japan, it was $14.40—85 percent less. It was even cheaper in other rich countries: $12.00 in Canada, $9.08 in France, $6.94 in Australia. The Australian price is just 7 percent of the cost in the United States![127]

"The differences were especially stark when the researchers looked at rapid-acting insulin, which makes up about a third of the U.S. market," reports Rand. "Its average price in other countries was just over $8. In America, it was $119." In other words, the average price in other rich countries was less than 7 percent of the extortionate U.S. charge.

In general, drug corporations know they can't pull the same tricks in other countries that are permitted in the United States, so their business model relies on gouging U.S. consumers and taxpayers. Based on its review of internal company documents, the House Oversight Committee reported that Pfizer "targeted the U.S. market for price increases. A draft internal Pfizer presentation from 2016 explicitly linked Pfizer's global profitability to its ability to raise prices in the United States, noting that growth was driven by 'price increases in the U.S.'"[128]

Insulin expenses are an enormous burden on Medicare, rising from $1.4 billion in 2007 to $13.3 billion in 2017—not because the population has expanded, but because drug company monopolists have been able to spike prices for a 100-year-old drug.[129]

Most poignantly, super-high insulin charges place impossible burdens on insulin users. Researchers have invented the term "catastrophic spending" to refer to people forced to spend more than 40 percent of their post-subsistence family income just on insulin. For 2017 and 2018, they found 14 percent of insulin users—or 1.2 million people—had reached catastrophic

Figure 8. Medicare Spending on Insulin

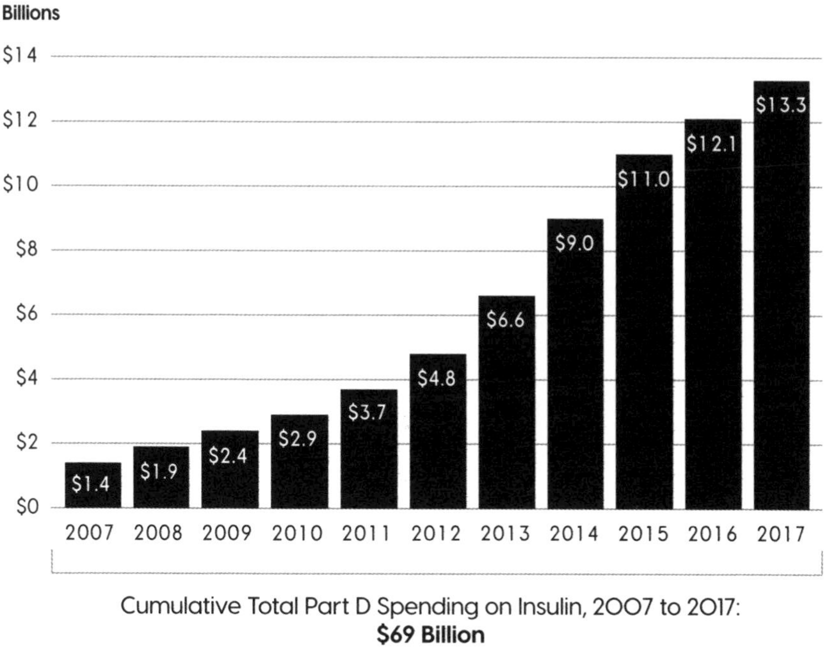

Billions

$14

$12

$10

$8

$6

$4

$2

$0

2007	2008	2009	2010	2011	2012	2013	2014	2015	2016	2017
$1.4	$1.9	$2.4	$2.9	$3.7	$4.8	$6.6	$9.0	$11.0	$12.1	$13.3

Cumulative Total Part D Spending on Insulin, 2007 to 2017:
$69 Billion

Source: Kaiser Family Foundation.

spending levels during the course of one year.[130] Many rationed their life-saving medication. Some, like Alec Smith, did not survive.

Insulin users, their families—like Alec Smith's mother, Nicole Smith-Holt, and allies like Public Citizen publicized the toll of death and suffering and demanded action. Even in the face of Big Pharma's power, that mobilization eventually made a difference. In 2022, Congress passed the Inflation Reduction Act which capped monthly insulin co-pays at $35 for the three million people with diabetes covered by Medicare. Then, in 2023, came even more momentous change. Eli Lilly, one of the three main insulin manufacturers, slashed the price of key insulin products and pledged that patients could access insulin for no more than $35 a month—a cap applied both to those with and without insurance.[131] Within weeks, Novo Nordisk and Sanofi—the other major insulin makers—followed suit.[132]

The sudden reduction in insulin pricing was an important reminder that, as powerful as Big Pharma is, the companies are still vulnerable to organizing and public pressure. And, if We the People can defeat Big Pharma, we can challenge and overcome any industry.

The Vioxx Disaster

It's not as if people in power didn't know about the impending calamity—what David Graham, a Food and Drug Administration (FDA) drug safety official, called "maybe the single greatest drug-safety catastrophe in the history of this country."

It involved Merck's arthritis drug Vioxx. Testifying before a Senate committee in November 2004, Graham put the number in the United States who had suffered heart attacks or stroke as a result of taking the drug in the range of 88,000 to 139,000.[133] And as many as 40 percent of these people, or 35,000 to 55,000, died as a result, Graham said.

Merck's own trials had shown extremely elevated risk for cardio events from the drug as early as 2000, but the company explained away the problem. By 2001, Public Citizen was urging patients not to use the drug because of the heart attack risk.

In March 2004, another study found elevated risks compared to Vioxx's leading competitor (itself a dangerous drug). Then Graham did an FDA study that found Vioxx increased the risk of heart attack 3.7-fold for high-dose regimens and 1.5-fold for low-dose, compared to its main competitor.

Merck withdrew Vioxx from the market on September 30, 2004 after a trial sponsored by the company itself found a doubling of the risk for heart attack or stroke among those who took the medicine for 18 months or more.

Merck insisted it had disclosed all relevant evidence on Vioxx safety as soon as it acquired it, and pulled the drug as soon as it saw conclusive evidence of the drug's dangers.

"Over the past six years," Merck CEO Raymond Gilmartin told the Senate Finance Committee at the same November 2004 hearing where Graham spoke, "since the time Merck submitted a New Drug Application for Vioxx to the FDA, we have promptly disclosed the results of numerous Merck-sponsored studies to the FDA, physicians, the scientific community and the media and participated in a balanced, scientific discussion of its risks and benefits."[134]

Until the September 2004 clinical trial results came in, Gilmartin said, "the combined data from randomized controlled clinical trials showed no difference in confirmed cardiovascular event rates between Vioxx and placebo and Vioxx and nonsteroidal anti-inflammatory drug (NSAIDs) other than naproxen. When data from the APPROVe study [the September results] became available, Merck acted quickly to withdraw the medicine from the market."

But there is evidence that strongly suggests a different version of the story.

The unacceptable cardiovascular risks of Vioxx were evident as early as 2000—a full four years before Merck finally withdrew the drug from the market, according to a study released by *The Lancet*, the British medical journal.

"This discovery points to astonishing failures in Merck's internal systems of post-marketing surveillance, as well as to lethal weaknesses in the U.S. Food and Drug Administration's regulatory oversight," *The Lancet* editors wrote.

Authors of the *Lancet* study pooled data from 25,273 patients who participated in 18 clinical trials conducted before 2001. They found that patients given Vioxx had 2.3 times the risk of heart attacks as those given placebos or other pain medications.[135]

These findings came in the wake of disclosures suggesting Merck was aware of Vioxx's risks by 2000. *The Wall Street Journal* revealed e-mails that confirm Merck executives' knowledge of their drug's adverse cardiovascular profile—the risk was "clearly there," according to one senior researcher.[136]

Merck's marketing literature included a document intended for its sales representatives that discussed how to respond to questions about Vioxx. It was labeled "Dodge Ball Vioxx"—as in how to dodge questions about its safety.

Documents obtained by the Associated Press showed that Merck researchers recognized the risk by 2000 and explored options to combine Vioxx with other products to reduce the heart attack risk.[137]

As Merck internal documents were provided to litigants in lawsuits, other evidence emerged suggesting that Merck gave the FDA an incomplete accounting of deaths in a clinical trial of Vioxx in people with mild dementia. Merck denied any improper conduct.[138]

While it was brushing aside safety concerns, Merck was pulling out all the stops to market its new painkiller.

Merck's promotional strategy relied heavily on doctors. NPR obtained documents that showed the company tracking details about particular doctors they were targeting for marketing, reporting such items as: "…2,400 prescriptions per year…also known nationally… Writes for a lot of rheumatology textbooks."[139] "Merck's vast army of sales representatives gathered intelligence on what it would take to win over individual doctors," NPR reported. For example: "Will speak for us only at certain restaurants and high honorarium… Likes to feel important… He needs the VIP treatment."

The documents and NPR reporting told a remarkable story about Merck's marketing and efforts to quiet critics. One of the doctors Merck recruited to promote Vioxx was Gurkirpal Singh of Stanford University. Singh had been the senior researcher on a study establishing a need for painkillers that were gentler on the stomach.

Singh agreed to promote Vioxx. He was paid up to $2,500 per talk and gave 40 talks in a seven-month period. "One setting, which is where I was speaking predominantly, was in the grand-round situation in hospitals, or in medical schools, or in the universities, where like you're giving a formal lecture to the physicians," Singh told NPR. "It's always lectures to physicians. And then the other set is usually these evening programs that drug companies arrange, where you also present your research, and then there's often a dinner with it."

But when early studies emerged about the heart risk from Vioxx, Singh grew concerned. He asked to review the underlying data. Merck put him off. Eventually, Singh started raising concerns with regulators and in his medical talks. Merck cut him off completely.

Singh would turn to promote Vioxx's main rival product, Celebrex, while continuing to raise concerns about Vioxx. Merck salespeople closely tracked his comments and actions.

A Merck executive placed a series of calls to Singh's superiors. "I received a call from a medical director at Merck, stating that someone on my staff had been making wild and irresponsible public statements about the cardiovascular side effects of Vioxx," James Fries, a professor of medicine at Stanford, told NPR. Fries said the Merck executive "hinted there would be repercussions for Fries and Stanford if Singh's statements didn't stop," NPR reported. Fries was left with the sense that Merck's financial support to Stanford was at risk.[140]

The Merck executive told NPR that he only made calls when he thought doctors were being unfair to Merck and acting unprofessionally. "I never, never made any threats to withdraw funding or hamper anyone's faculty appointment," the executive told NPR. "Under no circumstances did I ever do that."

Merck would eventually settle lawsuits with those alleging they had been injured by Vioxx for $4.85 billion.[141] It pled guilty to a charge of selling a mislabeled drug and settled civil charges by the Department of Justice that it improperly marketed Vioxx. Altogether, it paid nearly $1 billion in fines and penalties to the federal government.[142]

At the 2004 Senate hearing, Dr. Graham, the federal drug-safety reviewer, said that Vioxx was not the only unsafe drug that companies were selling—and which the compromised FDA permitted them to sell. He said that at least five medications currently on the market pose such risks that their sale ought to be limited or stopped.

Vioxx was an especially egregious case, but Graham was right that it was not unique. Since 2000, at least 20 prescription medicines have been removed from the market because of safety concerns.[143]

Other medicines may provide benefits to a specific group of patients, but are prescribed too frequently or marketed for purposes other than their approved use. Side effects are not just a matter of discomfort. They often involve serious conditions, some of them permanent. And, far more often than is generally appreciated, they result in death. Adverse drug reactions cause some 100,000 deaths a year in the United States, and nearly 1.5 million people are injured so seriously by adverse drug reactions that they require hospitalization.

The Pharma-Created Opioid Epidemic

The evil genius of the Sackler family that founded and ran the opioid maker Purdue Pharma lies in marketing.

Opioids have been around and used for pain relief for millennia. The Sacklers didn't invent a particularly novel product with OxyContin. They invented a new marketing strategy.

Others would follow in their wake, sometimes employing even more unethical marketing strategies. Drug companies, distributors and drugstores all got in on the act: a lot of money could be made selling opioids, if you were willing to look the other way and ignore the fact that it was abuse, not legitimate use, that drove sales.

It took decades for law enforcement and the judicial system to catch up with the opioid makers and distributors and end their wrongdoing. By the time they did, the opioid addiction epidemic was raging. Illegally manufactured drugs, especially illicit versions of the super-powerful opioid fentanyl, simply replaced the FDA-approved opioids on the street.

From 1999 to 2020, more than 564,000 people died in the United States from opioid overdoses.[144] Fully 80,000 people died from opioid overdoses in 2021 alone.[145]

The modern opioid addiction epidemic in the United States traces to 1995 and the FDA's approval of Purdue Pharma's new opioid, OxyContin. "Regulators let the company make a claim for the drug that the agency officials have not allowed for any other drug before or since," writes Barry Meier in *Pain Killer: An Empire of Deceit and the Origin of America's Opioid Epidemic*. Published in 2003, Meier's book was one of the first major works to expose the roots of the opioid epidemic. "The FDA permitted Purdue to imply that OxyContin might pose a lower risk of abuse than traditional painkillers because it was a time-release narcotic."[146]

The claim of reduced addictiveness became the linchpin of Purdue's marketing strategy. The company launched an elaborate, sophisticated campaign to convince doctors that they had been under-treating pain— and that OxyContin was the answer to the problem they had failed to treat. The company invited thousands of doctors to junkets where Purdue spread its gospel. Purdue paid hundreds of doctors to participate in its speakers' bureau and persuade other physicians to join in prescribing OxyContin.[147]

By 1998, Purdue had hundreds of full-time sales reps pushing OxyContin. Their marketing push centered on OxyContin's purportedly less-addictive qualities.[148]

The campaign worked. Purdue's sales soared. Doctors casually wrote prescriptions for back pain and other chronic conditions. Dentists would order up a month's supply of OxyContin for dental work that might cause two days of significant pain. In the course of all this, a lot of people who were prescribed OxyContin ended up addicted to it. And as the drugs became plentiful, they started being shared for recreational use.

Some doctors and associated "pill mill" pharmacies started writing and filling scripts with reckless abandon. With a concentration in Appalachia and New England, the opioid addiction epidemic took off.

This is an ongoing public health catastrophe that was entirely preventable. Bad corporate actors knew what they were doing, but they didn't take account of the lives they were sacrificing, or simply didn't care. It was wicked. And we will be dealing with the consequences for many, many years to come.

It's now clear that Purdue knew early on that OxyContin was being widely abused. A 2006 Justice Department memo obtained by Barry Meier concluded that although the company was aware of widespread abuse, Purdue continued "in the face of this knowledge" to market OxyContin as less prone to abuse.[149]

The Justice Department memo determined that Purdue's representatives used the words "street value," "crush," or "snort"—that is, references to opioid abuse—in 117 internal notes recording their visits to doctors or other medical professionals from 1997 through 1999. The report also cited emails showing top company executives were informed about abuse.

Purdue Pharma aimed to deflect worries about abuse away from the company and onto those addicted. Richard Sackler, who was chair and president of the company, wrote in a 2001 email that "We have to hammer on abusers in every way possible. They are the culprits and the problem. They are reckless criminals."[150]

Justice Department prosecutors wanted to charge top Purdue executives with felonies, but they were overruled by higher-ups. In 2007, Purdue and some executives pled guilty to misdemeanors. Prosecutors told the court approving the settlement that it would send a message to drug makers selling opioids to stop illegal sales.

In the six years that followed, the *West Virginia Gazette-Mail* found, "drug wholesalers showered the state with 780 million hydrocodone and oxycodone pills, while 1,728 West Virginians fatally overdosed on those two painkillers." Fewer than two million people live in West Virginia. "The unfettered shipments amount to 433 pain pills for every man, woman and child in West Virginia."[151]

Other companies followed Purdue Pharma's lead with their own products.

A company called Endo "wanted its own version of OxyContin and sought to outdo Purdue to establish a flagship opioid drug in the marketplace," according to a lawsuit filed by the state of Tennessee.[152] Endo launched a version of an opioid called Opana in 2006 and then a reformulated version in 2011.

Endo followed the Purdue Pharma playbook, emphasizing claims of abuse deterrence—in fact claiming it was superior to OxyContin for its abuse deterrent qualities—but its product was more potent than OxyContin. According to the Tennessee lawsuit, "Endo made sure that the active ingredient for Opana ER was twice as potent as OxyContin's active ingredient, hired more sales representatives than Purdue to make even more sales calls, pushed the high-strength doses of Opana ER, sought to poach OxyContin's high-dose prescribers, and called on Tennessee specialists with a suspect need to prescribe extended release opioids, like podiatrists, gynecologists, sleep doctors, medical geneticists, and pediatric or adolescent specialists, something that even Purdue was hesitant to do."

An Endo consultant advised the company at the time it launched its new product that it should put in place a crisis management strategy to respond to stories about abuse of Opana.

Endo would pull Opana ER from the market in 2017.

In the Tennessee case, the judge found that Endo and its lawyers had engaged in a "coordinated strategy" to withhold evidence and entered a judgment of liability against the company, leaving the issue of damages for trial. The company then settled for $35 million.[153]

Insys Therapeutics was another copycat company, selling a sublingual fentanyl spray called Subsys. It would eventually plead guilty to numerous counts of fraud and settle with the federal government other charges of wrongdoing.[154]

Insys' innovation was to bribe doctors directly to prescribe Subsys, as it admitted in its settlement. It laundered the bribes through a speaker's program. "Purportedly in exchange for a practitioner educating other prescribers about Subsys, Insys agreed to pay the speaker a fee, also referred to as an 'honoraria,' for each speaking event," the company acknowledged in a statement of facts as part of its settlement. According to the settlement:

The Speaker Program included certain speaker practitioners who had the potential to prescribe Subsys, and was used to induce them to write more medically unnecessary prescriptions in exchange for payment of money by Insys in the form of honoraria. Insys fashioned the payments to these certain practitioners as speaker fees, or honoraria, in order to hide the fact that they were in fact bribes paid to induce certain practitioners to write Subsys prescriptions.[155]

The bribe payments were contingent on the doctor recipients writing a sufficient number of Subsys prescriptions.[156] Insys founder and CEO John Kapoor would be found guilty for orchestrating the bribery scheme and was sentenced to more than five years in prison.[157]

Yet for all the outrageous misconduct of these small companies, it was much bigger players who moved the most pills. These included large generic manufacturers like Mallinckrodt, major distributors like Cardinal Health, and the leading drug store chains. In 2006, Purdue Pharma manufactured 130 million pain pills; Mallinckrodt made almost 30 times as many.[158]

"Keep 'em coming!" one Mallinckrodt sales rep wrote to another. "Flyin' out of here. It's like people are addicted to these things or something. Oh, wait, people are ..."

"Just like Doritos," came the answer. "Keep eating, we'll make more."[159]

Lawsuits would eventually turn up a lot of company information showing that the large companies, like the smaller opioid manufacturers, were very aware of the abuse epidemic that was ballooning their profits.

Executives at AmerisourceBergen, the third-largest drug distributor in America, circulated an email chain containing a "Pillbillies" parody of the theme song from the 1960s CBS sitcom "The Beverly Hillbillies." The song made light of the pill mills in Florida that were handing out opioids in large numbers and fueling the addiction crisis in Appalachia:

"Well, the first thing you know, ol' Jed's a-drivin' South," the parody went. *"Kinfolk said 'Jed, don't put too many in your mouth.' / Said 'Sunny Florida is the place you ought to be!' / So they loaded up the truck and drove speedily. / South, that is. / Pain Clinics, cash 'n' carry. / A Bevy of Pillbillies!"*[160]

Officials at the Drug Enforcement Administration (DEA) caught on to what the big guys were doing. They recognized that going after unethical individual doctors and pill mills would never solve the problem of opioids flooding the streets; they had to go after the big fish.

In *American Cartel: Inside the Battle to Bring Down the Opioid Industry,* *Washington Post* reporters Scott Higham and Sari Horwitz documented the response from the major players to DEA's increasingly aggressive enforcement strategy: They fought back.[161]

These weren't tiny corporations. They had economic and political power, and they knew how to play the Washington insider game. In 2016, the industry maneuvered to sneak through Congress a change in DEA's enforcement authority, crafted by a former top DEA lawyer hired by the industry. The change affected when DEA could issue an "immediate suspension order" shutting down a facility until a court hearing. Prior to the change, DEA could act in the face of "imminent" danger. After the change, it had to show "immediate" danger—an extraordinarily difficult standard when a factory or drug company is making or selling a drug that is hurting people far away and distant in time. After the change, Higham and Horwitz report, the DEA never again used this most potent tool.

To ease pressure from the DEA, the industry also hired high-powered lawyers, many of whom had previously worked for the DEA or Department of Justice, including Jamie Gorelick, a former deputy attorney general during the Clinton administration. These industry lawyers went to top officials in the Justice Department to complain about the DEA's enforcement activity. Eventually, an industry-friendly administrator was named to head the DEA. In 2015, he forced out of the agency the man who had led DEA's crackdown on the manufacturers, distributors and drug stores—Joe Rannazzisi, the head of the DEA's Office of Diversion Control.

Rannazzisi didn't go quietly. He teamed up with the lawyers who had started filing hundreds and then thousands of lawsuits against the industry on behalf of local and state governments and others who had suffered many billions in economic damages as a result of the industry-caused addiction epidemic. That litigation, along with the heroic advocacy of families affected by the epidemic, eventually led to a clampdown on industry supply of easy-access opioids.

In many ways, however, it was too late. Not only had the industry directly inflicted vast damage, it had built a huge market. When legally manufactured pills dried up on the streets, they were quickly replaced with the illegal opioids now washing over the country.

CHAPTER 5

Big Pharma's Political Influence Machine

At the turn of the century, Big Pharma was facing a serious problem: The public was furious about high drug prices and it looked like Congress might actually do something about it.

In what would become a pattern, however, the industry used its power to perform a master act of political jujitsu, turning threat into advantage—and making hundreds of billions of dollars in the process.

Apart from military contractors, Big Pharma is arguably the industry sector most dependent on the federal government. It relies on the massive investments the U.S. government makes in biomedical research. It benefits from exclusive licenses to government-funded medicinal inventions, with no reciprocal obligations to keep prices reasonable. Its business model relies on government-granted monopolies, in the form of patents and various marketing exclusivities. It needs the Food and Drug Administration (FDA) to approve its products in order to give them a Good Housekeeping seal of approval—but it doesn't want the FDA to be too tough. And it depends on Medicare as the biggest purchaser of drugs in the world—a purchaser barred by law from negotiating prices, with only a few exceptions.

With so much riding on government decision-making, it's not surprising that Big Pharma invests heavily in obtaining political influence. While the industry is a significant election campaign spender, it is also, by far and every year, the biggest lobbying spender in Washington. The industry gains influence as well by cultivating medical professionals and doctors to promote its wares and preferred policies. And unique among other Big Business sectors, it funds an array of patient groups—representing or purporting to represent people with specific diseases—to serve as a grassroots force amplifying its demands.

All this makes a difference—a big difference—in Washington. There may be widespread fury in the nation over high drug prices, with overwhelming public support for very aggressive measures to restrain drug pricing. But it takes the most heroic public campaigns and decades of work to achieve even modest price reforms.

That's not all. Big Pharma helped craft legislation that makes it a direct, major funder of the FDA, the agency that is supposed to regulate it. Every five years, the FDA and Big Pharma engage in negotiations, with very modest participation by consumer advocates, over how much Big Pharma should pay the agency and what policies the agency should adopt or adjust for reviewing new drug approvals.

Marauding Medicare

The problem for Big Pharma at the turn of the century centered on widespread distress over ever-escalating drug prices, especially the impact on seniors, who were increasingly unable to afford needed medicines. Drug coverage was part of the original scheme for Medicare, but it was dropped in 1965 out of concern even then that it would be too expensive.[162] Over the subsequent decades, pressure to add a Medicare drug benefit ebbed and flowed but grew intense in the 1990s and into the 2000s. The issue was hotly debated in the 2000 election.

Big Pharma feared a Medicare drug program that would control prices. Seeing grave political risk, the industry deployed its political power. In the 2002 midterm election, the industry spent heavily for Republicans, receiving—and taking—credit for enabling the Republicans to gain seats in the midterms, something that had not occurred for the party of a first-term president since the Civil War.

"Having spent more than $30 million to help elect their allies to Congress," reported *The New York Times,* "the major drug companies are devising ways to capitalize on their electoral success by securing favorable new legislation and countering the pressure that lawmakers in both parties feel to lower the cost of prescription drugs, industry officials say." Despite the rising public pressure for action on drug pricing, "the industry's hand appears stronger now than at any other time in recent years," the *Times* noted.[163]

In 2003, in a shift from its prior posture, the Bush administration called for a Medicare drug benefit. The debate over whether and how to create a new benefit fell largely along party lines, but it was Republicans who pushed for the plan eventually adopted. Democrats opposed the plan, arguing it both failed to provide sufficient benefits to consumers and would also unjustifiably fatten Big Pharma's bottom line by failing to include cost-containment measures.

Medicare Part D came into effect, but only as the result of extraordinary maneuvers. In the early hours of November 22, 2003, it appeared the bill creating the new prescription drug benefit would fail on the House floor. At 3 a.m., after the normal 15 minutes of voting, opponents had 15 more votes than supporters. Republican House leaders held the vote open for three hours. They strong-armed members; Secretary of Health and Human Services Tommy Thompson came onto the House floor to lobby members;

President Bush made early-morning calls; rumors would later emerge of political gifts offered in exchange for votes.[164] The heavy-handed tactics worked, and the bill passed. After a transition period, the full-fledged program began in 2006.

Medicare Part D did create a drug pricing insurance program for seniors, but it was a deeply flawed one. Seniors still had to make substantial payments for their drugs and, until a recent reform, were stuck paying thousands of dollars annually when in the "donut hole"—after they had hit the limit of their insurance coverage and before catastrophic coverage kicked in.[165]

For Big Pharma, Medicare Part D was a total winner. It created a new market for sales, it let the air out of the protest movement demanding pricing reform and, crucially, it included virtually no pricing restraint. This was a stunning achievement for the industry. Medicare Part D would become (and now is[166]) the world's largest drug buyer—and it was forbidden to negotiate prices.

Under the Medicare Modernization Act that created the Medicare drug benefit, Medicare Part D is not allowed to "interfere with the negotiations between drug manufacturers and pharmacies and [Part D plan] sponsors."[167] While Medicare Part D plan sponsors can obtain substantial rebates from both drug manufacturers and pharmacies, the federal program is prohibited from leveraging its purchasing power to realize economies of scale, due to this "noninterference" clause.

This prohibition on negotiation is completely irrational—and the direct result of the corrupting political influence of Big Pharma. It was House and Energy Committee Chair Billy Tauzin, R-Louisiana, who ensured that the new Medicare Part D drug purchasing program would prevent Medicare from negotiating drug prices.[168] Then, as the Medicare Part D legislation was being signed into law, he negotiated a new job heading up PhRMA, the industry trade association, with a reported annual salary of $2 million.[169]

Yes, you read that right: The guy who ensured this enormous gift for Big Pharma left Congress immediately afterwards and went on to head the industry's trade association.

Predictably, prohibiting negotiation with monopolists leads to price gouging and dramatic overspending. The excess profits for Big Pharma—and costs to taxpayers and consumers—have been jaw-dropping.

In 2019, the House of Representatives passed a Medicare drug price negotiation bill, the Elijah E. Cummings Lower Drug Costs Now Act. All 228 Democrats voted for the bill. Two Republicans voted for it; 191 opposed.[170] The bill would stall in the Senate.

The 2019 bill authorized negotiation for the most expensive pharmaceuticals, but not all; and it did not include the most effective method (licensing of generic competition) for lowering prices of drugs when manufacturers refuse to agree to a reasonable price. Still, the Congressional Budget Office estimated that it would have saved taxpayers $456 billion over 10 years.[171] That's an awful lot of money. It's money that comes out of taxpayers' hides and goes directly into Big Pharma's coffers.

Serious health costs, as well as well as monetary costs, result from inflated drug prices under Medicare Part D. Remember, almost one in three Americans are rationing prescriptions because they can't afford them. The result is needless suffering from treatable conditions and frequently worsened health and increased medical costs, as conditions that are preventable with drug treatment require more aggressive interventions.

In August 2022, Congress finally passed and President Biden signed into law a package that, for the first time, authorized Medicare negotiation of drug prices. Every Republican voted against the bill. Even this measure, however, is incredibly modest. It permits Medicare to negotiate prices only for a limited number of drugs, and only after they have been on the market—with no price restraint—for a number of years. Big Pharma price gouging is so severe that even this limited measure is projected to save taxpayers more than $150 billion over 10 years. But it is a testament to Big Pharma's extraordinary influence that the Democrats could not unite on a more aggressive package. Instead, a handful of Pharma-aligned Democrats sabotaged the more aggressive approach that the House had passed in 2019.[172]

Compromising Drug Safety

Before people can pay for overpriced medicines, the drugs must first receive approval from the FDA. Big Pharma has compromised that process too, exerting startling influence over the agency that is supposed to regulate drug companies and protect Americans from unsafe medicines.

The process by which the FDA evaluates and approves medicines for sale has long been regarded as the world's gold standard. Medicines must go through an extensive trial process.[173] Drug makers first test a new product on animals and show it is not toxic. Then they may seek authorization from the FDA to begin trials in humans. They must undertake early-stage trials to show that medicines are relatively safe for humans, and then must show that they actually work to treat a disease or condition, and do not have severe side effects. Then they undertake larger trials to show that the drug works and to monitor for common adverse reactions. Once they have gone through this lengthy process, a drug maker can seek approval for a new product, submitting all of its clinical trial data. The FDA reviews the data and often convenes an expert advisory panel to assess the drug approval application. Taking into account any panel's recommendation, the FDA makes a final determination.

The FDA's precautionary approach to approving medicines has served Americans well. Its quintessential success, perhaps, was protecting Americans from thalidomide, a drug widely prescribed in Europe in the 1950s for insomnia and morning sickness. The drug caused thousands of babies to be born with severe disabilities. That situation was largely averted in the United States because Dr. Frances Kelsey, a drug reviewer at the FDA, refused to approve the drug (though as many as 20,000 Americans received the drug in trials).[174] The thalidomide story, in fact, generated momentum for reforms that created the modern framework for FDA drug approval.[175]

Unfortunately, the FDA's gold standard of approval has been badly tarnished in recent decades. Big Pharma does not share patients' interest in careful and deliberate FDA review of drug approvals. Drug companies want their products approved as quickly as possible. Their profit interest pushes them to seek approval for drugs that may be unsafe or are of dubious efficacy. And for the last 30 years, the industry has succeeded in compromising the FDA.

The transformational change happened in 1992, with passage of the Prescription Drug User Fee Act (PDUFA). On its face, the idea behind PDUFA might have seemed reasonable at the outset. The FDA was underfunded. Drug companies needed and benefited from FDA approvals of their product. Why not make the drug companies pay directly? That was the idea behind "user fees"—payments from drug companies to fund the drug review process.

The problem, however, was embodied in the name of the law: Are drug companies really the "users" of the FDA? Does the FDA exist to serve the drug companies who submit drug approval requests, or is its purpose to protect patients and the public interest?

The PDUFA process has provided Big Pharma with enormous direct leverage over the agency that is supposed to regulate the industry. And it's not just that Big Pharma is literally paying the agency. Congress authorizes PDUFA for five-year periods. The reauthorization for another five-year period is considered "must-pass" legislation, because the agency is now dependent on its user fee revenue. In advance of the reauthorization, FDA enters negotiations with the industry over changes to the drug approval process. Consumer groups like Public Citizen now have some modest role in this process, but it remains basically a negotiation between FDA and Big Pharma. The result of the negotiations is passed on to Congress, which generally rubber-stamps the negotiated deal.

Think about that: Big Pharma is negotiating the terms for drug approvals—and it has leverage, because it is footing the bill. Big Pharma and other user-fee funding now accounts for nearly two-thirds of FDA's funding that is focused on human drug issues.[176]

Figure 9. FDA Spending, by Source, Fiscal Year 1992–Fiscal Year 2020

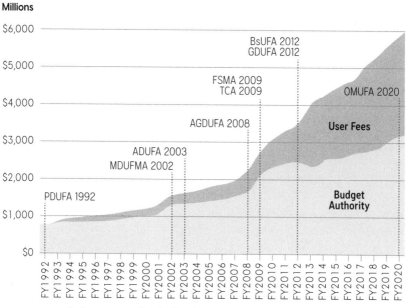

Millions

BsUFA 2012
GDUFA 2012

FSMA 2009
TCA 2009

OMUFA 2020

AGDUFA 2008

User Fees

ADUFA 2003
MDUFMA 2002

PDUFA 1992

Budget
Authority

Budget sources data by fiscal year; laws by calendar year of enactment.

Source: Congressional Research Service.

These five-year approvals function primarily as a means for the industry to extract concessions. Provisions in the 1997 deal, for example, launched direct-to-consumer advertising (the TV ads for pharmaceuticals that now blanket the airwaves) and made it possible for drug companies to promote drugs for "off-label" purposes—other than the purpose for which they were approved by the FDA.

One recent review concludes: "The majority of policy changes enacted through PDUFA legislation have favored industry through decreasing regulatory standards, shortening approval times, and increasing industry involvement in FDA decision-making. FDA's budgetary dependence on the industry, the urgency of each PDUFA reauthorization's passage to maintain uninterrupted funding, and the industry's required participation in PDUFA negotiations may advantage the industry."[177]

And the problem is even worse than that. Since the start of PDUFA, the FDA has more and more come to view drug corporations as its clients, rather than as businesses it is supposed to regulate.

The culture shift at FDA in favor of greenlighting drugs happened right away. In 1998, Public Citizen sent a detailed, confidential survey to the 172 reviewing medical officers in the FDA center that reviews and approves drugs.[178] Roughly a third (51) replied. Thirty-four of the medical officers stated that the pressure on them to approve new drugs was "somewhat greater" or "much greater" compared to the period prior to 1995. They reported that drugs were being approved that should not be. One medical officer stated, "We are in the midst now to approve everything but to describe drug weaknesses in the label. As one high-ranking official said, 'Everything is approvable. We can use the labeling creatively to lower the problems.'"

It was inevitable that this new approach would lead to dangerous and inappropriate drug approvals, and that happened quickly. Between June and November 1997, the FDA approved the heart drug Posicor; the anti-inflammatory painkiller Duract; and the antibiotic Raxar. All had known safety problems prior to approval. All were redundant: multiple other options were available to patients and physicians for the conditions these drugs were approved to address. Posicor was the ninth member of the calcium channel-blocker family of high blood pressure lowering drugs. Duract was the 20th nonsteroidal anti-inflammatory drug (NSAID) on the market. Raxar was the eighth fluoroquinolone antibiotic cleared for marketing.

All three of these drugs killed and injured patients before they were withdrawn from the market within two years of approval, between June 1998 and October 1999. Public Citizen testified in 2002: "We do not believe that these drugs would have been approved in the pre-user fee era."[179]

A top priority for Big Pharma was to speed up the review process. To be clear, there are undoubtedly cases where expedited review is appropriate on health grounds—and FDA innovated processes for accelerated review starting with HIV/AIDS medicines (and before PDUFA came into effect). When it comes to faster reviews based on lesser standards of evidence, however, Big Pharma's concern is profit, not health.

In the current era, accelerated approvals have become normal even in the absence of strong public health rationales. Nine medical officers in the 1998 Public Citizen survey identified 19 new drugs that they had reviewed in the previous three years that they said had been inappropriately shifted to the accelerated approval track. Even more troublingly, a dozen medical officers identified 25 new drugs that they reviewed in the previous three years that in their opinion had been approved too fast.

In practical terms, accelerated drug review means that medical officers don't have the time to demand more information from drug corporations. Instead, they are pressed to greenlight drugs in the face of uncertainty. Making matters worse, Big Pharma has maneuvered for expedited review of drugs that don't meet priority health needs. Patient health is inevitably compromised in the process.

Drugs with priority review have been forced off the market or required to make major revisions to their product labeling. For example, a drug for Type-2 diabetes, Rezulin, was granted a priority review and approved in January 1997, even though numerous other drugs were available for the treatment of this disease. Three years later, the drug was withdrawn after reports of 90 cases of liver failure, including 63 deaths and seven organ transplants.[180]

One major problem with the FDA's accelerated approval process that was pushed by Big Pharma is that it allows drugs to be approved based on surrogate markers, rather than on actual impacts against a disease or condition. The idea is that a drug's efficacy can be judged by whether it affects a bodily condition that *correlates* with a disease, especially where it may be difficult to measure impact on the underlying disease or condition. The problem, of course, is that people don't care about the surrogate marker—they care about their health problem.

The inappropriate reliance on surrogates played a key role in one of the worst FDA decisions in its history, the 2021 approval of Biogen's drug aducanumab for the treatment of Alzheimer's disease. The FDA took this action despite the nearly unanimous conclusion of an independent panel of experts the agency convened in November 2020—and of many other scientists, neurologists and geriatric specialists—that there was inadequate evidence that the drug is effective in slowing cognitive decline in patients with Alzheimer's.[181]

Biogen stopped aducanumab's clinical trials early because a preliminary analysis found that they were unlikely to show benefits for Alzheimer's patients. In an unprecedented move, however, the FDA and Biogen collaborated to salvage the drug. They jointly relied on dubious analyses that overemphasized the results of one trial that suggested a high dose of the drug might provide minimal benefit on one measure of cognitive function, but they disregarded data from the other trial, which showed no benefit at any dose. For the meeting of the FDA's independent panel of experts, the agency and Biogen co-authored an unprecedented joint briefing document on aducanumab that was heavily biased in its favor.

The independent panel harshly rejected Biogen's proposal for approval. It was unprecedented for a drug trial to be stopped in midstream for failing, and then for one of two trials to be reinterpreted and the other simply ignored. This kind of data "cherry picking" is exactly what the FDA approval process is designed to prevent.

One member of the panel, Dr. Scott Emerson, Professor Emeritus of Biostatistics at the University of Washington, said, "This analysis seems to be subject to the Texas sharpshooter fallacy, a name for the joke of someone first firing a shotgun at a barn and then painting a target around the bullet holes."[182]

But then the FDA simply disregarded the views of the expert panel—a rarity—and approved the Alzheimer's drug anyway. Using its accelerated approval pathway, the FDA based its approval on findings that aducanumab reduced amyloid plaques in the brains of Alzheimer's disease patients—a surrogate endpoint. The agency claimed that "it is expected that the reduction in amyloid plaque will result in a reduction in clinical decline."[183] However, other experimental drugs that reduced amyloid plaques in the brain of Alzheimer's patients failed to provide any clinical benefits, nor had any such benefit been seen in the two phase 3 trials of aducanumab.

It gets worse. Biogen's studies evaluated aducanumab only in subjects with mild Alzheimer's disease, yet the FDA inexcusably approved the drug "for the treatment of Alzheimer's disease," period, meaning Biogen can market the drug for use in any patient with Alzheimer's, regardless of disease severity. Patients with more severe disease may well be more susceptible to the adverse brain effects.

Then, compounding the outrage, Biogen announced an exorbitant price for aducanumab—$56,000 a year. Given the size of the Alzheimer's population—500,000 Americans—Medicare determined that it would need to raise premiums at roughly twice the rate it otherwise would have, just to cover this one drug.[184] The Kaiser Family Foundation estimated an annual cost to Medicare of $30 billion.[185]

Under pressure, Biogen lowered its price. But the biggest blow against the company's drug came in 2022, when the Centers for Medicare and Medicaid Services determined that Medicare would not pay for the drug at all, except for individuals enrolled in high-quality clinical trials.[186]

It was a welcome but still shocking development: Americans found that they could not rely on the compromised FDA to make evidence-based decisions on a critical drug application. The agency has become too compromised despite its reputation, and is now a paper tiger. Instead, Americans had to be rescued from the Biogen decision that would have offered false hope to hundreds of thousands of patients and their families, potentially endangered some, and imposed tens of billions in annual extra costs on Medicare.

CHAPTER 6

Plunder and Pillage: Big Pharma's Corporate Welfare

Government funding contributes to the invention and development of virtually every new drug.[187]

Think about that for a moment. Government spending in biomedical research and development (R&D) is the foundation for everything Big Pharma does.

So how does Big Pharma repay the favor? By making *us* pay—and pay and pay—for the very medicines that we taxpayers helped develop.

This is a colossal rip-off, but it's a lot more than that. People need essential medicines. As we've seen, when they can't afford the drugs, they can face financial ruin. Or they can choose to ration their prescriptions or not fill them at all. When poorer countries can't afford expensive medicines or when supplies are short, epidemics can intensify or, as we've now seen with Covid-19, pandemics can persist.

If the U.S. government helped pay for medicine development, isn't it reasonable to demand that drug corporations set prices taxpayers can afford? If drug companies can't produce enough of the needed medicines, shouldn't the government step in to alleviate shortages?

Those commonsense approaches are not how the system works.

Instead, the U.S. government invests a ton of money in biomedical R&D, then transfers exclusive, unconditional control over the inventions it funds to drug corporations.

Giving Away Taxpayer-Funded R&D

The U.S. government spends tens of billions of dollars every year supporting biomedical research, primarily through the National Institutes of Health (NIH). The NIH budget in fiscal year 2022 was $45 billion; that funded the NIH's own research and supported research grants to universities across the country.

NIH supports basic research—the building block research that expands global knowledge and creates the foundation for new inventions. Corporations completely depend on this research, but they won't fund it directly, because it is too many steps away from commercial application.

NIH also supports applied research—efforts to take general scientific knowledge and address specific problems. This is the research that most often leads to patentable inventions, though especially with the rise of biotechnology, the lines between basic and applied research are no longer as clear as they once were.

NIH also spends an increasing amount of money on development—clinical trials to test drugs or other inventions and get them to market.

All this research is absolutely fundamental to Big Pharma. In 2018, researchers at Bentley University found that "NIH funding contributed to published research associated with every one of the 210 new drugs approved by the Food and Drug Administration from 2010-2016."[188] *Every one!*

"Collectively," they found, "this research involved more than 200,000 years of grant funding totaling more than $100 billion."[189] That's a lot of public support.

When the government funds basic research, it puts the results in the public domain; the research is available for anyone to read, incorporate into their work, build on, and so on.

Things are different when the government pays for research that leads to patentable inventions. If the government funds don't lead *directly* to a new invention, the government doesn't claim any ownership rights. This is a choice. When the government provides a research grant, it could claim rights in inventions it helps to bring into being. But this doesn't happen.

Instead, only when government funding leads *directly* to an invention does the government claim ownership rights. But under current law and practice, NIH manages its ownership rights (often called "intellectual property") only with the goal of getting new drugs to market—without regard to whether drug corporations will charge reasonable prices for the medicines invented with public funds.

The main law that determines what happens with the fruits of federally sponsored R&D is known as Bayh-Dole (after its senate sponsors, Democrat Birch Bayh of Indiana and Republican Bob Dole of Kansas). In 1980, Bayh-Dole and related laws created a system where the National Institutes of Health and the universities it funds license their government-funded inventions to drug corporations on an exclusive basis. In other words, the licenses confer monopolies for each new drug.

Under Bayh-Dole, agencies and universities could require licensees to agree to price products reasonably, but they almost never do. In fact, in 1995, the NIH ended the use of the "reasonable pricing" clauses it had included in some licenses. "Eliminating the clause will promote research that can enhance the health of the American people," said the then-head of NIH, Dr. Harold Varmus.[190]

That claim was untrue then, and it's not true now. But it does show how much sway Big Pharma has exerted over federal research agencies. The corporations have convinced the federal research administrators that merely requiring the companies to be "reasonable" would diminish the companies' readiness to invest in R&D. Of course, the idea of creating an alleged incentive for R&D ignores the fact that the federal government has already done the hardest work, performing basic research and identifying promising new inventions.

There's nothing inevitable about this corrupt way of doing business, as a quick historical tour shows.

The Bayh-Dole Act represented a significant shift from previous policy. Following the creation of a major federal role in research sponsorship in World War II, the Justice Department concluded in 1947 that "where patentable inventions are made in the course of performing a Government-financed contract for research and development, the public interest requires that all rights to such inventions be assigned to the Government and not left to the private ownership of the contractor." The Justice Department recommended also that "as a basic policy all Government-owned inventions should be made fully, freely and unconditionally available to the public without charge, by public dedication or by royalty-free, non-exclusive licensing."[191] In other words, all people and businesses should have equal access to use and further develop government-funded inventions.

The Justice Department offered what remains a compelling case for non-exclusive licensing: "Public control will assure free and equal availability of the inventions to American industry and science; will eliminate any competitive advantage to the contractor chosen to perform the research work; will avoid undue concentration of economic power in the hands of a few large corporations; will tend to increase and diversify available research facilities within the United States to the advantage of the Government and of the national economy; and will thus strengthen our American system of free, competitive enterprise."

Even in 1947, the Justice Department position was not uniform within the federal government. The Defense Department consistently maintained a policy of allowing contractors to gain title to government-sponsored inventions, so long as the Pentagon was able to maintain a royalty-free right to use the invention. In the ensuing decades, government policy evolved unevenly between different agencies, with some gradual increase in exclusive rights transfers to private parties.

Beginning in the mid-1970s, Big Business, in collaboration with partners at major research universities, began lobbying for a major transformation in government patent policy. Based on highly questionable evidence, the business-university alliance argued that exclusive licensing was necessary to spur private sector innovation and development of government-funded inventions.

In 1980, Congress passed the Bayh-Dole Act, which authorized universities and small business contractors to take title to government-sponsored inventions. Universities were in turn permitted to license exclusively to private corporations, including big businesses. In 1983, President Ronald Reagan issued a Presidential Memorandum that instructed executive agencies to grant exclusivity on inventions to contractors of all sizes. In 1986, Congress passed the Federal Technology Transfer Act, which authorized federal laboratories to enter into exclusive contracts with corporations to develop and market inventions originating in the federal labs.

The Bayh-Dole Act was contentious from before its passage. Other alternatives proposed at the time included a suggestion by Admiral Hyman Rickover that government inventions be licensed non-exclusively for a period of six months; and that if no party had indicated an interest in commercialization, that the patent then be open to competitive bidding for an exclusive license. A proposal by President Carter, which passed the House of Representatives prior to passage of the Bayh-Dole Act, would have limited the exclusive license granted by the government to designated "fields of use."

In the many hearings and years of debate that preceded Bayh-Dole, three intertwined concerns were preeminent. First was concern about whether the government was getting repaid for its investment. Second was a concern that licensees would obtain windfall profits. The public had paid for the invention, cutting the investment costs of the company that would obtain control over the invention, but would the pricing fairly reflect the public subsidy? Would the monopoly patent rights enable the licensee to earn unfair super-profits? Third was the impact of the licensing arrangements on market competition and market structure. Patents provide monopolies for the covered invention, and patent protection is in perpetual tension with antitrust policies. Would the conferment of exclusive rights to publicly funded inventions create or deepen market concentration? Would it enable licensees to engage in anti-competitive behavior?

Senators Bayh and Dole acknowledged the concern about windfall profits. They favored measures for "recoupment," so that the government would be repaid for its R&D expenditures. But this idea was dropped.[192]

Other measures were included and did remain in the statute to address potential abuses. One safeguard was to give the federal government a license to use any invention it had helped fund. At the time of the Bayh-Dole debates, the federal government's paid-up license to use subject inventions was considered the most basic governmental right.

A second key protection was the right of the government to "march in" and issue licenses to parties other than the contractor or a university licensee, including in circumstances when the federally sponsored invention was not achieving practical application, or to meet health needs, or when public use needs were not being met. In the debates leading up to Bayh-Dole's passage, march-in rights were advocated as a key tool to restrain pricing or patent abuse.[193]

Unfortunately, the concerns that Bayh-Dole would give rise to abusive behavior were prescient. Even more unfortunately, the government has largely failed to exercise the safeguards that Congress included in the statute, as we will see.

The result is a public policy outrage, and a public health tragedy. U.S. taxpayers pay to fund R&D. The government turns the fruits of the research over to pharmaceutical and biotechnology companies, which then price-gouge U.S. consumers and even the government itself. Thus the industry executes a double swindle of the public.

And, this double swindle imposes huge public health costs. Let's look at a few cases.

The cancer drug Xtandi: Xtandi (generic name: enzalutamide) is a medicine to treat advanced prostate cancer, sold by Astellas and Pfizer. Xtandi is exorbitantly priced by any measure. In 2020, it cost $129,000 per year, or close to $90 per capsule.[194] The price of Xtandi is three to five times higher in the United States than in other rich countries. In 2020, Astellas and Pfizer made more money selling Xtandi in the U.S. than from the rest of the world combined.[195] The year before, Medicare spent more than $1 billion on the drug before rebates. A Canadian manufacturer once offered to sell generic enzalutamide to the U.S. government for $3 per capsule, but the offer was declined.[196]

Patients can't afford the sky-high price. For one patient who was briefly placed on the treatment, filling just one prescription cost $625 out-of-pocket. "Drugs like Xtandi force families to focus on and worry about price tags," he wrote in a submission to the Department of Health and Human Services. "Please allow American prostate cancer patients the same right to access affordable care as patients around the world."[197]

The high price of Xtandi also raises concerns about health equity. Black men die from prostate cancer at twice the rate of white men and may have a disproportionate need for the exorbitantly priced drug.[198]

Xtandi was invented at University of California, Los Angeles (UCLA) with U.S. government grants provided by the National Institutes of Health and the U.S. Army. U.S. government funds also helped pay for the early-stage clinical trials of the drug.

In 2016, Knowledge Ecology International and the Union for Affordable Cancer Treatment petitioned the NIH and Department of Defense to exercise their Bayh-Dole "march-in" rights and license other manufacturers to make generic versions of enzalutamide. The petition argued that "it is unreasonable, and indeed outrageous, that prices are higher in the United States than in foreign countries, for a drug invented at UCLA using federal government grants."[199]

In their petition, the groups said Xtandi was a classic case for government action: "The Bayh-Dole Act was passed with the promise that the federal march-in rights or the federal government royalty-free rights in patents would be available to protect the public from the unreasonable use of patented inventions. This is such a case."[200]

NIH and the Department of Defense did not agree.[201] Their logic: Xtandi is available for purchase.

Yes, that's what they really said! According to NIH and the Defense Department, the only obligation of a drug company licensee is that they try to develop a drug and put it on the market. Bayh-Dole actually requires drug companies to make their licensed drugs "available to the public *on reasonable terms*" (emphasis added), but NIH and the Pentagon ignored this requirement. And that is how NIH has treated every march-in request it has received.

Prostate cancer patients revived the request to the Department of Defense and NIH in 2021.[202] In 2023, the Biden administration rejected the request, echoing the faulty logic of the earlier refusal.

The multiple myeloma drug Revlimid: Revlimid (generic name: lenalidomide) is a drug for the treatment of multiple myeloma and other forms of cancer. It was made and sold by a biotech company called Celgene until 2019, when Celgene was acquired by Bristol Myers Squibb. It is another super-expensive cancer therapy, costing more than $16,000 a month.

Revlimid was the subject of an extraordinary study by the House of Representative Oversight and Government Reform Committee. The committee staff reviewed 50,000 pages of internal company documents.[203] They found outrage after outrage—compounded by the fact that Celgene had depended heavily on publicly funded research for the breakthroughs in the Revlimid development process.

"After launching Revlimid in 2005," the committee found, "Celgene raised the price of the drug 22 times—as many as three times in a single year. Through those price increases, Celgene more than tripled the price of Revlimid—from $215 per pill at launch to $719 per pill in 2019. After acquiring Celgene, Bristol Myers Squibb (BMS) further increased the price of Revlimid to $763 per pill. In 2005, a monthly supply of Revlimid was priced at $4,515. Today, the same monthly supply is priced at $16,023."

Internal documents obtained by the committee showed that pricing decisions were determined by two things. The first was the need to hit earnings goals. In one case in 2014, Celgene's CEO Mark Alles orchestrated an "emergency" price increase. "I have to consider every legitimate opportunity available to us to improve our Q1 [first quarter] performance," he wrote.

The other factor driving prices was executive compensation. For the Celgene chair and CEO, performance bonuses were larger than their base salary. To get those bonuses, they had to hit earnings targets.

Prohibited from negotiating prices, Medicare is the biggest sucker in this deal. From 2010 to 2018, Medicare Part D paid $17.5 billion to Celgene, more than $4 billion in 2018 alone.

But the worst victims are patients who couldn't afford the medicine. The Kaiser Family Foundation found the average out-of-pocket cost for Medicare patients in 2019 was more than $14,000.[204] Celgene was and is well aware of patient hardships, but that hasn't changed anything.

To rationalize its outrageous prices, Celgene has fallen back on the industry trope of blaming the high cost of R&D. That claim is ridiculous. Celgene has generated more than $50 billion in revenues on Revlimid, so it long ago recovered any research costs it had.

But the claim is even more appalling because Celgene relied so heavily on publicly funded research. At every stage of the drug's development, government funding drove the breakthrough findings—Celgene just followed along:[205]

- Celgene acquired the rights to Revlimid's precursor drug, thalidomide, from Rockefeller University. Thalidomide had been a disaster as a drug prescribed to pregnant mothers, but Rockefeller University researchers—funded in part by the U.S. Public Health Service—found it could be helpful for HIV/AIDS and some cancers.

- Later, researchers at Boston Children's Hospital discovered thalidomide and a chemical analog worked to suppress tumor growth. They convinced colleagues at the University of Arkansas Medical Center. This led to a larger, government-funded study that showed thalidomide was effective in treating multiple myeloma. "It was only after learning of the initial success of this study that Celgene decided to invest in larger trials that would be needed to receive FDA approval to sell thalidomide as a treatment for multiple myeloma."

- Then researchers at the Dana Farber Cancer Institute, funded by NIH, published research showing that thalidomide analogs (chemically similar versions)—including the compound that would be named Revlimid—were more effective than thalidomide itself. "It was only after these three federally funded studies demonstrated positive results for Revlimid that Celgene invested in additional trials to obtain FDA approval to sell Revlimid to patients with multiple myeloma."

- The story repeated itself again with studies for newly diagnosed patients with multiple myeloma. Government-supported researchers produced the first promising results; only after those early results did Celgene start investing in follow-on research.

- And it happened yet again with research on using Revlimid as a maintenance therapy for multiple myeloma patients who had stem cell transplants. It was publicly financed research that demonstrated this purpose for Revlimid.

In sum, the committee found, Celgene "contributed very little to the science first establishing that drugs like Revlimid could be an effective treatment for multiple myeloma. Rather, Celgene benefited from the acquisition of a decades-old product, academic and non-profit research, and at least eight federally funded studies."

And it paid back American taxpayers by price-gouging Medicare and American patients.

HIV/AIDS medicines: When HIV/AIDS first emerged as a disease of prevalence in the 1980s, an AIDS diagnosis was understood to be a death sentence. The toll in the United States, especially among gay men, was staggering.

In the early 1990s, effective AIDS medications were discovered. By the mid-1990s, scientists had shown that combining medicines led to very effective treatment. Death rates in the United States fell sharply.

But the disease globalized, with Africa the epicenter of an intensifying epidemic. Millions more people were being infected every year and drug treatments were almost wholly unavailable.

The reason? They were too expensive. Combination therapy cost $10,000 a year per person or more. In the United States, this cost was largely covered by insurance, including a new government insurance initiative through the Ryan White HIV/AIDS program.

In developing countries, the $10,000+ price tag was simply unaffordable. It was utterly unimaginable in African countries with per capita incomes of $800 or less. Unaffordable medicines meant that HIV/AIDS remained a death sentence in Africa and other developing regions—even though life-saving medicines were available.

Making this all the more scandalous: The first generation of AIDS drugs relied very heavily on government investment. Five of the earliest AIDS drugs were patented by NIH or research institutions reliant on NIH funding.[206]

Under the terms of Bayh-Dole, the U.S. government maintained rights in the drugs it had invented or helped fund. One of those rights was an automatic right to use the inventions for itself, or to license them to international organizations. That meant the U.S. government could have licensed the medicines in which it had rights to the World Health Organization, which could have had them manufactured cheaply. NIH declined to take this step, however.

Drug company monopolies and high prices led to millions of people dying needlessly. That's a tragic fact we know with certainty because we have the counterfactual evidence.

In 2001, Cipla, an Indian generic manufacturer, announced that it could manufacture a generic version of triple-drug therapies for $350 per year.[207] That was a game changer. African countries maneuvered around global patent rules to find ways to access generic AIDS drugs.[208] Generic prices would eventually fall to below $100 a year.

The more affordable prices spurred the Bush administration to create the President's Emergency Plan for AIDS Relief (PEPFAR). PEPFAR would go on to channel billions into HIV/AIDS treatment and prevention in developing countries. It was joined by a new Global Fund to Fight AIDS, Tuberculosis and Malaria, which also transferred billions into the fight.

As a result, global AIDS deaths have declined steadily from a peak in 2004 at 2 million a year, now down to 650,000 annually. More than 28 million people around the world are receiving life-saving AIDS therapies.[209]

Still, as new HIV/AIDS therapies have been developed, new problems have arisen.

Descovy is a two-drug combination used as preventative (PrEP) treatment for HIV, in addition to being used as part of HIV treatment regimens. Gilead Sciences is currently the only company selling Descovy in the U.S. Gilead charges more than $2000 a month—or $24,000 per year—for Descovy and is generating $1.7 billion annually in U.S. sales.[210]

Over 1.1 million people need PrEP in the United States, but less than a quarter are currently able to access it; just 9 percent of Black people for whom PrEP is recommended are taking it.[211]

Again, here's the kicker: The U.S. government conducted and paid for foundational research on the use of the drug as HIV PrEP. The U.S. government patented its research. To date, Gilead has not paid a dime for its use of the U.S. government's patented technology, despite earning many billions from sales of HIV PrEP. In November 2019, the Department of Health and Human Services sued Gilead Sciences for patent infringement.[212]

Figure 10. PrEP Coverage in the U.S. by Race/Ethnicity, 2019

PrEP is highly effective for preventing HIV from sex or injection drug use. Overall, **only 23%** of people who could benefit from PrEP were prescribed PrEP in 2019.

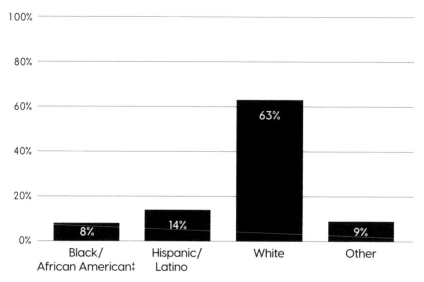

Source: Centers for Disease Control and Prevention.

Covid Vaccines: Many lessons were available from the global HIV/ AIDS experience. They included:

- Governments cannot permit corporate monopoly control over life-saving technology in the face of a global public health crisis.
- The U.S. government must leverage its investment in biomedical research to expand access to critical medicines and vaccines.
- Generic production can dramatically lower price and enhance production capacity.

Unfortunately, these lessons were not learned. Although the circumstances were not identical, history repeated itself with the Covid-19 pandemic: taxpayers were gouged and, even more importantly, millions of people died needlessly.

Covid was not the first infectious disease caused by a coronavirus. In the previous two decades, coronaviruses caused severe acute respiratory syndrome (SARS) in 2002 and Middle East respiratory syndrome (MERS) in 2012. In response, drug companies did almost no research into vaccines or treatments. Instead, that mantle was taken up by NIH, which invested $700 million in coronavirus research in the two decades after SARS. In

2019, before Covid, there were only six active coronavirus clinical trials involving pharmaceutical companies. All of them depended crucially on public funding.[213]

The federal government's early investment in coronavirus research laid the foundation for the rapid response to Covid-19, helping accelerate the development of many leading vaccine candidates.[214]

Coronavirus spike proteins—with the crown-like appearance that gives coronaviruses their name—play a critical role in viral infection, helping the virus fuse with human cells. NIH scientists engineered a new way of "freezing" coronavirus spike proteins in their pre-fusion shape, enabling vaccines to generate an antibody response.

Most of the leading first-generation Covid-19 vaccine candidates—including those by Pfizer/BioNTech, Johnson & Johnson and Moderna—relied on the NIH's approach. One vaccine scientist noted that we were "very lucky, actually" that scientists had earlier developed the method for freezing coronavirus spike proteins.[215]

Among the vaccine makers, Moderna uniquely benefitted from federal support. "We did the front end. They did the middle. And we did the back end," said Dr. Barney Graham, a former top NIH official, referring to the process for designing the spike-protein sequence, manufacturing vaccines and running clinical trials.[216]

Moderna tried to file patents on certain vaccine technologies that had been co-invented with NIH. After Public Citizen drew attention to the maneuver,[217] Moderna backed down.[218]

The Biomedical Advanced Research and Development Authority, an arm of the government, gave large-scale grants to Moderna to complete clinical trials and scale up manufacturing.[219]

Altogether, the U.S. government spent roughly $2.5 billion on the vaccine that would be called—misleadingly—the Moderna vaccine. It should rightly have been called the NIH-Moderna vaccine (or perhaps simply the NIH vaccine). The U.S. government paid the entire cost of its development, save for a relatively tiny donation ($1 million) from the singer Dolly Parton.[220]

All this spending and co-invention status gave the U.S. government powerful authority to condition how Moderna behaved and to share the technology. It did not do so.

Moderna generated tens of billions in sales—a huge portion from the federal government—and several of its executives became billionaires.[221]

Meanwhile, the world went for more than a year with an insufficient vaccine supply. Developing countries were unable to obtain enough vaccines for their people. When they could get access, it was often to lower-quality vaccines, not the high-quality mRNA vaccines of Moderna or Pfizer.

That delay in vaccination almost certainly cost hundreds of thousands and probably millions of lives.[222] It also made it more likely that new variants would emerge and that Covid would evolve into an endemic disease.[223]

If we had learned the lessons from the fight against AIDS, this tragedy could have been avoided. It was entirely possible to share the mRNA technology controlled by Moderna and scale up vaccine manufacturing in order to have vaccinated the world quickly.[224]

Even though the development of vaccine technology depended so heavily on U.S. government support—and entirely, in the case of the NIH-Moderna vaccine—that was the road not taken.

Instead, the U.S. and other governments deferred to and relied on Big Pharma. We all paid the price—and will continue to do so for many years to come.

PART III

Big Oil

CHAPTER 7

Fueling Disaster

The world's Big Oil companies have been very lucky lately.

When the global economy began emerging from the worst of the Covid pandemic in 2021, and then when the Russians invaded Ukraine in February 2022, world oil prices spiked. From $52 a barrel at the start of 2021, oil prices topped $110 a barrel in June of 2022.[225]

For Big Oil—the giant, integrated companies that drill, refine and market oil and oil products—this was an historic stroke of luck. The skyrocketing prices didn't cost ExxonMobil, Chevron, BP or Shell a dime more in production expense, but they could sell oil at prices twice as high as they had the previous year.

The result was huge profits. In 2022, the big four corporations reported a combined $163 *billion* in profits.[226] Again: $163 billion!

Consumers were the suckers in this deal, but they had nowhere to turn. If you drive, you need gas, and there weren't any companies selling gas that reflected only their cost of production, rather than the global price.

Well, there might have been one place to turn: the federal government.

The natural government response to companies earning windfall profits—those due to sudden changes in supply and demand, unrelated to anything the companies did—is to impose a windfall profits tax. That's the

Figure 11. Big Oil Profits and CEO Compensation, 2018-2022

Corporation Name	Profits, 2018-2022	CEO Compensation, 2018-2022
BP	$57.5 billion	$48.2 million
Chevron	$63.3 billion	$128.9 million
ConocoPhillips	$37.7 billion	$125.7 million
Exxon/Mobil	$91.5 billion	$117.4 million
Shell	$79 billion	$60.7 million
TotalEnergies	$53 billion	*(inadequate data)*

Source: Public Citizen compilation based on companies' Securities and Exchange Commission filings.

by-the-books policy response, even where companies aren't bad actors, as the oil giants surely are.

Many members of Congress, along with outside advocacy groups, did call for a windfall profits tax, with the proceeds to be returned directly to taxpayers.[227] It was an extraordinarily popular proposal, garnering 80 percent support among voters, including 73 percent among Republican voters.[228]

But the idea never went anywhere, despite its popularity.

Why not? It wasn't just luck this time. Many politicians are simply in the pocket of Big Oil. But many who are not also failed to demand or even lend support to a windfall profits tax. For them, Big Oil's political power was presumably too great even to contemplate such a measure.

For more than a century, that behavior has been the norm in the United States and around the world. Giant oil corporations have provided the fuel to run the global economy, yes, but they have inflicted enormous, avoidable harms. They have polluted communities; suppressed competition; poisoned the air, land and water; undermined democracy; and been complicit in shocking human rights abuses. And of course, as discussed in some detail in the next chapter, they have blocked action on the greatest challenge now facing humanity: the climate crisis.

BP'S Oil Gusher

On April 20, 2010, the BP-operated oil rig Deepwater Horizon exploded in the Gulf of Mexico, killing 11 workers and opening an oil gusher on the floor of the Gulf. It created the largest oil spill in U.S. history.

Major oil spills are not infrequent in the United States—occurring over 40 times since 1969[229]—though they have become less frequent since Deepwater Horizon sparked reforms in both government regulation and industry practices.[230]

The Deepwater Horizon disaster was an "accident" in the sense that no one wanted or intended it to occur. But it was no accident in the sense of being random or unavoidable. The explosion was the direct result of a pattern of reckless and negligent decisions and a corporate culture that devalued safety and encouraged excessive risk. It was a management-created disaster.

BP would eventually plead guilty to felony manslaughter, environmental crimes and obstruction of Congress, and paid $4 billion in criminal fines and penalties,[231] plus tens of billions more in private settlements for the damage it inflicted.

The immediate and long-term damage from the spill was gargantuan, starting with the 11 lives lost. The spill undermined the health of people living in communities along the Gulf; they reported spikes in dizziness, wheezing and burning lungs.[232] Tens of thousands of clean-up workers experienced significant exposure to toxic chemical dispersants—which BP misleadingly told workers were completely safe[233]—with long-term health effects, including impaired kidney and liver functioning, respiratory ailments, headaches and more.[234]

The economic impact on the nearby region was devastating, starting with the commercial and tourist fishing businesses. Academic researchers concluded that the Deepwater Horizon spill cost more than 25,000 business and fishing-related losses, especially among shrimpers.[235] Tourism also took a big hit, hurting everyone from local restaurants to hotels, tour guides and the shops that serve tourists.[236]

As the oil spread throughout the Gulf, the environmental harm and toll on sea life was distressingly far-reaching. A compilation assessment from the Center for Biological Diversity "found that the spill likely harmed or killed about 82,000 birds of 102 species; about 6,165 sea turtles; as many as 25,900 marine mammals; and a vast (but unknown) number of fish—from the great bluefin tuna to our nation's smallest seahorse—plus oysters, crabs, corals and other creatures."[237] The center reported that "oiled marine mammals have been collected from west of Cameron, Texas, to Port St. Joe, Fla. Researchers reported carcasses washing up daily—half being stillborn or dead infant dolphins. This oil spill could impair marine mammal reproduction in the Gulf for decades, as some orca whales that were exposed to the *Exxon Valdez* oil spill haven't been able to reproduce since that spill in 1989."[238]

BP's CEO Tony Hayward evidently didn't get the memo. "I think the environmental impact of this disaster is likely to have been very, very modest,"[239] he said. He was wrong.

The massive destruction in the Gulf region was avoidable, as BP acknowledged in court. In pleading guilty to an array of charges, the Justice Department explained, "BP has admitted that the two highest-ranking BP supervisors onboard the Deepwater Horizon, known as BP's 'Well Site Leaders' or 'company men,' negligently caused the deaths of 11 men and the resulting oil spill. The information details that, on the evening of April 20, the two supervisors … observed clear indications that the Macondo well [the name of the Deepwater Horizon well site] was not secure and that oil and gas were flowing into the well. Despite this, BP's well site leaders chose not to take obvious and appropriate steps to prevent the blowout. As a result of their conduct, control of the Macondo well was lost, resulting in catastrophe." BP also lied to Congress about how severe the spill was; the blowout was discharging 10 times more oil into the Gulf than the company admitted while the spill was ongoing.[240]

BP's systemic failures were far worse even than it acknowledged in its guilty plea. The problem was not limited to the night of the deadly blowout.

In January 2011, the National Commission on the BP/Deepwater Horizon Oil Spill and Offshore Drilling, convened by President Barack Obama, issued a detailed report that walked through the events that led to the tragedy. The commission highlighted a series of decisions and actions in which BP and its contractors chose the quicker and cheaper course in each case, ultimately with deadly and tragic consequences. Each of these was a lost opportunity to prevent or at least mitigate the effects of the blowout.[241]

"Whatever irreducible uncertainty may persist regarding the precise contribution to the blowout of each of several potentially immediate causes, no such uncertainty exists about the blowout's root causes," the commission found. The problem wasn't "aberrational decisions" by "rogue" officials. Instead, "the missteps were rooted in systemic failures by industry management (extending beyond BP to contractors that serve many in the industry), and also by failures of government to provide effective regulatory oversight of offshore drilling."

Those regulatory failures tracked directly to improper industry influence. This issue was at least partially addressed by subsequent reforms and the creation of an offshore oil drilling safety agency with more independence from industry.

Concluded the commission: "The most significant failure at Macondo—and the clear root cause of the blowout—was a failure of industry management. Most, if not all, of the failures at Macondo can be traced back to underlying failures of management and communication."

BP, the commission found, recklessly ignored risk. "BP's management process did not adequately identify or address risks created by late changes to well design and procedures. BP did not have adequate controls in place to ensure that key decisions in the months leading up to the blowout were safe or sound from an engineering perspective." Key "decisions appear to have been made by the BP Macondo team in ad hoc fashion without any formal risk analysis or internal expert review. This appears to have been a key causal factor of the blowout."

And here's the bottom line from the commission: "Whether purposeful or not, many of the decisions that BP, Halliburton, and Transocean made that increased the risk of the Macondo blowout clearly saved those companies significant time (and money)."

In other words, this wasn't a problem of incompetence. The risks that were taken, the failures to communicate, the shortcuts pursued, the warning signs ignored were the result of a culture that prioritized profit over safety.

Eleven workers paid for that with their lives, as did the Gulf ecosystem and the regional economy.

Contaminating Communities

Spewing oil into the ocean is the most dramatic way in which Big Oil pollutes the planet, but it's not the only way, or even the most consequential.

Oil pipelines leak. A lot.[242] More than 350 leaks occur in the United States annually.[243] It can take quite some time before leaks are detected—on average nine hours, with five more hours needed for operator response—and the amount of oil spilled can be quite consequential. Some of the problems can be attributed to poor construction quality,[244] but if you decide to build a pipeline, some substantial risk of leaks is probably unavoidable.

The environmental impacts of pipeline spills are lasting. Researchers find that 85 percent of spilled oil remains unrecovered, causing soil contamination in half of all cases and impacting environmentally sensitive areas about 40 percent of the time. Leaks and spills from pipes crossing waterways almost always involve uncased pipes. About 10 percent of leaks contaminate water supplies.[245]

Pipelines crisscross the United States, moving oil and natural gas from often remote locations to refineries in urban centers, often in coastal areas. With fracking and the sharp rise in U.S. domestic production of oil and gas—along with tar sands production in Canada—oil and gas corporations continue to propose and construct new pipelines. Very often, these pipelines cross indigenous lands.

Pipelines, refineries and petrochemical plants create severe, localized harms everywhere they go. And because pipelines so frequently run across indigenous lands, and because petro plants are almost always located in communities where people are mainly low-income and of color, they are the people who bear the overwhelming brunt of the pollution and risk.

Native communities rely more heavily on the land for survival than many others; and many Native groups claim a special spiritual relationship to the land and water. This is in large part why Native communities have been such leaders in opposing the Keystone, Dakota Access, Mountain Valley, Enbridge and many other pipeline proposals in the United States (as well as around the world). They are literally on the front lines.[246]

Pipelines don't bring only the risk of environmental contamination to indigenous communities, however. There are shocking social hazards as well. Building pipelines in remote, rural, low-population areas often relies on "man camps," temporary housing built for construction workers, who are overwhelmingly male. These man camps and oil development have been associated with spikes in violent crime, especially against indigenous women.

One study of the Fort Berthold reservation in North Dakota concluded that "with the combination of economic hardship, an influx of temporary workers, historical violence against Native women, a lack of law enforcement resources, and increased oil and gas development, Fort Berthold has become the perfect place for th[e] heinous crime of sex trafficking."[247] An already startling problem of missing and murdered indigenous women and girls in the United States—who are murdered at 10 times the rate of the general population—is only made worse by oil development and man camps.[248]

Oil refineries and petrochemical plants follow a very similar ecological pattern as pipelines: They pose significant local environmental and public health risk, with impacts felt most heavily in low-income and people of color communities. In southern Louisiana, for example, the lower Mississippi River area is known as "Cancer Alley." The petrochemical plants in Cancer Alley have "not only polluted the surrounding water and air, but also subjected the mostly African American residents in St. James Parish to cancer, respiratory diseases and other health problems," found a United Nations team of human rights experts.[249]

Cancer Alley is not unique but representative. "Thirteen refineries exceeded EPA's 'action level' in 2020 for the 12 months ending on December 31, 2020, reporting annual benzene concentrations that range from 9.36 micrograms to more than 31 micrograms for the year," documented the Environmental Integrity Project. "More than 530,000 people live within three miles of these refineries, with 57 percent being people of color and 43 percent living below the poverty line, according to U.S. Census Bureau and EPA data."[250] Benzene is a carcinogen and contributes to lung disease. It also is associated with the presence of other dangerous air pollutants.

Think about this for a moment: More than half the people downwind from these refineries are people of color and more than four in 10 live below the poverty line. For comparison, about a third of the U.S. population consists of people of color. Only one in 10 Americans live below the poverty line, so poor people are wildly overrepresented in this endangered population.

It all makes sense, right? An oil refiner or petrochemical company would never dare locate a plant in a wealthy neighborhood. If they tried, the community would rise up and stop it.

By contrast, oil, gas and petrochemical corporations are able to bulldoze communities with less political power. It's a central theme to the story of corporate power abuses.

But no one can escape the damage inflicted by Big Oil. While localized pollution from pipelines, refineries and chemical plants is an especially acute concern, everyone is breathing air polluted by fossil fuels. Burning coal is a big part of the story, but so is petroleum refining and the burning of oil and gas. In the United States, particulate matter—which includes soot—causes as many as 200,000 deaths every year, disproportionately affecting communities of color,[251] but a hazard from which no one is safe. The dollar cost of fossil fuel illness in the United States may total as much as $600 billion annually.[252] The world suffers as many as 4.5 million premature deaths annually from fossil fuel air pollution.[253]

Planetary Predators

Big Oil's footprint is global. The harms in the United States are mirrored around the world—except they are often much worse in poor nations.

Big Oil has a sordid record around the world of consorting with and financing authoritarian regimes, benefiting from or even facilitating human rights abuses in order to protect drilling projects, and subjecting poor and indigenous communities to shocking levels of environmental violence.

While discoveries of oil and gas wealth should supercharge economic development in poor countries, it has, over and over, instead led to the deepening of authoritarianism, the enrichment of an oligarchic class, and the perpetuation of poverty. This phenomenon is so widespread that it has a name: the "resource curse."[254] But it might as well be called the "corporate curse," because the story so frequently involves multinational corporations exploiting institutional weaknesses in developing countries in order to boost profits, without regard to the social consequences.

- In Burma, the Yadana natural gas pipeline was operated by a consortium in which Unocal (now owned by Chevron) was a lead partner. It was constructed with forced labor and associated with brutal human rights abuses by the Burmese military. Unocal and its project partners relied on the Burmese army for pipeline security, and those forces pulled thousands of villagers from their homes and forced them to work on the project. In the course of these abuses, the Burmese military committed torture, rape and murder. Unocal never acknowledged knowledge of the military's crimes. In 2003, it was forced to settle a major lawsuit, led by EarthRights International, on behalf of victims of the pipeline development project.[255]

  Further, income from the pipeline project has been a lifeline for the brutal Burmese military,[256] which has maintained its grip on power for decades under various governmental forms. Natural gas revenues continue to provide about $1 billion in foreign currency annually for the military-led government.[257]

- In Nigeria, oil drilling led by Shell, Chevron and other oil giants has polluted vast areas, inflicted social, economic and environmental distress on local communities, supported military and corrupt governments and undermined democratic movements.

Internationally renowned playwright and activist Ken Saro-Wiwa, a member of the Ogoni people in the Niger Delta, helped lead a campaign against Shell, demanding it clean up the region it had trashed. In 1995, the Nigerian government responded: it arrested and then hanged Saro-Wiwa and eight of his colleagues.

"Just weeks before the men were arrested," according to Amnesty International, "the Chairperson of Shell Nigeria had met with then-president General Sani Abacha, and raised 'the problem of the Ogonis and Ken Saro-Wiwa.' This was not the first time Shell had engaged with military and security forces to frame the Ogoni protests as a 'problem.' Shell also repeatedly reminded the authorities of the economic impacts" of the Ogoni protests.[258]

Decades later, the Ogoni would receive a modicum of justice when a lawsuit filed by Environmental Rights Action/Friends of the Earth Nigeria in the Netherlands found Shell responsible for oil spills in three Ogoni villages, forcing the company to pay compensation and clean up its mess.[259]

But hundreds of spills occur every year in the Niger Delta. "We have groundwater polluted with benzene 900 times above the WHO [the World Health Organization] level, we have farmlands with poor yields, rivers that are barely fishable, neonatal deaths numbering thousands yearly as a result of spills. We have reduced neuroplasticity of the brain as a result of oil pollution," Niger Delta activist Saatah Nubari told CNN. "The Niger Delta is a graveyard of the living."[260]

- In Ecuador, oil drilling in the Oriente, a vast Amazonian tropical rainforest area, led to monumental environmental pollution. For two decades starting in 1972, Texaco—now absorbed into Chevron—controlled 90 percent of these operations. A 1991 report by environmental investigator Judith Kimerling estimated that oil operations discharged 4.3 million gallons of toxic wastes into the Oriente environment every day. The New York-based Center for Economic and Social Rights documented toxic contaminants in drinking water at levels reaching 1,000 times the safety standards recommended by the U.S. Environmental Protection Agency. Local health workers report increased gastrointestinal problems, skin rashes, birth defects and cancers, ailments that they believe to be related to this contamination.[261]

Oil development—involving the trashing of lands and waters and the influx of outsiders—devastated indigenous populations in the area. One group, the Tetetes, disappeared altogether. The Cofan population declined by more than 75 percent.[262]

Although an Ecuador court ordered Chevron to pay $9.5 billion in compensation and clean-up costs to the communities injured by oil drilling in the Oriente, the company has not paid anything. Instead, it has waged a scorched-earth legal campaign in U.S. courts, estimated to have cost more than $1 billion, which resulted in criminal contempt-of-court charges against the Ecuadorians' lawyer.[263]

Big Oil and Climate Change

Of course, Big Oil's most devastating global impact has been to accelerate the world's race toward climate catastrophe.

Big Oil and its apologists like to point out that we have all benefited from reliance on fossil fuels and to suggest, implicitly and explicitly, that we all share equal responsibility for whatever harms accompany the benefits of burning oil and gas.

This is not true.

It's not just that in a fossil fuel-driven world, most consumers have had no viable alternative. It's that Big Oil has suppressed and denied the truth about climate change, obstructed efforts to transition the world away from fossil fuel reliance, and sabotaged politicians who tried to address the problem. It arguably constitutes the most deadly and dangerous exertion of corporate political power ever.

It is to this shameful history that we now turn.

CHAPTER 8

Big Oil's Political Influence Machine and the Fate of the Planet

Denying and covering up evidence of threats that major corporations pose to the public is part and parcel of the corporate playbook. The industries that make asbestos, plastics, chemicals, lead paint and other dangerous substances carried out long-running campaigns to suppress the science that showed how their products kill and sicken their workers and the public. Time and time again, auto companies hid deadly product defects, as have many other corporations. And, of course, Big Tobacco lied for decades about the science of tobacco, health and addiction, aggressively attacking critics and profiting from millions of preventable deaths.

Big Tobacco's full-court, multi-pronged, take-no-prisoners campaign strategy provided the template for Big Oil's effort to block progress against catastrophic climate change—the greatest threat, alongside nuclear war, that humanity has ever faced.

The science of the climate crisis is well established and beyond dispute: Burning fossil fuels generates greenhouse gas emissions, including carbon and methane, that act like a blanket wrapped around the Earth, trapping the sun's heat and raising temperatures.[264] Other human activities are helping to rush us to climate chaos, including forest destruction, but forestalling the most frightening climate change scenarios will require the world to transition quickly away from fossil fuels and rely instead on renewable energy sources.

Big Oil knows this. In fact, it turns out that Big Oil-employed scientists identified the ways burning fossil fuels would drive climate chaos around the same time that a scientific consensus started to emerge on the issue. But Big Oil kept quiet about its internal findings. Instead, it funded an array of climate change-denying scientists who proclaimed themselves "skeptics." It backed think tanks, universities and advocacy groups that spread doubts about climate science and opposed measures to slow global warming. It spent millions on a decades-long public relations campaign to spread climate disinformation. It deployed its lobbyists on Capitol Hill and in state houses across the country. And fossil fuel moguls deployed hundreds of millions in Dark Money to support their allied political candidates and—more importantly—to intimidate politicians from taking necessary measures.

Every person alive will pay the price for this campaign, as will generations to come.

If the world had acted when the scientific consensus around climate science solidified—certainly by the early 1990s—we could have managed a much cheaper, orderly and slower transition to a clean energy future.

Instead, we wasted decades—and we're barely making progress now. As a result, the transition will be much, much costlier and much more disruptive. The costs are hard to fathom. Depending on how quickly we move and how severe we let climate chaos become, estimates suggest the dollar costs could be 11 to 14 percent of total global economic output by 2050.[265]

That's trillions of dollars every year. And worse scenarios are very possible.

What is certain is that humanity is going to experience vast and needless suffering—almost all of which could have been avoided with timely action. Even in the more optimistic scenarios, millions will die, hundreds of millions will be forced to emigrate, livelihoods will be uprooted, food and water shortages will plague vast regions, new diseases will emerge, economies will be devastated. Ecosystems will be destroyed, countless species will be wiped out, the surface of the earth will be remade. These impacts are all occurring now and they are going to accelerate.

It didn't have to be this way.

Exxon Knew, Big Oil Knew

The science of climate change goes back longer than you might think. Two women were pioneers in the field. In 1856, physicist and women's rights advocate Eunice Foote presented a scientific paper, "Circumstances affecting the heat of the sun's rays." In 1896, a Swedish scientist named Svante Arrhenius discovered feedback loops that could accelerate climate change. Others also had early insights into the science in the 1800s.[266]

Climate science continued to evolve in the early 1900s, and the prospect of human-induced climate change gained widespread acceptance in scientific circles by the 1970s.

Exxon's scientists were among those who came to and built that scientific understanding, as *Inside Climate News* detailed in breakthrough reporting on internal industry documents.[267]

In 1977, a senior company scientist, James F. Black, told Exxon's Management Committee that "there is general scientific agreement that the most likely manner in which mankind is influencing the global climate is through carbon dioxide release from the burning of fossil fuels." A year later, Black told company scientists and researchers that humanity "has a time window of five to ten years before the need for hard decisions regarding changes in energy strategies might become critical."[268]

Exxon responded the way you might hope, at least at first, report Neela Banerjee, Lisa Song and David Hasemyer of *Inside Climate News.* The company "launched its own extraordinary research into carbon dioxide from fossil fuels and its impact on the earth. Exxon's ambitious program included both empirical CO_2 sampling and rigorous climate modeling. It assembled a brain trust that would spend more than a decade deepening the company's understanding of an environmental problem that posed an existential threat to the oil business."[269]

It wasn't just Exxon. In the 1980s, Shell scientists accurately forecast the coming climate crisis. They predicted substantial sea-level rise and warned that disintegration of the West Antarctic Ice Sheet could result in a world-wide sea level rise of "five to six meters." They predicted the "disappearance of specific ecosystems or habitat destruction," destructive flooding and water shortages. Global changes in air temperature would also "drastically change the way people live and work." Shell concluded, "the changes may be the greatest in recorded history."[270]

As early as the mid-1960s, the president of the American Petroleum Institute (API)—the oil industry's trade association, which later played a leading role attacking climate science—publicly credited scientific reports on climate change.[271]

In short, Big Oil has long known the planet is burning. In a parallel universe, it might have continued building its own climate science and then led the way to a transition to renewable energy. But in this universe, that's not how things happened.

By the end of the 1980s, Exxon had shut down its climate investigative work. Exxon and the industry instead decided to launch a campaign to deny the reality of climate change and forestall action that would imperil not just their profits but their entire business model. The nature of the campaign has morphed over time, but it continues to this day.

Climate Obfuscation

At this same time, in the late 1980s, pressure was growing for an international agreement to deal with the global challenge of climate change. Big Oil, along with utilities, manufacturers and others organized by the public relations firm Burson-Marsteller, formed the Global Climate Coalition (GCC) to lobby at international negotiating meetings and counteract the emerging scientific consensus that global warming was real.

The coalition had great success. Its strategy was to spread doubt about climate science and demand that policymakers be "realistic" about the potential costs of transitioning to renewables. Its policy focus was to block any binding cuts on carbon emissions.

As one of its key players, E. Bruce Harrison, would later write, "GCC has successfully turned the tide on press coverage of global climate change science, effectively countering the ecocatastrophe message and asserting the lack of scientific consensus on global warming."

When the world's governments gathered in Rio de Janeiro, Brazil, for the Earth Summit in June 1992, the top agenda item was to negotiate a climate treaty to reduce greenhouse gas emissions. Big Oil was well represented in the government of George H. W. Bush, a former oil man, and the industry succeeded in taking control of the U.S. negotiating position at the summit.

The world was ready to establish specific and binding emission reduction targets in a treaty on climate change. But responding to Big Oil demands, the United States blocked the proposal. Then the United States succeeded in watering down the agreement itself. The final pact called on countries to make their best effort to reduce greenhouse gas emissions, but did not set a goal of achieving 1990 levels by the year 2000—a standard around which all countries but the United States had reached consensus.[272]

"The GCC has provided constructive input into United Nations-sponsored negotiations to establish an international 'Framework Convention' on climate change through contacts with the U.S. negotiating team and attending the first two negotiating sessions," reported the National Association of Manufacturers, a GCC convenor, in a self-congratulatory "business activity report."[273]

How would the United States follow through on the voluntary commitments it had made at Rio?

Big Oil and the GCC knew how to answer that. The GCC's Harrison explained that the coalition had "actively influenced" congressional debates over carbon taxes to avoid "strict energy taxes," and had affected the Clinton administration's decision "to rely on voluntary (rather than mandatory) measures" to reduce emissions in its 1993 National Action Plan, which was required under the Rio agreement.

Deadly Disinformation

Throughout the 1990s and beyond, Big Oil continued to spread climate disinformation. As Pulitzer Prize-winning journalist Ross Gelbspan explained in his furious and prescient 1997 book *The Heat Is On:* "To carry out their mystification campaign, the industry's public relations specialists have made extensive use of a tiny band of scientists whose views contradict the consensus of the world's experts. The deep-pocketed industry lobby has promoted their opinions through every channel of communication it can reach. It has demanded access to the press for these scientists' views, as a right of journalistic fairness."[274]

This disinformation found industry-backed allies in Congress who were ready to amplify it, Gelbspan explained. But most importantly, "the campaign has had a narcotic effect on the American public. It has lulled people into a deep apathy about the crisis by persuading them that the issue of climate change is terminally stuck in scientific uncertainty. It is not."[275]

In fact, as we now know, the industry was not only aware of the scientific consensus, its own scientists had been sounding the alarm for decades.

Here's one example of how all this played out.[276] Big Oil-backed climate skeptics created petitions led by so-called experts to spread the seeds of scientific doubt about climate change. The web site of climate skeptic Fred Singer's Science and Environmental Policy Project listed four such petitions, including the "Oregon Petition." That document was first circulated in a bulk mailing to tens of thousands of U.S. scientists in April 1998. The mailing included what appeared to be a reprint of a scientific paper in the exact same typeface and format as the official proceedings of the National Academy of Sciences (NAS). Ex-NAS president Frederick Seitz provided a cover note that made it appear that the paper, which claimed to show that pumping carbon dioxide into the atmosphere is actually a good thing, was an official NAS publication.

In fact, the paper had never been peer-reviewed or accepted for publication anywhere. Its author was widely discredited for having declared in 1994 that ozone depletion was a hoax, and the NAS ended up issuing a blunt statement distancing itself from the petition. Nonetheless, it received 15,000 signatures within a month. (To show how lax the management of the petition had been, environmental activists added to it the names of fictional characters, such as "B.J. Honeycutt" of the TV series M*A*S*H, and Geraldine Halliwell, also known as Ginger Spice of the Spice Girls, whose field of scientific specialization was listed as "biology.")

The petition may have been a hoax as representing expert views, but mainstream opinion pieces on global warming would cite it, and politicians such as Nebraska Senator Chuck Hagel referred to it as a basis for opposing the Kyoto treaty on global warming. Signed in 1997 as an elaboration on the 1992 Earth Summit deal, the Kyoto Protocol established binding obligations to reduce carbon emissions.

Meanwhile, Big Oil's trade group API was working furiously to undermine the public's understanding of the scientific consensus. In 1996, API published a book claiming that "no conclusive—or even strongly suggestive—scientific evidence exists that human activities are significantly affecting sea levels, rainfall, surface temperatures or the intensity and frequency of storms."[277] An API internal media plan explained, "victory will be achieved when […] average citizens 'understand' (recognize) uncertainties in climate science; recognition of uncertainties becomes part of the 'conventional wisdom.'"[278]

API and the industry made a priority of preventing the United States from ratifying the Kyoto Protocol. In 1998, *The New York Times* reported on an API draft of a multi-million dollar plan to defeat Kyoto. API aimed to provide "a one-stop resource on climate science for members of Congress, the media, industry and all others concerned," with the express intention of countering the scientific consensus put forward by the Intergovernmental Panel on Climate Change, which had included almost all the world's leading climate scientists.

"A proposed media-relations budget of $600,000, not counting any money for advertising, would be directed at science writers, editors, columnists and television network correspondents, using as many as 20 'respected climate scientists' recruited expressly "to inject credible science and scientific accountability into the global climate debate, thereby raising questions about and undercutting the 'prevailing scientific wisdom.'"[279]

Deny, Deny, Deny

In 2001, the George W. Bush administration announced that it had "no interest" in the Kyoto Protocol. "POTUS rejected Kyoto, in part, based on input from you," read the talking points prepared for a meeting between White House staff and the Global Climate Coalition. Its mission accomplished, the coalition disbanded in 2002.[280]

The Bush II administration was very good to Big Oil. Vice President Dick Cheney had previously served as CEO of the oil fields service company Halliburton. Cheney drove Bush administration energy policy, creating an industry-reliant task force to develop a National Energy Plan that matched Big Oil's wish list and pointedly did nothing about climate change. At least one executive order that came from the task force closely matched text provided by the American Petroleum Institute.[281]

The industry continued to fund a vast array of organizations to spread disinformation and block climate action. A 2020 report from Senate Democrats on the climate crisis found a network of between 160 and 200 anti-climate groups that were loosely coordinated and were "created, dissolved, and then restarted under new names in a rolling shell game that makes it hard to identify who is actually behind the scheme." ExxonMobil alone has funded dozens at a time.[282]

"There is big money behind this operation," the Senate Democrats concluded. "An analysis of 91 anti-climate groups revealed that they collectively reported more than $7 billion in funding over an eight-year period, or more than $900 million per year on average."[283]

If anything, climate obstructionist spending is intensifying. Dylan Tanner, the executive director of InfluenceMap, testified to the U.S. Senate in 2019 that "since the Paris Agreement negotiations in 2015, the five Oil and Gas Majors alone (ExxonMobil, Shell, BP, Chevron and Total) have spent over $1 billion on misleading climate branding and wide-ranging lobbying efforts. We found these efforts to be overwhelmingly in conflict with the goals of this landmark global climate accord and designed to maintain the social and legal license to operate and expand fossil fuel operations."[284]

On top of this comprehensive disinformation campaign came a new superpower for Big Oil and fossil fuel interests: the 2010 Supreme Court *Citizens United* decision, which freed them to spend on electioneering. They immediately invested heavily in super PACS and Dark Money groups. Suddenly, politicians faced the prospect of serious political risk if they decided to follow the science and support policies to address climate chaos. The risk was particularly severe for Republicans, who were acutely aware that supporting climate policies might generate a primary challenger backed by millions in Dark Money.

The results were very tangible. As the Senate Democratic report explained, "Prior to *Citizens United,* there had been a long history of bipartisanship on climate. In the 2000s, several bipartisan climate bills were circulating in the Senate, and one Republican senator even ran for president with a climate action pledge as part of his platform. But after that decision, bipartisan activity on comprehensive climate legislation collapsed as Republicans legislators fled from engagement."[285]

In 2010, shortly after *Citizens United* was decided, South Carolina Republican Representative Bob Inglis lost his primary race by a 3-1 margin—to a fossil fuel-backed challenger. Inglis' home district support collapsed because he supported taxing carbon pollution.[286]

You may wonder how smart some politicians are. But know this: They care about winning elections. When candidates like Inglis get bulldozed by fossil fuel interests, they learn their lesson.

Under Donald Trump, Big Oil had its greatest feeding frenzy yet, capturing the government like never before. The industry spent more than $100 million in the 2016 election and was well rewarded. The Trump administration was stuffed with officials from the oil and gas industry or who had represented it. Among many others, these included U.S. Secretary of State and former ExxonMobil CEO Rex Tillerson; the Environmental Protection Agency senior deputy general counsel, who provided legal counsel to the American Petroleum Institute; and the deputy counsel to the president, who had previously provided legal services to Chevron Corp.[287]

Industry allies were hard at work. The Trump administration rolled back or stalled the modest steps forward the Obama administration had made on climate, opened up new lands and water to oil drilling and generally did Big Oil's bidding. While Trump mocked the idea that climate change was even occurring, the climate crisis accelerated.

Delay, Delay, Delay

Big Oil has mostly softened its messaging now. It's no longer plausible to deny that climate chaos is occurring. The worldwide heat waves, intense hurricanes, out-of-control fires, severe rain and flooding are just too much to ignore.

Now Big Oil claims to be part of the solution. But as two House committee chairs concluded, "rather than outright deny global warming, the fossil fuel industry has 'greenwashed' its record through deceptive advertising and climate pledges—without meaningfully reducing emissions."[288] Summarizing findings from their extensive investigation, Oversight Committee Chair Carolyn Maloney and Environment Subcommittee chair Ro Khanna explained that:[289]

- Contrary to what their pledges imply, fossil fuel companies have not organized their businesses around becoming low-emissions, renewable energy companies. They are devoted to a long-term fossil fuel future.
- Big Oil's climate pledges and green advertising focus on unproven technologies the companies have privately admitted are decades away from implementation.
- Oil and gas companies have tried to create the impression that they are taking ambitious steps to reduce emissions—without actually doing so.
- Big Oil relies on accounting gimmicks, tricky language and delay tactics to claim the mantle of climate leadership while continuing to be a primary cause of an ongoing climate catastrophe.

And, perhaps even more importantly, Big Oil continues to deploy all its political power to sabotage or obstruct measures to speed the transition to clean energy. Notably, as a CNN headline explained, Big Oil went "all-out to fight climate rules" proposed as part of President Biden's Build Back Better package. "We're leaving everything on the field here in terms of our opposition to anti-energy provisions," Mike Sommers, president and CEO of the American Petroleum Institute, told CNN.[290]

Big Oil's work helped undermine and defeat the Build Back Better package. The replacement Inflation Reduction Act contains meaningful measures to reduce carbon emissions, but not at the scale of Biden's original proposal—and not at the scale scientists tell us is needed to avert climate catastrophe.

It is truly hard to wrap your head around the severity of the crisis and the calamity that Big Oil is forcing on us. But to put all this in terrifying perspective, consider just one likely impact if emission trends continue. In the 2030s—the next decade—we can expect 10 million deaths every year from exposure to excessive heat.[291]

That carnage could have been avoided if Big Oil and fossil fuel interests hadn't run their decades-long campaign to block climate action. It still could be curtailed dramatically with urgent action—if We the People muster the political power and energy to overcome Big Oil.

CHAPTER 9

Plunder and Pillage: Big Oil's Corporate Welfare

Making Big Oil's sordid record all the more infuriating is this fact: The industry couldn't survive without taxpayer-funded subsidies, tax breaks and other privileges from a captured government.

The biggest subsidy that the United States and other countries confer on Big Oil firms is permitting them to externalize costs. "Externalize" is the term economists use when a corporation imposes costs on society rather than "internalizing" or absorbing them itself.

Big Oil and other fossil fuel corporations have inflicted the costs of air pollution and climate chaos on all of us. These costs are enormous. Experts estimate it at about $600 billion annually in the United States and nearly $3 trillion for the entire globe.[292] Costs include deaths, hospitalizations and lost work. Even those astounding figures pale compared to the startling costs that the climate crisis—for which Big Oil and the fossil fuel industries deserve a great deal of responsibility—is imposing and will continue to impose on us. With current policy pathways, economists say, the cost could be 10 percent of U.S. GDP by the end of the century; lost revenues and increased expenses for the federal government alone could total $2 trillion annually.[293] Other scenarios present costs that are even greater or accrue more rapidly.

That's not all. Since World War II and especially since the 1970s and the oil crises, the United States has conferred a giant subsidy on Big Oil by maintaining a bloated Pentagon budget and major military presence in the Middle East and Persian Gulf. The primary reason the Middle East has "strategic importance" is its oil reserves. The U.S. military presence and war-fighting in the Middle East have been extraordinarily expensive: Just maintaining our military presence in and oriented to the Persian Gulf costs tens of billions annually.[294] U.S. costs of the post-9/11 wars—primarily in Iraq but also including major expenses in Afghanistan, Pakistan and else-where—totaled around $8 *trillion* over a 20-year period, according to the Cost of War Project at Brown University.[295]

These unfathomably large subsidies have provided the foundation for Big Oil's global operations and super-profitability over many decades. That they are indirect subsidies—costs absorbed or expenses incurred, but not money provided directly—is no reason to ignore them.

Big Oil also has long benefited from a host of direct subsidies in the form of discounted access to public resources and a series of complicated tax benefits. Big Oil has deployed its lobby teams and political power for decades to protect these public gifts, only occasionally experiencing policy setbacks.

A Royal Rip-off

The most straightforward U.S. giveaway to Big Oil is just that: a give-away of the rights to drill on public land for a ridiculously low royalty rate.

For a century, starting in 1920, the U.S. government has allowed oil and gas companies to drill on public lands by paying a rock-bottom rate of 12.5 percent of the value of oil and gas produced. For example, if a fossil fuel company sells $1 million in oil in any given month, it would owe the government $125,000 under a 12.5 percent rate. That low royalty rate remained in place for more than a century.

It is far below the rates imposed by major oil and gas producing states, including Texas (20-25 percent), Louisiana (20-25 percent), Pennsylvania (20 percent), Colorado (20 percent), New Mexico (18.75-20 percent), Montana (16.67 percent), and Wyoming (16.67 percent).[296] The federal government also charges more itself—18.75 percent—for offshore drilling on federal waters.

The Inflation Reduction Act, passed in August 2022, will bump the royalty rate to 16.67 percent, an improvement, but still too low.

The century-old discount royalty rate helped boost the bottom line of oil and gas companies at the direct expense of taxpayers. Over the last decade, the public lost up to $13.1 billion to Big Oil. Lost potential revenue hit a record high of $2.3 billion in 2021, due to the dramatic increase in oil prices, according to Taxpayers for Common Sense.[297]

To identify which companies have benefited the most from this blatant taxpayer rip-off, Public Citizen analyzed Interior Department data to calculate how much extra money the companies could have paid if a rate of 18.75 percent had been in place when leases were sold.[298]

Public Citizen's analysis found that:

- From 2013 through 2021, 20 U.S. oil and gas companies doing the most drilling on public lands would have returned up to $5.8 billion to U.S. taxpayers under an 18.75 percent royalty rate. That's about half the $11.8 billion total lost royalty revenue during this nine-year period, according to Taxpayers for Common Sense's statistics.
- The five companies that have taken the most advantage of the failure to charge fair royalty rates from 2013 to 2021 were: Oklahoma

City-based Devon Energy, (up to $1.09 billion in avoided royalties), Houston-based EOG Resources (up to $896 million), Denver-based PureWest Energy, formerly known as Ultra Petroleum, (up to $493 million), Houston-based ConocoPhillips (up to $470 million) and Denver-based Ovinitiv (up to $329 million).

- In 2021, President Biden's first year in office, the 20 U.S. companies that did the most drilling on public lands would have returned up to $1.3 billion in extra royalties under an 18.75 percent rate. That's more than half the amount that all onshore drillers paid in royalties last year.
- The five companies that have taken the most advantage of the failure to charge fair royalty rates last year were: EOG Resources (up to $304 million), Devon Energy (up to $263 million), Mewbourne Oil (up to $106 million), Hilcorp (up to $73 million) and PureWest Energy (up to $68 million).

Of course, given the climate crisis, the U.S. government should stop leasing federal lands or waters for new drilling altogether, no matter the royalty rate. Permitting more drilling, whether or not at a fair market rate, is facilitating Big Oil business as usual, when that's exactly what we can't afford.

Under former President Donald Trump, the federal government did the opposite, engaging in a massive giveaway of our public resources to oil, gas and mining interests.[299] During this fire sale, the Bureau of Land Management sold leases on 5.6 million acres of public lands,[300] locking in global warming emissions. It was an especially reckless move, given that Big Oil emissions from public lands and waters make up about a quarter of U.S. carbon emissions each year.[301]

Candidate Joe Biden promised to end fossil fuel subsidies and additional drilling on public lands, stating in one debate: "No more subsidies for the fossil fuel industry, no more drilling on federal lands, no more drilling, including offshore, no ability for the oil industry to continue to drill, period, ends."[302]

Legal challenges from the oil and gas industry, as well as a difficult political climate resulting from high gasoline prices, have challenged Biden's effort to move away from fossil fuels. Shortly after taking office, Biden paused the sale of new federal oil leases, pledging to conduct a comprehensive review of the federal oil and gas program. The oil and gas industry and several Republican-led states sued to block the pause, and a federal judge in 2021 sided with the oil industry, issuing a ruling that ordered the Biden administration to resume lease sales.[303]

The administration then published a report endorsing reforms to the federal oil and gas leasing program and supported similar changes in the

Build Back Better legislation, but that stalled in Congress.[304] The Inflation Reduction Act that eventually passed did not include those reform measures, and in fact required the federal government to *speed up* offshore oil and gas leasing.[305]

Lubricating the Tax Code

Like many powerful industries, the oil and gas industry has deployed its political power to win and maintain special tax treatment. A relatively modest investment in lobbying expenses yields huge rewards in tax rules that save the industry billions. Big Oil has been among the most effective at exploiting the complexity of tax rules to win esoteric provisions with enormous benefits. It's no accident that these provisions have no direct relevance to regular taxpayers and are incredibly hard to understand if you're not a tax lawyer. It's easier for oil drillers to accrue tens of billions in subsidies if regular Americans don't know what's happening.

Altogether, analysts estimate the value of direct federal subsidies to oil and gas companies at around $20 billion a year.[306] The Organization for Economic Cooperation and Development, an association of the world's richest nations, estimates that U.S. government subsidies for oil and gas jumped by almost a third between 2017 and 2019.[307]

One special tax benefit for Big Oil is known as "intangible drilling costs."[308] Under regular tax rules, a company can deduct the cost of its investments over the period while the investment is expected to generate profits. If you pay $1 million for a roof on your factory that will last for 10 years—and therefore help your business for 10 years—you can deduct $100,000 a year in expenses. Under the intangible drilling costs rule, oil and gas companies get treated differently and are able to deduct most of their investment costs right away. That works out to reduce their tax bills very significantly, saving oil and gas companies—and costing taxpayers—more than a billion dollars annually.[309]

Another similar tax benefit is known as percentage depletion. Under regular tax rules, when a business uses up a resource on which it relies, it can deduct from its revenues the lost value of the resource. Normally, if you use up 10 percent of the resource, you can make a deduction equivalent to that depletion. The special percentage rules available to oil and gas producers, however, permit them to make deductions greater than the amount they are actually depleting. This benefit throws an extra $500 million to $1 billion to oil and gas producers every year.[310]

You get the idea: Oil companies are experts at rigging—especially the tax system.

Here's one last example that shows the system's rewards for size, influence and tax-escaping audacity. Experts at the Institute on Taxation and

Economic Policy explain: "Each year, corporations publicly state that some of the tax breaks they claim are unlikely to withstand scrutiny from tax authorities. And each year, corporations report that they will keep some of the dubious tax breaks they declared in previous years simply because the statute of limitations ran out before tax authorities made any conclusions."[311] Publicly traded companies are required to report "uncertain tax benefits"—tax breaks that authorities are likely to disallow. "The biggest single beneficiary of uncertain tax benefits that ran out the clock in 2020," reports the Institute on Taxation and Economic Policy, "was ExxonMobil, with $237 million in tax savings."[312]

Can you imagine announcing on your personal tax return that you were reducing your tax payment by $10,000 for reasons you know the IRS is unlikely to accept? And that you'd get to keep the money if the IRS didn't quickly get around to reviewing your return and your dubious claim?

The double standard in that comparison tells you everything you need to know about the injustice of corporate welfare.

PART IV
Big Tech

CHAPTER 10
Colonizing Our Minds

The great promise of the internet was to connect people, build community and foster greater understanding. And it has in fact done those things.

But under the direction of Big Tech corporations, it has also done the opposite. Increasingly, it feels like the internet is isolating individuals, dividing communities, fostering hate and serving up consumers as mere collections of data to be surveilled, marketed to and exploited.

The bad is not an inevitable price of accepting the good. As Tim Berners-Lee, credited as the founder and inventor of the World Wide Web, argues, the internet could "easily be safer and more humane, if the people who build big platforms thought more carefully about their users." How the internet functions, he argues, depends on design decisions—such as whether control over your data rests with you or Big Tech companies.[313] The problem, over and over, is that the Big Tech business model has pushed the internet, the web and social media in the direction of being more toxic, more commercialized and more predatory.

Facebook Knew: Social Media Hurts Kids

Anyone with a teenage kid, or who works with or knows teenagers, or who is a teenager, knows something profound is going on in the culture. It's not just that kids spend so much time interacting with social media

Figure 12. Big Tech Profits and CEO Compensation, 2018-2022

Corporation Name	Profits, 2018-2022	CEO Compensation, 2018-2022
Amazon	$87 billion	$253.2 million
Apple	$366.7 billion	$240.2 million
Facebook/Meta	$132.3 billion	$125.2 million
Google/Alphabet	$241.4 billion	$522.2 million
Microsoft	$234.1 billion	$217.9 million

Source: Public Citizen compilation based on companies' Securities and Exchange Commission filings.

or gaming versus other possible activities. It's that all that online time is changing how they think and feel.

In addition to an endless series of anecdotes, a growing academic literature identifies very significant harms to adolescent self-identity. Not everyone is negatively impacted, to be sure, but a great many teens are. One overarching problem is that more time on social media correlates to greater feelings of isolation and loneliness.[314] Despite the term "social" media, engaging on Instagram is not like hanging out with friends. In fact, engaging on social media has negative emotional effects that are roughly comparable in scale to (or greater than) the positive feedback from in-person interactions.[315]

For teenage girls, in particular, there's lots of evidence that social media drives feelings of insecurity, concern about body image and self-doubt. One particular problem is girls comparing themselves to idealized pictures, often of models, frequently airbrushed, on Instagram and other social media feeds.[316] Virtually no one can measure up to these artificial images, which are normalized on social media. Lots of evidence suggests that the resulting negative self-image fuels emotional distress and eating disorders. One study found "the association between poor mental health and social media use among girls is larger than the association between mental health and binge drinking, hard drug use, marijuana use, lack of exercise, early sexual activity, being suspended from school, being stopped by police, and carrying a weapon."[317]

Despite the mounting evidence of harm, doubts persist. The internet and social media obviously do help people get connected in lots of ways. Is social media really fueling isolation? There have always been depressed kids. Body image issues for girls are not new. Is social media really responsible for new problems?

It turns out there were definitive answers to these questions—in the files of the world's leading social media corporation, Facebook (now calling itself Meta). We know this because of disclosures from the Facebook whistleblower Frances Haugen. The Facebook documents Haugen shared with *The Wall Street Journal* and other media outlets showed that, yes, social media—particularly Facebook's Instagram—is causing serious emotional distress among teenaged girls. The documents also showed that Facebook knew about the problem but chose not to act.

Based on far-reaching surveys and access to user data—a research trove far richer than what most independent researchers might access—Facebook researchers discovered and shared within the company that:[318]

- "Thirty-two percent of teen girls said that when they felt bad about their bodies, Instagram made them feel worse. Comparisons on Instagram can change how young women view and describe themselves."

- "We make body image issues worse for one in three teen girls."
- "Teens blame Instagram for increases in the rate of anxiety and depression. This reaction was unprompted and consistent across all groups."
- Among teens who reported suicidal thoughts, 13 percent of British users and 6 percent of Americans traced the desire to kill themselves to Instagram.
- Teens often reported feeling unable to stop viewing Instagram, even if they wanted to.

The researchers shared their findings with top executives at Facebook, including company CEO Mark Zuckerberg. But Facebook did not share these startling results with the world. Instead, it downplayed the harms that Instagram and social media cause.

Omnipresent Surveillance and the Erosion of Privacy

No one thinks that Facebook wants to inflict harm on teenaged girls. So why was the company so reluctant to take action? Probably because the problem wasn't exactly an accident—it was a direct outgrowth of the company's business model.

That model, shared by other Big Tech and social media companies, involves acquiring as much information about users as possible, keeping them engaged for as long as possible, and then marketing to them relentlessly.

Unfortunately, it turns out that this model is not just worsening a mental health epidemic among teenagers. It is undermining our privacy; intruding into our thoughts; opening us up to scams; spreading misogyny, hate speech and extremism; enabling racist business practices; and tearing apart the fabric of our democracy.

Let's start with the data-gathering issue. All kinds of companies engage in massive data collection now. But none can compare to the full-on surveillance of the Big Tech companies. The scale and scope of their surveillance is almost incomprehensible.

Most of us use Google to navigate the internet, and "to Google" has become a verb: to use its search engine. But Google is a lot more than a search engine. Its empire includes Chrome browsers, the operating system for Android phones, Gmail, Google Maps, Youtube, Google calendars and an array of other tools. All of these feed Google's data surveillance system.

From the Google app, the company gathers location information, your contact information, browsing history and more. From Gmail, the company takes in your purchase history, location, email address, photos and videos, search history, and more. Similarly, from Chrome, the company obtains your browsing history, purchasing record and more.[319]

To contextualize this, in 2018, a Vanderbilt University professor found that each Android phone communicated location information to Google 340 times in a 24-hour period. He concluded as well that Google could gather information about your use of apps and visits on others' websites and connect it to your real identity.[320]

Location information is especially important data for brick-and-mortar advertisers, who want to serve ads to people when they are near their storefronts. Google has lots of information about where you are and have been, whether you want to volunteer that information or not. A 2018 AP investigation found that Google tracked users' location even when they had turned location history off.[321] If a user keeps location history "on," Google will store their locations on a minute-by-minute basis. However, "even with Location History paused, some Google apps automatically store time-stamped location data without asking."[322] Google Calendar tracks not just the events a user adds to their calendar but also whether and when they went to these events.[323] "Using your location data, Google Maps can automatically determine the location of your home and workplace based on the frequency of your travel to those locations, how much time you spend there, and the time of day you visit."[324]

In 2022, the District of Columbia sued Google, claiming that the company's location surveillance is pervasive and practically inescapable. "There is effectively no way for consumers to prevent Google from collecting, storing, and profiting from their location data," according to the District's summary of its lawsuit. "Google's deceptive location tracking practices impact users of smartphones running on the company's Android operating system, but they also extend to consumers who use Google products, including Google search and Google Maps, on non-Android devices."

"Regardless of the settings they select, consumers have no option but to allow Google to collect their location data," the District alleged. "Even if a user adjusts settings in their account or their device that they believe will stop their location data from being saved or transmitted, Google can still collect and store their location through Google apps on the user's device, Wi-Fi and Bluetooth scans from the user's device, the user's IP address, or through other methods."

The story is very similar with Facebook. For its part, Facebook starts with the information that people volunteer, such as their names, employer and relationship status, across all its platforms, which include not just Facebook but also Instagram and WhatsApp. It tracks what people "like" and their Facebook activities. "Likes" alone provide Facebook with enormous insights, including highly accurate predictions about race, gender, sexual orientation and more. Even a decade ago, studies concluded that with data from 10 likes a computer model could define your personality and preferences better than a colleague. With 300 likes, the model could describe you better than a spouse could.[325]

That was a decade ago. And Facebook has a LOT more information than likes.

It collects biometric data without users' consent[326] and tracks pictures and faces across its platforms.

"Facebook's reach also goes way beyond Facebook itself. It has partnerships with a whole host of marketing firms and ad networks so that activities on other sites—including but not limited to logging into a third-party service with your Facebook account—can be combined with your Facebook profile."[327] A 2019 Privacy International study found that "at least 61 percent of apps we tested automatically transfer data to Facebook the moment a user opens the app. This happens whether people have a Facebook account or not, or whether they are logged into Facebook or not."[328] Researchers have found that Facebook can collect data from other browser tabs and pages that users—including children—open, and from the buttons they click and purchases they make.[329]

Facebook's Pixel program allows websites to embed a very tiny transparent image on their page in order to track users' activity, including, for example, adding an item to their shopping cart or making a purchase.[330] This information is also shared with Facebook.

Facebook captures enormous amounts of data about where you are and where you've been. It stores "every time you log in to Facebook, where you logged in from, what time, and from what device."[331] If a user has turned on Location History in the Facebook app, Facebook "will periodically log your precise location to your history, even when you aren't using the app." It will also track "when you're on the move" and "points along your journey." Facebook also collects IP addresses, and wifi, Bluetooth and check-in data to show targeted advertisements. Users cannot turn this feature off, and Facebook will gather this geographical information even if a user indicates on the app that they "never" want Facebook to acquire their information and if they never check in.[332]

As Facebook explained in a letter to U.S. senators, "Even if someone does not enable Location Services, Facebook may still understand information about their location based on information that they and others provide through their activities and connections through our services. For example, if someone responds to an event on Facebook for a local music festival, uploads a location-tagged post, or gets tagged by a friend in a check-in at a restaurant, these actions would give us information about that person's likely location."[333]

As unfathomable as the current Big Tech data surveillance system is, it may soon be dwarfed by the total information gathering system that may accompany the growth of the Metaverse, persistent virtual reality worlds. To enter the metaverse requires wearing a helmet, glasses or some immersive device. This technology will likely enable Big Tech companies to track everything we see, say and do in the Metaverse, and even where we direct our eyes and how we move our heads in the real world. Warns one group of researchers:

> [Engaging with the Metaverse] requires pervasive user profiling activities at an unreasonably granular level, including facial expressions, eye/hand movements, speech and biometric features, and even brain wave patterns. ... It can facilitate the analysis of physical movements and user attributes and even enable user tracking. For example, the motion sensors and four built-in cameras in [Facebook's] Oculus helmet help track the head direction and movement, draw our rooms, as well as monitor our positions and environment in real time with submillimeter accuracy.[334]

Against this monstrous surveillance and monitoring system, consumers' single protection is the privacy policies of the Big Tech companies themselves. With limited exceptions for certain health and financial data, and for information related to children 13 and under, U.S. law does not require corporations to provide any particular privacy protections. However, when companies do make promises to users through their privacy policies, they are required to abide by them.

Big Tech can work around the promises it makes, however, simply by changing those privacy policies. That's something that Facebook in particular did frequently, as it transformed from a company that promised to let users control their data to an information-gathering leviathan that makes billions by vacuuming up that data. Journalist Matthew Keys surveyed Facebook's evolving privacy policies and identified 11 changes in privacy policy or practices over the decade from 2008-2018. He concluded: "Users who became invested in Facebook as a lifeline may have complained about all of those changes, but almost all of them acquiesced. Facebook always came out on top."[335]

Even with constantly changing privacy policies, however, Facebook has repeatedly failed to adhere to the voluntary commitments it made. In 2011, the company agreed to a consent decree with the Federal Trade Commission (FTC), finalized in 2012, to settle charges that the company repeatedly violated its own privacy policy. As the FTC complaint summarized:

- In December 2009, Facebook changed its website so that certain information that users may have designated as private—such as their Friends List—was made public. They didn't warn users that this change was coming or get their approval in advance.

- Facebook represented that third-party apps that users installed would have access only to user information they needed in order to operate. In fact, the apps could access nearly all of users' personal data—data the apps didn't need.
- Facebook told users they could restrict sharing of data to limited audiences—for example, with "Friends Only." In fact, selecting "Friends Only" did not prevent their information from being shared with third-party applications their friends used.
- Facebook had a "Verified Apps" program and claimed it certified the security of participating apps. It didn't.
- Facebook promised users it would not share their personal information with advertisers. It did.
- Facebook claimed that when users deactivated or deleted their accounts, their photos and videos would be inaccessible. But Facebook allowed access to the content, even after users had deactivated or deleted their accounts.
- Facebook claimed that it complied with the U.S.-EU Safe Harbor Framework that governs data transfer between the U.S. and the European Union. It didn't.[336]

You might have thought that getting called out like that would force Facebook not to repeat the pattern. But you would be wrong.

Eight years later, Facebook would enter into another privacy settlement with the FTC, this time paying $5 *billion* in fines and penalties, by far the largest ever imposed for privacy violations. This settlement covered the practices that led to the Cambridge Analytica scandal, when the political consulting firm was able to access personal data from millions of Facebook users without their consent.

In that 2019 settlement, the FTC said in its summary that Facebook violated its commitments under the 2012 agreement. It alleged:

- Facebook violated the 2012 order by deceiving its users when the company shared the data of users' Facebook friends with third-party app developers, even when those friends had set more restrictive privacy settings.
- In May 2012, Facebook added a disclosure to its central "Privacy Settings" page that information shared with a user's Facebook friends could also be shared with the apps used by those friends. Soon after, the company removed the disclosure, even though the practice continued.
- Facebook launched various services that claimed to help users better manage their privacy settings, but failed to disclose that, even with the most restrictive setting, Facebook could still gather and share information about an app user's Facebook friends.

- Facebook announced in April 2014 that it would stop allowing third-party developers to collect data about the friends of app users, but waited more than four years—until at least June 2018, after the Cambridge Analytica disclosures—to end the practice.
- Facebook failed to screen app developers or their apps before granting them access to vast amounts of user data.
- Facebook misrepresented users' ability to control the use of facial recognition technology with their accounts.[337]

This is an utterly astounding record.

But it turns out that companies regularly violate their privacy policies in consequential ways. The FTC has filed many dozens of such cases.[338]

And the 2022 District of Columbia case against Google—with parallel actions filed in Texas, Washington state and Indiana—makes claims similar to those lodged against Facebook. Since at least 2014, the D.C. complaint contends, Google has misled Google account users into believing they can control the information Google gathers about them through their account settings. For example, D.C. argues, from 2014 to 2019, Google told users that turning off location history would mean that "the places you go are no longer stored." D.C. says, "That is false. Even when Location History is off, Google continues to collect and store users' locations."

The purpose of all this information data gathering is to enable advertisers to very precisely target their marketing messages. Advertisers can target you through demographics—including education, employment, marriage status, homeownership—or demonstrated interests. They can target consumers based on what they are researching or planning, or what major life events they are experiencing or nearing, such as graduations, marriage or moving.[339] They can target "psychographics"—beliefs, values and aspirations.[340] Travel-related companies can target ads based on where a user plans to go.[341] Facebook permits advertisers to target a specific address and those in the immediate vicinity. Advertisers can further target based on those who live at, recently were in, or are traveling to a location.[342]

Google similarly enables advertisers to target precise advertisements by location, enabling advertisers to target people who have searched for a location, are regularly located at a place, or both.[343] Google enables advertisers to target users based on products and services for which they are actively searching.[344] Facebook's pixel program lets advertisers target users based on what they have previously searched for on the advertisers' website, including knowledge of what they placed in a shopping cart but did not ultimately purchase.[345]

It's important to note that Amazon also vacuums up an enormous amount of data with little user awareness, but its means of profiting from the data is different than that of Facebook and Google, as we'll see later in this chapter.

Facebook and Google treat this surveillance and targeted marketing system as a public good: it means consumers are being shown advertisements for the things that most interest them. There is an element of truth to this, though even "useful" targeted marketing can feel disturbingly creepy, as most of us can attest.

But this grain of truth ignores the big picture. As we have seen, to facilitate narrowly targeted advertising, Big Tech companies need to surveil everything we read, write, think and imagine. They surveil where we go and what we do. They intrude into our innermost thoughts, they know our secrets and they peek into our intimate lives. To construct this system of total surveillance, they often deceive us about their information-gathering practices. They are stealing our privacy, tricking us along the way, and, as individuals, there's virtually nothing we can do about it.

Spreading Hate, Enabling Scams

As serious as all that is, it's not just about privacy.

The data surveillance system requires all of us ("users") to keep feeding information to Big Tech and the advertising system requires us to stay connected so we can be hit with advertisements. As Columbia University law professor Tim Wu characterizes it, Facebook, Google and their compatriots are "attention merchants," scrambling to control our attention and minds.[346]

The companies have learned that often the best way to hold our attention is to play to our fears, anxieties and worst selves. That's why the problem of Instagram increasing teens' sense of isolation and profoundly worsening teenage girls' body image anxiety is not random. And it's not something that Facebook/Instagram can easily remedy. It's a direct outgrowth of the Big Tech business model.

The problem is not limited to teenagers.

Facebook and other social media companies do not exist as passive platforms for the transmission of posts, videos and other content. Their algorithms make decisions about what content to share widely. Although this has been understood generally, the companies are very proprietary about how their algorithms work, so it's hard to know exactly what's going on. But Facebook whistleblower Frances Haugen's disclosures changed that, at least for Facebook.

The Facebook papers show that the company studies in extreme detail how tiny changes to its algorithms affect user engagement. When it has found that extremism and misinformation increase engagement, it has let the problem persist. For example, in 2019 it created a "dummy" account for a conservative mother in North Carolina. Within five days, the Facebook algorithm directed her to QAnon. Yet Facebook let QAnon continue to operate on its platform more than a year after the FBI declared it a domestic terrorist threat.[347]

The company has discovered that anger maintains engagement. For a period of years, Facebook's algorithm gave a user clicking on an anger emoji (a small digital image, like a face) five times the weight for someone clicking "like." This continued even though Facebook knew posts were disproportionately connected to "civic low-quality news, civic misinfo, civic toxicity, health misinfo, and health antivax [anti-vaccination] content."[348]

Similar problems have persisted at YouTube, owned by Google. In 2018, for example, a *Wall Street Journal* investigation "found YouTube's recommendations often lead users to channels that feature conspiracy theories, partisan viewpoints and misleading videos, even when those users haven't shown interest in such content. When users show a political bias in what they choose to view, YouTube typically recommends videos that echo those biases, often with more-extreme viewpoints."[349]

There's a lot going on in America right now that is driving right-wing extremism, hate speech, virulent racism and sexism, conspiratorial thinking and threats to democratic functioning. Social media is not responsible for all this on its own, but there's little doubt it is a significant contributing factor. It's not just that the platforms are available to purveyors of hateful speech, it's that the platforms amplify, reward and incentivize extremism, spreading it to wider audiences and drawing sympathizers in closer.

And then there's the problem of the Big Tech data surveillance/target marketing system doing what it is supposed to do—but for bad actors:

- **Junk food purveyors:** YouTube, TikTok, Instagram and other social media outlets mesmerize young users for hours on end. Notwithstanding privacy and data protections for people under 13, marketers are deluging teenagers and young children with both overt and disguised advertisements. Notable among them are junk food companies. Concludes the Center for Digital Democracy in a groundbreaking study on junk food marketing and the childhood obesity epidemic: The "constant immersion in digital culture has exposed them to a steady flow of marketing for fast foods, soft drinks, and other unhealthy products, much of it under the radar of parents and teachers. Food and beverage companies have made digital media ground zero for their youth promotion efforts, employing a growing spectrum of new strategies and high-tech tools to penetrate every aspect of young peoples' lives."[350]

- **Scammers:** At a conference for sketchy marketers, participants told a *Bloomberg* reporter, Zeke Faux, that "Facebook had revolutionized scamming. ... Facebook's targeting algorithm is so powerful, they said, they don't need to identify suckers themselves—Facebook does it automatically." A scammer might sell junk diet pills. They advertise on Facebook, Facebook's algorithm discovers the kind of person who clicks on the ad, and then targets the ad at the right set of people. "They go out and find the morons for me," a marketer who sells deceptively priced skin-care creams with fake endorsements from Chelsea Clinton said.[351]

- **Predatory Lenders:** The target marketing tools of social media platforms enable predatory lenders to home in on the most vulnerable consumers. To their credit, Google, TikTok and Facebook have banned payday and other high-interest lending ads,[352] but there is evidence of payday lenders working around the bans.[353] The Better Business Bureau reports that the ads are targeting TikTok's and Facebook's younger users, who may be particularly susceptible to the misleading promises of high-interest lenders.[354]

Discrimination by Algorithm

Big Data offers corporations and governments the promise of automated, instant and precise decision-making about a wide range of issues. The accumulation and analysis of vast troves of data can reveal patterns, predilections and associations that are otherwise hidden.

Unfortunately, Big Data information gathering and analysis does not occur in laboratory conditions. We live in a society with profound income, wealth, racial and gender inequality. Computer programmers live in that society, and they almost unavoidably embed the assumptions, biases and values that flow from that inequality into the programs and algorithms they create. Moreover, even when they create "neutral" algorithms, the algorithms themselves may reflect social inequality.

For example, if there's more street crime in lower-income neighborhoods, an algorithm may recommend that people who live in those neighborhoods pay higher auto insurance premiums. That kind of algorithmic discrimination—irrespective of the intent or good-heartedness of the people who developed the program—turns out to be widespread.

- Algorithmic decision systems have been demonstrated to replicate and worsen racial bias in the following ways:[355]
- Making auto insurance more expensive for communities of color: Communities of color pay 30 percent more for auto insurance than whiter communities with similar accident costs.[356]
- Lowering credit scores: White home buyers have credit scores 57 points higher than Black home buyers, and 33 points higher than Latino home buyers.[357]

- Making mortgages more expensive or inaccessible: Higher, discriminatory mortgage prices cost Latino and Black communities $750 million each year. At least 6 percent of Latino and Black applications are rejected but would be accepted if the borrower were not a part of these minority groups.[358]
- Denying needed care to patients: White patients were assigned higher algorithmically determined risk scores than Black patients with the same level of illness. As a result, the number of Black patients eligible for extra care was cut by more than half.[359]
- Making the criminal justice system more punitive: Black defendants are 45 percent to 77 percent more likely to be assigned risk scores indicating a higher likelihood of recidivism—that is, that they will commit crimes in the future—than white defendants.[360]
- Facilitating over-surveillance and over-policing of communities: Predictive policing algorithms have targeted Black communities for drug-related policing at twice the rate of white individuals. Other communities of color were targeted at a rate 1.5 times that of white neighborhoods. But the actual pattern of drug use by each race is comparable across the board.[361]

Crushing Competition

The monopoly power of the Big Tech companies makes all these problems worse—and creates additional, profound economic and political difficulties.

In 2020, the U.S. House of Representatives antitrust subcommittee issued a 450-page report on Big Tech monopolization, the result of the most thorough congressional antitrust investigation in decades. The report documented the illegitimate ways Big Tech companies have gained and maintained monopoly power, and showed what that means for small businesses, consumers and American democracy. Based on hundreds of interviews and a review of more than a million company and other documents, the subcommittee report didn't just make sweeping accusations; it provided a detailed, play-by-play account of how Big Tech corporations deploy their market power to undermine competitors, injure small business, slow innovation, leverage all that data they collect on us and limit consumer choice.

Each of the Big Tech companies has maneuvered ruthlessly to squash competition, the antitrust subcommittee found:[362]

- At Facebook, "a senior executive at the company described its acquisition strategy as a 'land grab' to 'shore up' Facebook's position, while Facebook's CEO said that Facebook 'can likely always just buy any competitive start-ups." Among many other purchases, Facebook did buy two of its major competitors: Instagram and WhatsApp.

- Google grabbed and maintained a stranglehold over internet search by aggressively defeating "vertical" search providers—tools to search within particular sites—including by misappropriating data from other sites, the subcommittee found. Google also entered into contracts to lock in reliance on its search engine, including with cell phone makers.

- Amazon has made over 100 acquisitions, including key competitors like Diapers.com and Zappos, to become the dominant online retailer in the United States and around the world.

Big Tech Monopoly Power Matters

Small businesses cannot compete with these giants. This is most acutely the case with Amazon. Small businesses have no choice but to use the Amazon marketplace, since so many consumers search for products not on the broad internet, but on Amazon.com. And Amazon is not shy about using this power to disadvantage and extract money from small businesses, the subcommittee found.

For example, "CEO and Founder of PopSockets David Barnett testified about Amazon's bullying tactics, which he said were enabled by 'the asymmetry in power between Amazon and its partners.' (Popsockets are stands and gripping devices for mobile phones.) He stated that after the two companies decided on a minimum price at which Amazon would sell PopSockets, Amazon sold the products for a lower price and then demanded that PopSockets pay for the lost margin. As a result, PopSockets decided to end its relationship with Amazon Retail. When PopSockets communicated this intent to Amazon, its response was, 'No, you are not leaving the relationship.' PopSockets did sever its relationship with Amazon Retail for a period of time, but reestablished it about a year later. Mr. Barnett estimates that in 2019 his company incurred losses of $10 million in revenue from when he stopped selling to Amazon Retail and Amazon blocked one of his authorized distributors from selling on the marketplace."[363]

Monopolists typically deny choice to consumers, and that behavior is central to Big Tech's business model. At Facebook, for example, users invest huge amounts of time in uploading pictures, personal information, diary-like thoughts and much more. By design, it is very hard for users to take the information they have uploaded onto Facebook properties and transfer them to other social media platforms. "Facebook's internal documents and communications reveal that Facebook employees recognize that high switching costs insulate Facebook from competition," the subcommittee found.

There is "stickiness" to Facebook products, making it difficult to migrate. Although the company claims to facilitate data migration (known as "interoperability"), its tools for migrating data don't work well and the widespread use of Facebook information to create accounts on other services massively deters closing Facebook accounts. If consumers can't easily switch services, then rival companies have little incentive to develop new products that might compete directly. Yes, it is possible for a new social media platform like TikTok to emerge—but that is the exception that proves the rule. Users have little choice when it comes to social media, precisely because Facebook and others prevent competitors from emerging.[364]

Equally, monopoly control has blocked or deterred competitors from investing in new innovative technologies and products, harming consumers and the overall economy alike. One example involves Google taking content from other sites and displaying it directly as part of its search results. In doing this, Google keeps users on its site and away from the other sites. If users don't go to those sites, then the businesses running those sites can't generate revenue and can't invest in new products. One competitor told the subcommittee that "Google's conduct has sapped investment, as 'investors don't want to invest in companies that are producing content that relies on Google traffic,' resulting in 'less capital invested in companies reliant on traffic from Google.'"[365]

Brian Warner, the founder of Celebrity Net Worth, explained that his business has been hurt as Google directly displays information from his site rather than just supplying links. He wrote to the subcommittee, "It is my view that Google has removed essentially all of the oxygen from the open internet ecosystem. There is no longer any incentive or even basic opportunity to innovate as I did back in 2008. If someone came to me with an idea for a website or a web service today, I would tell them to run. Run as far away from the web as possible. Launch a lawn care business or a dog grooming business—something Google can't take away as soon as he or she is thriving."[366]

The Big Tech companies' size and market power also fuels the comprehensive surveillance and privacy intrusions we saw above. On the one hand, the companies' business models are structured around data accumulation and monetization. Their size and market power give them the ability to collect more information than competitors and maintain their stranglehold on the market. For example, the subcommittee found that the Android operating system, owned by Google and installed on most cell phones, "gives Google unparalleled access to data on its users and developers. This includes information that Google can monetize through its ad business, as well as strategic intelligence that lets Google track emerging competitors and general business trends."[367] On the other hand, because the Big Tech products are so inescapable and so "sticky," and because the Big Tech giants have bought up or squashed competitors, it's not practical for most users to give up Big Tech's privacy-intruding products and services and switch to competitor products that are more privacy protecting.

In short, the Big Tech companies' size and power intensifies surveillance and diminishes our privacy. The equation is that simple.

Social Unraveling

In the course of a few short decades, the internet, social media and digital technologies have remade our lives—increasingly under the control and direction of Big Tech goliaths.

We have all lived through this (the younger among us have never known anything else). We know how much time we devote to devices. We're aware of conveniences and wonders that were all but unimaginable a few decades earlier. We're able to maintain connections with family and old friends in ways that were once impossible; we can communicate globally with ease and at a low price; and we can access boundless information worldwide with a few clicks.

We know, too, that in the process our culture has changed in profound ways—not all of it bad, to be sure, and in ways not necessarily easy to identify. Many of these are paradoxical. We can connect with others like never before, but communities are weakening, feelings of isolation are worsening, and rates of anxiety and depression are rising sharply around the world. We can do many things that were once unimaginable, but many of us feel a loss of control. We can access all kinds of information, but lies, disinformation and conspiratorial thinking are all intensifying. The internet and social media have some inherently democratizing features, but inequality and authoritarianism are surging.

These broad, worrisome and often global trends surely have many causes—but Big Tech is driving many of them.

In her magisterial work, *The Age of Surveillance Capitalism,* Harvard Business School Professor Shoshana Zuboff aimed to capture these broad sweeping changes. In short, she says, "our lives are scraped and sold to fund their [Big Tech's] freedom and our subjugation, their knowledge and our ignorance about what they know."[368] She identifies dangers in the way major communications and information corporations care about the volume and flow of information, but not about what is communicated. Big Tech's "radical indifference" leads to the widespread dissemination of information "that would normally be viewed as repugnant: lies, systemic disinformation, fraud, violence, hate speech and so on."[369] Indeed, if those repugnant forms of communication generate more clicks and sustained interest—and they do—then Big Tech algorithms don't just permit but amplify them.

Even more, Zuboff points out, Big Tech doesn't just exploit its knowledge of our wants, thoughts, desires and insecurities to sell us things; the corporations use that knowledge to shape what we think, know and want. Of course, to some extent, TV networks and advertisers have always done this. But they never had the technology to analyze on an individual and micro-community basis, to personalize, and to target advertising and information in the ways that Big Tech companies can and do. They never had the ability to track where we were. They could not travel along with us. However ubiquitous TV once seemed, it never controlled and intruded into our minds in the way that Big Tech does.

Big Tech's concentration of economic, political and cultural power, indifference to values and control of our minds is antithetical to democracy. "Indeed," Zuboff concludes, "surveillance capitalism must be reckoned as a profoundly antidemocratic social force."[370]

CHAPTER 11

Big Tech Comes to—and Buys—Washington

In October 2020, the House subcommittee on antitrust concluded the most thorough investigation of Big Tech companies ever conducted. The report, as we have seen, detailed the manifold ways in which Amazon, Apple, Facebook and Google have used their market dominance to squash competitors, surveil consumers, undermine innovation and deny consumers meaningful choice.[371]

The report rocked the political establishment—and Big Tech. Antitrust action—competition policy aimed at preventing big corporations from using their market power unfairly to injure competitors and consumers—had been considered dead in Washington for decades. The report suggested it might be coming back to life.

And the next year, both the House and the Senate started debating far-reaching legislation to address the ever-growing power and influence of Big Tech. What made this time different was the fact that Democrats and Republicans alike were sounding the alarm. They highlighted somewhat different concerns, but they converged on many issues—especially the need to combat the companies' anti-competitive practices. Bipartisan antitrust legislation had broad support in both houses, and it appeared that the bills were fast-tracked to passage.

Then Big Tech struck back.

The corporations spent record amounts on lobbying. Amazon, Apple, Facebook and Google spent a combined $57.6 million on lobbying in 2021 and $32 million in just the first six months of 2022.[372]

They deployed their most effective lobbyists—the company CEOs who generally disdain visiting Washington. Google CEO Sundar Pichai, Amazon CEO Andrew Jassy and Apple CEO Tim Cook all directly lobbied senators in person and/or over the phone.[373]

Big Tech conjured up new front groups to advance their position. The Alliance on Antitrust, a new conservative grouping, loudly opposed antitrust reforms. It was funded by Google, as were many individual members of the new coalition. A whole host of industry-funded conservative groups jumped into the fray, aiming to persuade Republicans who had been critical of Big Tech not to support antitrust reform.[374]

With Democrats the party in power and more ready to restrain Big Business than Republicans, the Big Tech companies also doubled down on their influence game with the Democratic establishment. *Sludge* reported that "tech industry lobbyists and lobbying firms, as well as their owners, bundled more than $1 million for the Democratic Senatorial Campaign Committee."[375] An industry trade group, the Chamber of Progress, burst on the scene and started lobbying against antitrust reform. It was funded by Google, Amazon and Facebook, among others. It was founded by a Democratic operative who had previously served on the Google policy team.[376] To place TV ads, a lucrative business, Big Tech relied on Democratic Party-affiliated firms, presumably hoping to win points in Democratic circles.[377]

Over the previous decade, the Big Tech companies, especially Google and Facebook, had poured money into think tanks, advocacy groups and academics. Now they cashed in their chips. "Dozens of Washington advocacy groups and think tanks that receive funding from tech giants, including liberal and conservative organizations, have spoken out against the antitrust bills," *The Hill* reported.[378]

Big Tech even marshaled the national security establishment, with top former national security officials claiming that antitrust reform would undermine U.S. national security.[379] It was a preposterous argument: Exactly how is the United States stronger if the tech sector is less competitive and innovative? Well, it's fair to conclude the generals were not only motivated by merits arguments. They were all paid by Big Tech, a fact not revealed when they criticized antitrust reform.[380]

All of this was the industry inside game. Even more important was its outside game.

Big Tech flooded television airwaves and online channels with advertisements. "Don't Break Our [Amazon] Prime," "Don't Let Congress Break Google Maps," the ads proclaimed.

There were a lot of ads. A *Wall Street Journal* analysis concluded that, through early June 2022, "advocacy groups bankrolled by big technology companies have poured at least $36.4 million into TV and internet ads opposing antitrust legislation that would bar dominant tech platforms from favoring their own products and services."[381] By November, the Big Tech TV advertising blitz exceeded more than $120 million.[382]

The ads were heavily concentrated in states where senators were up for reelection in the 2022 cycle, particularly where Democratic incumbents had close races, including New Hampshire, Nevada and Arizona. The ads also targeted states like West Virginia and California, where Big Tech hoped they might persuade Democratic senators to oppose the legislation.[383]

It's not certain that the ads persuaded anyone. The ads weren't clear about what they were opposing. Polling showed continued strong support for antitrust legislation.

But persuading the public may have been a secondary goal. As much as anything, political ads like these served as a warning: If you vote the wrong way, senator, the next set of ads may be targeting you.

The Big Tech campaign blitz worked. With congressional support uncertain, the Senate did not move the antitrust legislation to the floor for debate.

It was a remarkable achievement, the culmination of a decade of political work by Big Tech in preparation for just such a moment.

Lobbying Behemoths

For a long time, the Big Tech companies eschewed Washington. They considered themselves above politics and just wanted to be left alone.

As the companies grew in size and power, however, Americans grew more concerned about the companies' conduct, and Congress and federal regulators started to take notice. They began to examine the range of issues discussed in the previous chapter: privacy, data gathering, hate speech, human rights violations, threats to democracy, worker rights, unfair competition and more.

As Washington started to take more notice of Big Tech, Big Tech started to beef up its presence in Washington, at first tepidly and then very aggressively.

Here's how that translated: In the 2009-2010 election cycle, the top four companies spent $19.2 million on lobbying and campaign contributions combined (including campaign contributions by their lobbyists). That figure topped $70 million for 2013-2014 and hit $124 million in 2019-2020.[384] That's up *more than 640 percent* over a decade!

By 2020, nearly all (94 percent) members of Congress on committees with jurisdiction over privacy and antitrust issues had received money from a Big Tech corporate PAC or lobbyist. Of course, the mere fact of a contribution from a corporation's employee does not automatically compromise a legislator. At the same time, there is no doubt companies direct their campaign funds in order to gain access and influence—and the overall picture of what's going on here is clear.

The four companies' lobbying spending skyrocketed from $7.5 million combined in 2009 to $57.6 million in 2021.

Facebook/Meta and Amazon are now the two biggest corporate lobbying spenders in the country, with Google/Alphabet number seven.

The four Big Tech companies have a giant lobbying force. From a mere 89 in 2009, the number rose to 333 in 2020. There are only 535 representatives and senators. What do all these lobbyists do all day, you might wonder?

Well, it helps to think about how corporate lobbyists exert influence. They may be charming and/or they may be policy experts, but those aren't the major sources of their power. One source is their employers' money. This is especially true for lobbyists who haven't worked in government recently (or at all).

Not surprisingly, many of these lobbyists are D.C. power brokers and major campaign contributors. Among the 10 lobbyists who were the biggest contributors to the 2020 election cycle, five of them lobby on behalf of at least one of the four Big Tech companies. Together, just these five lobbyists contributed over $2 million to the 2020 elections.

The other major source of lobbyist influence is their personal connections, particularly for those who have recently worked in Congress or an administrative agency. When you can call up your old friends and colleagues, it's easier to get your call returned. It's easier to ask for a favor. And you're better positioned to present your company's positions in a way that resonates with the person you're lobbying. For this reason, former members of Congress make the best lobbyists. But it's former congressional staffers who by dint of numbers most frequently travel through the "revolving door," moving from government service to lobbying—and, not infrequently, back and forth again with the shifting winds of election results.

The vast majority of Big Tech lobbyists have traveled through the revolving door. Six dozen revolving-door lobbyists are in their direct employ. More than 200 of the lobbyists Amazon, Facebook, Google and Apple hire through lobby firms have moved through the revolving door.

The companies' policy shop heads all hail from previous government service. From 2015 until July 2022, Jay Carney, former press secretary for President Biden, served as Amazon's Senior Vice President of Global Corporate Affairs. Joel Kaplan, a former aide to President George W. Bush, is Facebook's vice president of global public policy. Karan Bhatia, who worked at the Department of Commerce and Department of Transportation for George W. Bush, is Google's Global Head of Government Affairs & Public Policy. Tim Powderly, a former congressional staffer, is Apple's Vice President for Public Policy and Government Affairs for the Americas, and Lisa Jackson, who ran the Environmental Protection Agency under President Obama, is the company's vice president of Environment, Policy and Social Initiatives.

Many of the biggest Washington, D.C., insider names are on Big Tech's lobbying roster. These are the people who throw the parties, hold the fundraisers and make up the political establishment.

And then there are very targeted Big Tech hires. For example, in the summer of 2022, with antitrust reform legislative debate hitting a crescendo in the U.S. Senate, Amazon Web Services hired Judd Smith, a senior Republican staffer on the Senate Judiciary Committee. An aide to Ranking Member Chuck Grassley, Smith had helped draft the bipartisan bills under consideration in the Senate.[385] As *Politico* noted, Smith wasn't the first committee staffer working on the bills that Big Tech hired. Apple hired April Jones, a tech and telecom policy staffer for Senator Amy Klobuchar, the chair of the antitrust subcommittee and lead author of the antitrust bills, in fall 2021.[386]

Deep Lobbying

Along with its intense lobbyist- and advertising-led push to derail legislation it fears, Big Tech corporations have been masterful players of the long game of shaping policymaker attitudes.

The number-one way they have done this is by funding pro-Big Tech research and writing. When you have as much money as the Big Tech companies, this isn't hard to do. The academic field is rife with people who have received grant support from Big Tech—a potential conflict of interest that they only sometimes disclose.

As one example, Fiona Scott Morton, a Yale University economist who has published multiple influential articles on the antitrust cases against Facebook and Google, was found in 2020 to have received funds from Amazon and Apple—yet failed to disclose them until they were uncovered by reporters.[387]

There's lots of money to spread around. *The New York Times* opinion columnist David Brooks wrote about a Facebook-funded project on which he was working without disclosing publicly the payments he received, and he also praised Facebook as a guest blogger on the company's website.[388]

In the Washington, D.C., policy world, it's hard to escape Big Tech money. Amazon, Google and Facebook in particular fund nonprofits that advocate as hard for Big Tech positions as the companies do. They fund organizations whose work is adjacent to their interests—for example, those working on foreign policy. They even fund consumer and tech policy groups that are critical of them, presumably in order to soften the criticism.

The Tech Transparency Project is a project of the Campaign for Accountability, which has been funded by Oracle, a company antagonistic to the big four companies. It has compiled a database of nonprofits funded by Big Tech. According to the Project, "Amazon, Google, Facebook and Apple have funded over 900 third-party organizations since 2015, including not only tech- and science-based groups, but groups devoted to immigration, foreign relations, business development, minority and women's rights, health, education, transportation, tax reform, music, the wireless industry, retailers, addiction, and child protection. They include trade and advocacy groups, partisan organizations (both conservative and liberal), foundations, university programs—even downtown associations."[389]

Of course, the hundreds of millions of dollars spent on all these projects amount to a relatively small sum for the Big Tech goliaths.

But it's an awful lot of money in policy circles. What do the companies get for all this spending? They have constructed an awe-inspiring policy infrastructure, influence machine and political powerhouse. Plan A is to hold off legislation and regulatory initiatives overwhelmingly favored by the American people. Plan B will be to weaken those initiatives and slow their implementation to continue, as much as possible, business as usual.

Political money can't guarantee you victories, but it sure improves your odds.

CHAPTER 12

Plunder and Pillage: Big Tech's Corporate Welfare

It turns out that Al Gore never claimed to have invented the internet,[390] but the U.S. government really did invent it. The internet's origins trace to the programs of the Advanced Research Projects Agency (ARPA, later the Defense Advanced Research Projects Agency), the creation of an early computer network called ARPAnet, and the invention of internet protocols by ARPA researchers.[391]

Government investments also led to the invention of microchips, touch screens,[392] even the voice recognition application Apple uses for Siri.[393]

There is no Big Tech without U.S. invention and investment in the internet. Big Tech has never paid a dime for the fundamental infrastructure upon which all its operations run.

There's nothing wrong with that. It's a good thing that the government created the internet and made it available as a public asset. The open nature of the internet has allowed it to flourish and made it available for all kinds of users, from big companies to small nonprofits, from giant social media companies to individual bloggers, from U.S. presidents to young children.

Big Tech companies like to tell the story about how they grew out of college dorms and garages, built by young, visionary and driven founders who did it all on their own. The Big Tech companies do all in fact have impressive founding stories. But if we pull back a little, we can see the bigger picture: what these corporate founders built depended entirely on an infrastructure and inventions created by U.S. government investment.

Recognizing the central government role in building the sector is important for contextualizing the idea of entrepreneurship and under-standing the profoundly social nature of invention.

It's also crucial for this reason: The Big Tech companies are the wealthiest in America. By stock valuation, Apple, Microsoft, Amazon and Google are the nation's four richest companies, and Facebook has frequently ranked in the top five, as well. They owe that wealth in significant part to the investments of the taxpaying American people. But they are among the companies most aggressive at innovating ways to avoid paying their fair share of taxes.

The Tax Haven Racket

To make billions and pay nothing at all in taxes takes some work.

One trick corporations use is to shift their profits to offshore tax havens, such as the Cayman Islands, Bermuda or Ireland, which levy zero or very low taxes on corporate profits. Corporations may shift profits in this fashion by lodging ownership of patents and intellectual property in subsidiaries based in tax havens, and then paying high royalty rates to those subsidiaries. Or they may simply use elaborate subsidiary arrangements to move revenues to offshore havens. The Trump tax cut package permitted this practice to persist.

The Biden administration has negotiated a tax treaty that would establish a worldwide base level for corporate taxes of 15 percent. Congressional Republicans are trying to block that global agreement.[394]

Instead of shutting down the tax haven racket, the Trump tax package aimed to persuade U.S. companies that had booked profits overseas to "repatriate" the profits to the United States. The carrot for repatriation was a super-low rate for repatriated profits: as opposed to the 35 percent corporate rate that applied at the time the profits were generated, companies would pay a tax rate of just 15.5 percent on cash and 8 percent for non-cash assets.

In the first couple of years after the Trump tax cut went into effect, companies repatriated $1 trillion in order to reap these savings.[395] The cost to taxpayers, compared to the previous 35 percent tax rate, was just shy of $200 billion, with allowance for some variance with the detailed application of the tax rules.

An Institute on Taxation and Economic Policy (ITEP) analysis of the final Trump tax bill found that the tax holiday for repatriated profits would save corporations—and cost taxpayers—$413 billion.[396] This calculation was based on estimates that Fortune 500 companies had parked $2.6 trillion in profits overseas.

Based on publicly available information, ITEP and Public Citizen analyzed the impact of the Trump tax proposals on three industries that exploited offshore tax havens more than any other. Big Tech,[397] Wall Street[398] and Big Pharma[399] manipulated complicated corporate structures and intellectual property rules to lodge astoundingly large profits in overseas subsidiaries: The ITEP/Public Citizen analysis was necessarily incomplete, since not all relevant companies disclosed their overseas cash and profits.

Eight Wall Street firms were projected to save more than $22 billion, and four Big Pharma corporations were projected to reap $17 billion in tax savings. But Big Tech was the biggest winner from the deal, hands down.

Eight Big Tech corporations will pay $88 billion less in taxes when they repatriate their $502 billion in offshore profits, much of which is booked to their 94 tax haven subsidiaries across the globe.

The biggest winner was Apple, which the analysis projected would save $43.7 billion on an estimated $252.3 billion in profits in three offshore tax haven subsidiaries.[400]

Microsoft reaped $25 billion in savings and Oracle slashed its tax bill by $8.4 billion. Other tech giants such as IBM, Cisco Systems and Google also are known to book tens of billions in profits to offshore subsidiaries, but because they do not disclose their offshore tax rates, it is difficult to accurately estimate what they would owe under the proposed plan.

Amazon's Civic Shakedown

When it comes to corporate tax evasion, Amazon is, at minimum, giving Apple a run for its money.

Amazon uses legal methods to avoid billions in federal taxes on an ongoing basis. In 2021, Amazon paid a federal income tax rate of 6 percent on its profits—saving the company $5.2 billion compared to what it would owe if it paid at the 21 percent standard corporate tax rate. From 2018 to 2021, it reported a total federal tax rate of just 5.1 percent on over $78 billion of U.S. income.[401] (After passage of the Inflation Reduction Act in August 2022, it should be impossible for Amazon to pay less than 15 percent on its revenues.) Amazon's tax avoidance strategies, as detailed by ITEP, include: tax credits; deductions for granting stock options to executives, even though the options don't cost companies anything; and a Trump tax break on revenues from exports tied to intellectual property, like patents and copyrights on trademarks (the foreign-derived intangible income deduction).[402]

Figure 13. Amazon's Corporate Tax Avoidance Since 2018

	2021	2020	2019	2018	4 Years
U.S. Pretax Income	$35.1 billion	$19.6 billion	$13 billion	$10.8 billion	$78.6 billion
Current Federal Income Tax	$2.1 billion	$1.8 billion	$162 million	$-129 million	$4 billion
Effective Federal Income Tax Rate	6.1%	9.4%	1.2%	−1.2%	5.1%

Source: Institute on Taxation and Economic Policy.

But Amazon is not satisfied merely to escape from federal taxes. It has perfected the art of extracting massive tax subsidies from locales that are desperate for jobs.

In September 2017, Amazon made a grand announcement that it would open a second headquarters somewhere outside its home in Seattle. The corporation's operations there had become too big to house in a single place. "HQ2," it said, would be equal in scale to the Seattle headquarters. It said it anticipated $5 billion in construction and 50,000 new jobs.[403]

Where would this new headquarters be based? Amazon did not say. Instead, it proclaimed it was launching a search for a new location. It declared that it was opening the Amazon HQ2 Request for Proposal ("RFP"), with guidance for local and state leaders about what they should offer. The company said it wanted a metropolitan area of more than 1 million people and a "business-friendly environment." It encouraged cities to "think big and creatively when considering locations and real estate options."[404] That instruction translated into a request for local and state subsidies: subsidies in acquiring land, constructing supportive infrastructure and, especially, local and state tax abatements.

What followed was a sordid contest among cities across the nation to prostrate themselves in front of Amazon with gigantic subsidy packages … for one of the biggest and richest corporations on the planet. Many of the "finalist" cities that sought to lure Amazon made their offers public. Buzzfeed compiled the astounding set of legal bribe offers.[405] Here are a few lowlights of the subsidy packages:

- Atlanta offered $2 billion in incentives. It also offered to create an "Amazon Georgia Academy," a state university-affiliated education program featuring 24-week boot camp programs for company employees; an exclusive lounge and free parking for Amazon executives at the city's airport; and a possible additional car on its rapid transit trains to deliver Amazon products.
- Chicago proposed gifting $2.25 billion or more in incentives to Amazon, including $400 million in road, sewer and other infrastructure improvements. William Shatner, the actor who played Captain Kirk in the original Star Trek, narrated a proposal video, in an attempt to capitalize on Amazon chief Jeff Bezos' fandom.
- Montgomery County, Maryland, outside of Washington, D.C., offered $6.5 billion in tax incentives in what the *Baltimore Sun* said was the largest subsidy package the state had ever offered. The state promised an additional $2 billion in infrastructure and transportation improvements.

In the end, Amazon selected two sites: Alexandria, Virginia, outside Washington, D.C., and Queens, New York. Virginia offered $750 million in direct subsidies and an additional $1 billion to locate an "innovation campus," putting the overall value of the deal at $1.8 billion, according to the economic development group Good Jobs First. The value of the New York package totaled $2.8 billion, according to Good Jobs First.[406]

Many analysts surmised that the final selections were predestined from the beginning. Jeff Bezos and new Amazon CEO Andy Jassy reportedly overruled the recommendations of Amazon's internal selection team, for reasons that seemed personal and trivial. Jassy even reportedly said that he didn't want to be in Philadelphia because the city's football team was a rival of his preferred New York Giants. This was perhaps said jokingly, but the story seemed to suggest the arbitrariness of the process. One view was that Bezos preferred New York and the Washington, D.C., area because he already had homes in each place.[407]

Another, perhaps more plausible, theory is that the ultimate sites were predestined because they made business sense: New York to be close to the center of finance, and the Virginia site to be close to the Pentagon, now a major source of business for Amazon (think Amazon Web Services), and to Washington decision-making.

However, in a surprise to local political leaders and to Amazon, New Yorkers rallied against the extravagance of the incentive package. As opposition sustained and surged, Amazon decided that the negative attention was not worth the upsides of New York, and it canceled its New York expansion plan.[408]

The shabby tax incentive and bidding contest that Amazon triggered for its second headquarters was nothing new for the company. In locating warehouses, data centers and other facilities, the company regularly pits locales against each other in order to win escapes from local taxes. According to Good Jobs First, Amazon has extracted more than 100 separate local tax abatements and subsidy deals over the last 20 years, totaling more than $4.8 billion in lost revenue to communities.[409]

In the town of University Park, south of Chicago, for example, an Amazon representative approached the town's trustees with an offer of a $150 million warehouse, with 800 jobs—if they would keep the name of Amazon secret and deliver the subsidy within a matter of weeks. The trustees rammed through the proposal—in violation of their standard practice of debating such matters over three successive meetings. In the Chicago area, according to an analysis by WBEZ, most of the nearly $750 million in subsidies Amazon has extracted came overwhelmingly from communities with majority or large Black and/or Latino populations. By contrast, the company has opened at least seven facilities in mostly white communities with no tax incentives at all. [410]

The secrecy that Amazon demanded in University Park is typical. The company frequently operates with stealth before entering a community, and it often demands non-disclosure agreements with localities over the terms of the subsidies they are providing.

In August 2022, Niagara County, New York, agreed to provide Amazon $123 million in subsidies over spirited opposition. Argued Rethink Albany in opposing the deal: "As any public finance expert can tell you, there is no such thing as 'free money.' Whether on budget or off-budget, any subsidy for an e-commerce vendor is a bad investment of taxpayer dollars. Multiple studies have shown that when Amazon warehouses are built, warehouse wages actually drop, and new fulfillment centers do not produce a significant rise in broad-based employment."[411] Amazon made a non-binding promise to create 1,000 jobs at the new facility; but even if it does so, that will amount to a payment from the city of $8,200 per job per year—an extraordinary gift. And the critics noted that, with Amazon increasingly automating, the promise of 1,000 jobs should be viewed with skepticism. Still, as happens so often in an economically distressed area, local officials were willing to confer enormous subsidies in exchange for the lure of new jobs.[412]

The tax subsidies that local and state governments throw at big corporations like Amazon come with a very real cost: lost revenue for schools, social services, emergency medical technicians and more. Proponents of the deals say that communities actually come out on top; Amazon may not be paying its full freight, but it is paying something, giving the city more tax money that it would generate if Amazon didn't decide to locate there. The flaw in this argument is that Amazon and other large corporations do not generally make site decisions based on tax benefits; instead, they look to factors like infrastructure, workforce and local markets. The tax and other subsidies are typically just sweeteners that Amazon demands and gladly accepts—but not a decisive factor in site location determinations.

If we pull back from the local level, this point comes into sharp focus for a company like Amazon. Perhaps if University Park, Illinois had not agreed to the enormous gift package, Amazon would have set up its warehouse in a neighboring town that did. But there's no doubt that Amazon was going to open a warehouse somewhere in that area, in order to service the area market. In other words, the subsidies that towns like University Park offer Amazon do not create new Amazon jobs; at most, they exert a small influence over where those jobs are located, and they probably do not even do that.

Let that sink in: The typical argument for corporate welfare is that it creates new jobs, spurs new investment or offers some new public benefit—beyond what would take place without the subsidy. None of that is even plausibly true for the billions in local and state subsidies that Amazon has extracted.

The story is as simple as this: Amazon is big, rich and powerful and it leverages its size to squeeze as much out of communities as it can—especially from desperate communities least able to forego the revenue.

Coda: The Seattle Strong-Arm

It's not only more vulnerable communities that suffer. Amazon really hates paying its fair share anywhere.

Amazon made a spectacular attempt to reshape the City Council in its hometown of Seattle in order to escape new tax obligations. This ranks as among the most dramatic examples of a big corporation using its financial muscle to strong-arm local democracy.

In 2019, Amazon contributed $1.5 million to the Seattle Metropolitan Chamber of Commerce's super PAC—more than half of what the super PAC raised during the cycle[413]—to support the "pro-business" candidates the super PAC backed.

Drawing Amazon's wrath was a tax of $275 per employee on corporations with more than $20 million in annual earnings, designed to pay for affordable housing.[414] Before the tax's passage, Amazon engaged in negotiations with Seattle's government, lowering the tax from $500 per employee to $275,[415] an amount that reportedly would cost the corporation more than $10 million a year.[416]

Despite Amazon's involvement in negotiating a lower tax, soon after the Council passed it into law, the tech giant gave $25,000 to No Tax On Jobs, a referendum campaign organized to repeal the tax. The campaign also received $25,000 each from Starbucks, Kroger, Albertson's and Vulcan.[417] "Frankly, Amazon signaled they were OK with [the tax], and within 48 hours, reneged on that," Seattle Council member Teresa Mosqueda told *The Atlantic*.[418]

A pro-tax campaign formed but only raised $30,000. Public conflicts between the campaigns soured public opinion on the proposal, and the City Council repealed the tax itself.[419]

Then came city council elections, in which the Amazon-backed Chamber of Commerce endorsed seven candidates, including only one incumbent, for election to the nine-seat council.[420] The apparent objective was to take revenge on city council members for their pro-tax vote by replacing almost every single one with a more corporate-friendly member.

Amazon General Counsel David Zapolsky, who also personally contributed to the Chamber super PAC, made it clear that he hoped the campaign would discipline the city council: "There's a level of invective, and what I think is an unfortunate tone of some of the dialogue, that just makes it impossible to engage productively."[421]

Pouring more than $1 million into the Chamber's super PAC also upended reforms the city had enacted to reduce the influence of money in politics.[422] Seattle's Democracy Vouchers program offers public funds to candidates who meet certain thresholds of support—as long as those candidates agree to abide by strict limits on campaign spending. Candidates can opt out when their opposition has so much money that the public funds would be insufficient for running a competitive campaign. In 2019, the Amazon money forced 11 out of 12 candidates that previously participated in the voucher program to opt out.[423]

Few examples offer a purer illustration of how corporate welfare is a product of democratic dysfunction—and how corporate maneuvering for subsidies twists and subverts democracy itself.

PART V

Solutions

CHAPTER 13

Combating Corporate Power, Strengthening the Nation

If you've made it this far in this book, you're very likely convinced that excessive corporate power is undermining our democracy and siphoning our public resources, endangering the public and threatening the livability of the planet.

What can we do?

For starters, we have to keep a few ideas in our heads at once:

- First, there is no silver-bullet solution to the problem of too much corporate power.
- Second, there are lots of steps that will reduce corporate power and advance justice and democracy; we shouldn't dismiss any idea just because it won't do everything.
- Third, throughout American history, when social movements have organized and mobilized, they have shifted power from corporations to the people and made our country stronger, fairer, more sustainable and more just.

Indeed, it is those social movements which have been the great drivers of progress in our history.

Let's focus first on some measures that would work to meaningfully constrain corporate power. Our attention here is on measures that would affect corporations generally, not just specific industries or sectors, though we do try and incorporate some lessons drawn from our prior examination of Big Pharma, Big Oil and Big Tech.

Here are 10 ideas to reduce corporate power and strengthen the nation:

1. Overturn *Citizens United* and End Big Money Dominance

As we have seen, a very narrow class of super-rich individuals and corporations dominate campaign spending. They have a profound effect on who runs for office, who wins, what is debated in elections, what positions are considered "serious," and the policies that governments adopt at the federal, state and local levels.

Candidates should run on their ideas and vision, gaining strength from their ability to mobilize supporters, not their ability to raise megadollars from the super-rich and the corporate class. To level the playing field, we need a campaign funding system that provides candidates with a designated amount of publicly provided funding, imposes sharp caps on what individuals can spend beyond that, and ends all corporate spending.

Such a system is not possible while *Citizens United*—and another important Supreme Court decision, *Buckley v. Valeo*—are the law of the land. With no prospect of the Supreme Court reversing course on these decisions, we need a constitutional amendment to overturn them.

A large and growing movement is calling for just that. Large majorities of Americans support a constitutional amendment to overturn *Citizens United.* More than 800 cities and towns, and 22 states, have passed resolutions calling for an amendment. The proposed Democracy for All constitutional amendment has won majority support in both the House and the Senate.

The Democracy for All amendment would afford Congress and the states the freedom they need to appropriately limit campaign contributions and spending, including the power to distinguish between rights and privileges afforded to human beings and those available to corporations. It would solve all the Supreme Court-created, improper restrictions on campaign finance regulation elucidated above. It would, in fact, ensure democracy for all, by empowering legislative bodies to end Big Money's dominance of our elections.

It is hard, by design, to pass a constitutional amendment. It takes two-thirds of Congress and three-quarters of the states. But we've come far along this path already and are making steady progress to win this essential reform to recover our democracy.

And, yes, there are important steps we can take in the meantime. The For the People Act would have established a system of small-donor and public financing of elections. It would have ended Dark Money. It also would have protected the freedom to vote for all Americans, especially communities of color, and ended extreme partisan and racial gerrymandering. The For the People Act passed the House in 2021 but was unable to overcome a filibuster in the Senate.

2. End Corporate Capture

As we have seen, corporate political influence extends far beyond election spending. Corporations exert undue influence over the government agencies that are supposed to regulate them—known as "regulatory capture"—so that regulators enable rather than restrain them. We saw this with drug company influence over the Food and Drug Administration, Big Oil sending its former employees into the Trump administration to run key agencies, and Big Tech scooping up hundreds of former government officials to serve as its lobbyists and to influence policy.

Corporate capture involves many different strategies, starting with the "revolving door"—hiring people who once worked in agencies and in Congress, and also sending former company executives and lawyers into top positions at agencies. It's probably impossible to eliminate all corporate influence inside government, but we sure could reduce it.

A great many ideas that have percolated for a long time have been combined into a single piece of legislation, introduced by Senator Elizabeth Warren, D-Massachusetts, and Representative Pramila Jayapal, D-Washington, as the Anti-Corruption and Public Integrity Act, a portion of which was separately introduced by Jayapal as the Stop Corporate Capture Act.

This package of proposals would slow the revolving door, prohibiting cabinet secretaries or members of Congress from ever serving as lobbyists, and impose long cooling-off periods before other federal employees could become lobbyists. It would create an ombudsman's office to advocate for the public at agencies and offset the well-resourced efforts of corporate lobbyists. It would crack down on companies submitting sham studies and information to government agencies.

These and other measures in the bill would go a long way toward assuring agencies protect the public, not the corporations they are supposed to be overseeing.

3. Make Corporations Pay Their Taxes

As we have seen, among the most expensive forms of corporate welfare are tax subsidies and tax breaks. These loopholes are almost always justified as spurring investment and creating jobs, but those claims are typically just a fig leaf to rationalize corporate greed.

There is overwhelming public support for making corporations pay their fair share, reflecting a basic American sense of fair play and justice.

But with major media—outside of the business press—rarely reporting on corporate taxes, most people don't realize the scale of corporate tax avoidance or its consequences.

Politicians regularly say "we can't afford" to do what's right—to expand Medicare to provide hearing, vision and dental benefits; to guarantee childcare; to invest in the transition to a clean energy economy; to end homelessness; or to address other essential priorities.

Well, if we taxed corporations fairly, the government would have vastly more resources to make these investments. There is a direct connection between corporate tax evasion and avoidable human suffering.

Two broad pieces of legislation could help make corporations pay their fair share in taxes. First is to raise the corporate tax rate back to 35 percent (from the current 21 percent). The second is to root out general and specific tax escapes built into the tax code, such as the special provisions that enable oil and gas companies to avoid on the order of $20 billion a year in taxes.

It does make sense in some cases for the tax code to provide targeted subsidies, such as to encourage investments in energy efficiency and renewable energy. But there should be a high bar for such measures to ensure they are advancing the broad public interest and not narrow corporate profit grabbing.

4. Take on Corporate Welfare: Manage Public Resources and the Public Domain

Plundering the public domain is at the heart of the corporate welfare scam. It's time to put the public back in charge of the public domain—the things that We the People own in common.

A first and basic principle is that exhaustible public resources should not be given away at below-market prices. If mining corporations are going to mine on public land, or oil and gas companies are going to drill on public land, they must pay market-rate royalties for the privilege of doing so.

But truly *public* management of the public domain must do more than demand market-rate exchanges. As the public, our interests extend far beyond fair market exchanges. When it comes to natural resource exploitation, we need to decide if exploitation makes sense at all. It often makes sense to prohibit logging in the interest of preserving forests. And in light of the climate crisis, it is past time to end any new leasing of rights to drill for oil and gas on public lands.

Similarly, when it comes to the vast public investment in biomedical and other research and development (R&D), it makes sense to think about more than dollars and cents.

For drugs developed with federal funds, for example, our goal should not be to ensure the federal government gets its cut from overpriced medicines. Rather, the government should insist that beneficiaries of federally funded R&D charge reasonable prices. The government should also have a bias toward licensing the rights to use government-funded inventions on a non-exclusive basis. Non-exclusive licensing would promote both more innovation and more price competition.

5. Promote Competition and Break Up Monopolies

For the past several decades, one could be forgiven for thinking the United States had repealed its antitrust laws. We saw Exxon and Mobil combine into one company, along with Chevron and Texaco. The Department of Defense encouraged mergers in the 1990s, leaving just a few top military contractors. Once heavily decentralized, banking has progressively consolidated—and the Big Banks emerged from the 2008 financial crisis with vastly larger market shares. Hospitals, insurers, drug stores and health care companies have gobbled each other up. And the Big Tech companies have grown into goliaths atop the world economy, in large part through mergers and exertion of market power.

All this centralized power has meant more political influence and more economic power for the corporate Big Boys.

And meanwhile, antitrust enforcers by and large did nothing.

Yet this is changing. Federal and state enforcers are rising from their somnolence and beginning to crack down on abusive monopolistic practices, especially those of Big Tech.

To assist the newly energized antitrust enforcers, to maintain momentum and defend anti-monopoly law against a hostile judiciary, we also need new laws.

These laws should flat-out prohibit mergers among giant corporations. They should restore the rights of victims of anti-competitive practices—whether competitors or consumers—to sue monopolists. They should impose special duties on giant online platform companies—the Big Tech corporations—not to discriminate in favor of their products and services over competitors. They should give antitrust enforcers more power to break up established monopolies. Antitrust legislation should reinforce the authority of regulators to take into account the political power that accompanies concentrated economic power, and to block mergers on the grounds that they will trigger future mergers (a doctrine known as "incipiency").

As crucial as antitrust policy is, promoting economic competition must involve more. We have seen how government licensing of its inventions can promote competition (or monopoly). Net neutrality rules—ensuring that internet service providers do not discriminate between online service providers—advance competition. The Department of Agriculture has authority to protect farmers and ranchers from the abusive practices of meat industry processors.[424] Advancing competition as an antidote to concentrated corporate power should infuse government policy making.

6. Restore the Right to Organize Unions

Over the past 40 years, it has become progressively more difficult to organize labor unions.[425]

This is not because workers don't want to join unions. It is because corporations have become more aggressive at stifling union organizing drives, through mechanisms that are both legal and illegal. When employers run anti-union campaigns, as corporations almost always do, they regularly force workers into "captive" meetings to hear anti-union diatribes from anti-union consultants little constrained by facts. In nearly half of such campaigns, employers illegally threaten to close facilities or outsource work. In one in six cases, employers fire union supporters.[426] All of this makes a profound difference.

The Biden administration's National Labor Relations Board has valiantly tried to defend workers' rights—for the first time in decades—but it doesn't have sufficient resources or legal backing. U.S. labor laws need to be modernized to take into account and offset corporations' anti-union playbook.

Protecting workers' right to organize unions will enhance their bargaining power with employers, enabling them to win higher wages and better working conditions.

But the benefit of unionizing extends far beyond the workers who join the union. Once unions gain sufficient representation in an industry sector, they start to bring up the wages and improve the working conditions even of those not unionized, because non-union employers have little choice if they want to keep their workers. Unions also frequently hold their employers to account to improve overall social well-being, as when nurses' unions demand lower nurse-to-patient ratios to ensure patient safety, or when unionized teachers demand adequate resources to educate the kids in their classrooms.

Even beyond that, unions serve as the most consequential countervailing power to corporations. They bring together a constituency with shared interests to form permanent organizations with financial resources, robust staffing and political clout.

7. Take Urgent Action to Address the Climate Crisis

The climate crisis is more than a specific issue. As we have seen, even optimistic future scenarios that assume the world will take rapid action to shift to clean energy will be enormously costly in dollars, human lives and ecological well-being. The more extreme scenarios—which will occur in the absence of more aggressive action—will make vast areas of the planet uninhabitable and throw the world into chaos.

The climate crisis is, in many ways, a problem of corporate power. As we have seen, Big Oil and fossil fuel interests not only are endangering our well-being through their greenhouse gas emissions, they have also maneuvered for decades to block and delay a transition to a clean energy future.

Speeding that transition will require defeating the political power of Big Oil and the fossil fuel industry. It will require dismissing the arguments from a wide range of industries—from utilities to meat processors, from paper manufacturers to real estate developers, from banking to insurance— that what science demands is too expensive or will require more time. It will require stripping subsidies from Big Oil and investing massively in clean energy. It will require We the People to tell Big Business defenders what they must do.

Especially because of the immensity of what must be done, the details of how to transition to a clean energy future matter—and, of course, the transition must occur globally, not just in the United States.[427] The core concepts are simple enough, however, among them:

- There must be a rapid transition to 100 percent clean energy, with major restructuring of transportation, manufacturing and buildings to advance efficiency and eliminate reliance on fossil fuels.
- There must be major investments in soil-regenerative agriculture, transformation of the livestock sector and a serious commitment to reforestation.
- As the world undertakes a rapid economic transformation and adapts to the increasingly harsh effects of climate chaos, special attention must be paid to equity, within and among countries. Poor countries and poor communities in rich countries—who use less energy and have contributed less to the climate crisis—are both more vulnerable to climate impacts and less resourced to adapt to them.

Putting these principles into place will require subordinating some corporations' profit priorities to humanity's imperatives. There is no alternative.

8. End Data Surveillance

We focused earlier on how Big Tech has made user surveillance the core of its business model and how this has given the giant tech companies access to our most personal thoughts, the ability to direct our buying decisions, undue influence over our culture, and more.

As the world grows increasingly digitized, it is not just Big Tech that is surveilling us, undermining our privacy and using data to manipulate markets and culture. With almost no meaningful limits, businesses throughout the economy are watching us, trading our data and trying to exert top-down control over our individual decisions. This is true for everything from supermarkets[428] to auto companies,[429] vacuum cleaner-makers[430] to casinos.[431]

The data surveillance model does more than trash our privacy, as disturbing as that is. It takes our most personal information—with no meaningful opportunity for us to opt out—and transforms it into a corporate-controlled commodity. Then the corporations combine and trade that commodity to exert control over our lives—to determine what we will see, what products we are offered and the prices we are charged—to shape what we think, in ways that we can't possibly understand (and couldn't do anything about even if we did understand them).

Surveillance is not an inherent feature of a digital economy. It is simply one that benefits corporations and that our government has permitted. While much more must be done, the European Union has made very significant strides in protecting privacy and reducing surveillance,[432] yet somehow, Big Tech and other companies have survived the European protections and continue to make money. We could do the same here.[433]

9. Toughen Corporate Crime Enforcement and Penalties

Corporate crime imposes vastly greater harms on the nation than street crime, as horrific as street crime is.

All property crimes in the United States cost about $16 billion annually.[434] In contrast, corporate wage theft alone is estimated to cost at least $15 billion.[435] Health care fraud almost certainly costs more than $100 billion a year.[436] BP's oil spill settlements and restoration costs totaled $62 billion.[437] The 2008 Wall Street crash cost the U.S. economy a staggering $22 *trillion*.[438] The human toll of corporate crime is staggering as well. Workplace trauma and disease kill more than 50,000 Americans annually, and air pollution kills hundreds of thousands of Americans prematurely every year.

Corporate crime is preventable. Corporations are the ultimate rational actors: If the penalties for violating the law and the risk of getting caught are high enough, they will follow the law. If not, well, too often they will take advantage of the opportunity to line their pockets through illegal activity.

Unfortunately, corporate crime prosecution is at an historic low. The U.S. Department of Justice prosecuted 296 corporate crimes in 2000. By 2019, the number had fallen to 94, and dropped even further, to 90, in 2021.[439] Meanwhile, federal prosecutors have increasingly relied on leniency agreements, where they agree not to prosecute a company in exchange for pledges that it won't violate the law in the future. Not surprisingly, corporations regularly violate those pledges.[440]

We need a new paradigm to ensure society's most powerful actors follow the law. The Department of Justice needs to prioritize corporate criminal prosecutions, but it needs more resources to do so. It should end the policy of providing leniency agreements. Congress should act to significantly increase monetary policies for illegal corporation actions and to more systematically prohibit law-breaking businesses from obtaining government contracts. Congress should also act to make it a crime for corporations to recklessly endanger their employees or the public, or to suppress information about corporate hazards. The penalties should be tough, holding executives as well as corporations criminally liable.

10. Empower Citizens to Hold Corporations Accountable

Holding corporations accountable is essential to make them compensate the victims of their wrongdoing and, equally importantly, to deter them from engaging in misconduct in the first place.

Government prosecutors and regulators have a crucial role to play in holding companies accountable, but—even if they are committed, empowered and resourced, and even if the corporations don't capture them—they can't possibly catch and hold companies accountable for all their misdeeds.

That's why it is crucial that members of the public, starting with those injured by corporate wrongdoing, be empowered to sue them in court.

Corporations understand perfectly well how powerful the tool of civil lawsuits can be, which is why they have made a decades-long effort to thwart the ability of people to sue them.[441]

We need to restore the rights that have been stripped from the public. This means making it easier for people to join together in class actions when they have been similarly injured by corporations. It means prohibiting contract provisions ("forced arbitration" clauses) that require consumers and workers to forfeit their right to join together in class actions, or even to sue corporate wrongdoers in court. It means undoing a series of Supreme Court decisions that have made it more difficult to sue corporations—for example, when they violate statutes meant to protect consumers.[442]

We need to do more than restore rights taken away. Citizens should be given the power to act as "private attorneys general" and empowered to enforce the law against corporations that injure workers, rip off the public, pollute the environment or otherwise violate laws and regulations. Authorizing citizen groups to enforce the law and hold law-breaking corporations accountable in court would be transformative.

Hope is Realistic, Despair is Deadly

So while there may not be silver bullets to solve the problem of corporate power, there's no shortage of good ideas that would make a real difference.

Can we actually put them in place?

Yes!

Some of these ideas will be tougher to make real than others; some are on the precipice of becoming law; some are very far from enactment. And there are tougher and more moderate versions of each of the ideas presented here.

None of it will be easy.

It shouldn't be easy! We're talking about taking on corporate power. If the reforms are easily won, that's probably a sign that corporations don't much fear them.

Not easy, but definitely doable. How can we be sure of success? Well, one way is to look back at history—recent and not-so-recent—and see how citizen movements have restrained corporate power in the past and improved our country.

It's easy to despair and lose sight of this history, so let us now (ever so briefly) consider a range of examples:

- The progressive movement and then the labor movement beat Big Business and guaranteed a minimum wage, ended child labor and established limits on the length of the work week.[443] Our nation is vastly more just as a result.

- More recently, the worker-led "Fight for Fifteen"—demanding a $15-an-hour minimum wage—overcame opposition from fast food companies, nursing homes and other low-wage employers and raised wage standards in cities and states across the country, forcing companies like Amazon also to step up their salaries. The result has been $150 billion in additional pay for more than 25 million workers, with half the benefits going to workers of color.[444]

- The environmental movement overcame opposition from a broad swath of the corporate sector and won passage of the Clean Air Act, winning and preserving rules to improve our air's breathability, saving hundreds of thousands of lives annually.[445]

- Consumer advocates forced the auto industry to adopt safety technologies, including seat belts and air bags, that have saved more than 4 million lives in the United States alone.[446]

- Disability advocates won passage of the Americans with Disabilities Act, which empowered disabled persons by giving them improved access to public facilities and workplace opportunities.[447]

- Consumer advocates overcame Big Pharma and won passage of a law that created the modern generic drug industry, saving consumers and taxpayers tens of billions of dollars by facilitating competition among generic medicines.[448]

- Economic justice advocates beat Wall Street and won rules in the 1930s that for half a century, until the onset of financial deregulation, provided financial stability and a right-sized financial sector, helping create robust economic growth and shared prosperity.[449]

- Public health advocates took on Big Tobacco and won anti-smoking rules and policies that slashed smoking rates, saving at least 8 million lives in the United States alone.[450]

- Decades of campaigning by civil rights organizations and movements broke through in the 1960s and 1970s, overcoming business power in the U.S. South and throughout the nation, winning legal protections to ensure equal access to business-provided services, prohibitions against racial discrimination on the job, fair housing guarantees and obligations for banks to serve all communities.[451]

In every one of these cases, movements for justice refused to take no for an answer. They refused to despair or give up. They refused to be intimidated or cowed by the power of their adversaries. They set their eyes on the imperative of taking on corporate power to make our country more fair and just, safer and healthier, more democratic, better.

We can do the same.

APPENDIX

Talking Points to Take On Corporate Power

THE AMERICAN PEOPLE OVERWHELMINGLY SUPPORT POLICIES TO CONSTRAIN MEGA-CORPORATIONS AND THE BILLIONAIRE CLASS

- Roughly 90 percent of Americans want Medicare to negotiate drug prices.[452]
- More than 80 percent of Americans want to end Dark Money—secret spending—in elections.[453]
- In fact, there's virtual unanimity among the public about the need to transform the campaign funding system. The only debate is between those who favor "fundamental changes" and those who think it should be "completely rebuilt."[454]
- Three-quarters of Americans want stricter limits on smog.[455] Even given the false choice between environmental protection and economic growth, voters overwhelmingly favor environmental protection.[456]
- By a greater than a 2-1 margin, voters support empowering Americans to sue mega-corporations directly when they violate federal regulations.[457]
- More than 3 in 4 Americans believe CEOs should be held accountable for the crimes their companies commit, including being sent to jail, because there should be real consequences to corporate wrongdoing.[458]
- Eight in 10 Americans think the minimum wage is too low, and a strong majority favor raising it to $15 an hour (more than double the current federal minimum).[459]
- Four in 5 Americans support a requirement for paid family and medical leave.[460]
- Three quarters of Americans want the government to do more to protect online privacy.[461]

BIG MONEY FROM THE CORPORATE CLASS IS OVERWHELMING ELECTIONS

- Big Money exerts a huge influence on who runs for office, who wins, what is debated, what is considered "serious," which proposals get air time in Congress and what legislation is passed.
- While there was far too much Big Money dominance of elections previously, the Supreme Court's outrageous 5-4 decision in *Citizens United* in 2010—finding a constitutional right for corporations to spend whatever they want to influence elections—opened a floodgate that is drowning our democracy.
- Outside spending by corporations and the super-rich to influence elections has skyrocketed since *Citizens United:* from $70 million in 2006 to $309 million in 2010, the first post-*Citizens United* election, to more than $1.4 billion in 2022.[462]
- An incredibly small number of donors are powering this outside spending. *Just 25 people were responsible for almost half of all super PAC spending between 2010 and 2018.*[463]
- The campaign finance system disadvantages people of color. As one indicator, majority-white zip codes gave nearly $2.8 billion to super PACs—more than 25 times the amount from majority-minority zip codes.[464]
- *Citizens United* spurred a surge in corporate spending in election— though we don't know true numbers, because most corporate spending runs through secret, Dark Money organizations.[465]
- The reality and threat of huge outside spending by industry interests exerts a major chilling effect on political debate and policymaking.

CORPORATE WELFARE FOR BIG COMPANIES IS OUT OF CONTROL

- Corporate welfare—giveaways of taxpayer-funded assets, below-market sales of government-owned resources, access to government-funded research and development, bailouts for failing companies, tax breaks, escapes and loopholes, loans and loan guarantees, overseas marketing assistance, grants and direct subsidies, sweetheart contracts, privatization, immunities from liability and many other government subsidies—cheats the public of its wealth.
- Corporate exploitation of political power to feed at the public trough degrades our democracy and breeds cynicism.
- Corporate welfare drains public funds at the expense of the priority needs of the nation, everything from health care to addressing climate change to investing in housing to child day care, and much, much more.
- Politicians who denounce basic government functioning or the expansion of crucial services to middle- and lower-income families as "socialism" routinely and hypocritically support corporate welfare handouts.
- Corporate welfare is big money, totaling hundreds of billions annually.
  - The Trump tax cuts were estimated to be a $750 billion savings for mega-corporations, though this total should be somewhat reduced by the Inflation Reduction Act.[466]
  - The prohibition on Medicare drug price negotiation costs taxpayers more than $400 billion over 10 years. Even after passage of the Inflation Reduction Act, persistent restraints on Medicare negotiation will cost taxpayers on the order of $300 billion or more.[467]
  - Partial privatization of Medicare—through Medicare Advantage—will cost taxpayers hundreds of billions over the next decade.[468]
  - Even by a conservative estimate, defense contracting bloat constitutes at least $500 billion over a decade.[469] The Pentagon itself has identified more than $100 billion *of waste* in its own budget.[470]
- Compare corporate welfare to programs to benefit regular people: Poor children, for example, don't have the lobbying clout of Boeing, Pfizer or Amazon—and they don't fare nearly as well in Congress, despite being far more deserving. Instead, a program like the expanded Child Tax Credit—which reduced child poverty by a third—is criticized for including middle-class children and canceled because it is too expensive. Yet there's no means testing for corporate welfare, and the budgetary effects are routinely ignored.

THE BIG PHARMA RAP SHEET

Big Pharma Price Gouging Forces Rationing

- Three in 10 Americans report rationing their prescriptions because of high prices.[471]
- Prior to reforms in the Inflation Reduction Act and pressure campaigns that dropped insulin charges for most patients to $35 a month, 1.3 million Americans were rationing insulin due to cost.[472]
- Drugs are far more expensive in the United States than other rich countries, all of which have some system of cost control in place. Brand-name drugs are three-and-a-half times more expensive in the United States than other rich countries.[473]

Big Pharma Sells Dangerous Drugs, Sparks the Opioid Epidemic

- Adverse drug reactions kill more than 100,000 people in the United States every year— and many of these involve drugs that should not be on the market or are improperly labeled and marketed. One drug alone, Vioxx, killed as many as 50,000 people before being removed from the market.[474]
- The opioid addiction epidemic—a direct outgrowth of illegal and improper sales techniques by drug companies—killed more than 75,000 Americans in 2021.[475]

The Biggest Lobbying Industry, Big Pharma Benefits from Massive Public Subsidies

- Big Pharma is the biggest lobbying industry by far, spending $2 billion more on lobbying than its nearest competitor over the last two decades.[476]
- Big Pharma lobbied to prevent Medicare from negotiating prices for drugs it pays for, costing taxpayers at least $300 billion over the next decade, even after some recent reforms.[477]
- Every one of the 210 new drugs approved by the U.S. Food and Drug Administration from 2010-2016 received federal government research and development support.[478] But the companies that benefit from this support are free to charge whatever they want for these publicly backed drugs.
- The U.S. government paid for almost all the research and development costs for the Moderna Covid-19 vaccine.[479] Moderna's executives made billions[480] and, as the pandemic emergency waned, announced plans to quadruple the price of the vaccine.[481]

THE BIG OIL RAP SHEET

Big Oil is Taking Consumers to the Cleaners

- Big Oil raked in windfall profits after the Russian invasion of Ukraine, recording record revenues while integrated companies' costs remained flat. In 2022, the big five oil corporations reported a combined $200 billion in profits. U.S. policymakers failed to impose a windfall profits tax.[482]

Big Oil Poisons the Planet, Enables Authoritarians

- The 2011 BP oil disaster in the Gulf of Mexico cost 11 workers their lives, poisoned the Gulf ecosystem and imposed tens of billions in economic damage on the region. The disaster was due to BP's recklessness, and was preventable, as BP itself acknowledges.[483]
- Pipelines, refineries and petrochemical plants cause leaks, transgress wildlands and spew toxics into the air. The public health harms are concentrated in low-income communities and disproportionately poison people of color.
- From Nigeria to Burma, Ecuador to Chad, Big Oil has a sordid record around the world of consorting with and financing authoritarian regimes, benefiting from or even facilitating human rights abuses in order to protect drilling projects, and subjecting poor and indigenous communities to shocking levels of environmental violence.

Big Oil Created and Covered Up the Climate Crisis

- Big Oil has known that burning fossil fuels causes climate change since at least the 1970s, yet it has perpetrated a campaign of denial, deceit and delay that for decades blocked action on the greatest threat, alongside nuclear war, that humanity has ever faced.
- Big Oil and Dirty Energy-fueled climate chaos will cost Americans trillions of dollars, result conservatively in millions of deaths and impose untold disruption in America and around the world on communities and vast regions.

Big Oil Hits a Corporate Welfare Gusher

- Big Oil is a master of rigging tax codes, saving the industry billions every year.
- For decades, Big Oil has ripped off taxpayers by paying too little for oil drilled from public lands.
- Direct federal subsidies to oil and gas companies total around $20 billion a year.[484]

THE BIG TECH RAP SHEET

Big Tech is Injuring Teens' Sense of Self

- Social media is driving feelings of insecurity, concern about body image, and self-doubt among teens. From Facebook's own researchers: "Thirty-two percent of teen girls said that when they felt bad about their bodies, Instagram made them feel worse."[485]

Big Tech Has Stripped Away Our Privacy

- Big Tech has created a comprehensive data surveillance system that has stripped away our privacy. There's almost no way to escape this system. Most of the time, we have no idea that Big Tech is collecting data about us.

Big Tech's Business Model is Driving Hate and Scams, and Worsening Racial Bias

- Big Tech's data surveillance system is driving right-wing extremism and hate speech.[486]
- Big Tech's targeted marketing tools are empowering junk food purveyors, scammers and predatory lenders, among others.[487]
- Big Tech's algorithmic decision systems are replicating and worsening racial bias.[488]

Big Tech is Leveraging its Power to Defend its Monopoly, Prevent Regulation

- Big Tech companies have maneuvered ruthlessly to squash competition, hurting small business, denying choice to consumers and entrenching the corporations' data surveillance systems.
- To forestall regulation and antitrust action, the Big Tech companies have become the biggest lobbying corporations in Washington, D.C.

Flush With Cash, Big Tech is Avoiding Taxes

- Big Tech's reliance on offshore tax havens—combined with kid glove treatment in the Trump tax bill—will enable Big Tech to escape $88 billion in federal taxes.[489]
- In the last two decades, Amazon has extracted more than 100 separate local tax abatements and subsidy deals, totaling more than $4.8 billion in lost revenue to communities.[490]

CORPORATE CRIME IS SERIOUS AND GOES UNPUNISHED

Corporate Crime Costs Vastly More Than Street Crime

- Corporate crime imposes vastly greater harms on the nation than street crime, as horrific as street crime is. All property crimes in the United States cost about $16 billion annually.[491] In contrast, corporate wage theft alone is estimated to cost at least $15 billion.[492]
- The 2008 Wall Street crash—a direct result of Wall Street recklessness and widespread fraud—cost the U.S. economy a staggering $22 trillion.[493] Only one, low-level bank executive went to jail.[494]

Corporate Crime Kills and Injures Far More People than Street Crime

- Between 5 million and 8 million people are injured on the job every year. Roughly 125,000 people die annually from workplace accidents or occupational diseases. Yet there's barely any enforcement of workplace health and safety laws. The federal worker health and safety agency has enough inspectors to visit each workplace once every 236 years. In 2021, the Department of Labor referred nine cases for criminal enforcement.[495]
- Corporate crime and violence conservatively kills 300,000 people in the United States annually—including from dangerous products, environmental toxins, workplace injuries and disease and more—far more than roughly 22,000 lives lost to criminal homicide.[496]

Corporate Crime is Commonplace

- Corporate crime occurs with alarming frequency. A Harvard Business School analysis concluded that major firms are engaging in misconduct at least twice a week—the overwhelming number of which will never be sanctioned.[497]

Corporate Criminal Prosecutions are Infrequent

- Corporate crime prosecution is at an historic low. The U.S. Department of Justice prosecuted 296 corporate crimes in 2000, 94 in 2019, and 90 in 2021.[498]
- Unlike street criminals, corporate criminals can deploy their political muscle to define the law itself, as well as to impact the resources available to corporate crime enforcement agencies.

STRENGTHENING AMERICA BY CONFRONTING MEGA-CORPORATIONS: IT CAN BE DONE

Overturn *Citizens United* and end big money dominance: A constitutional amendment would overturn the Supreme Court's heinous decision empowering corporations and the super rich to spend whatever they want on elections. A system of small-donor and public financing of elections would end Big Money dominance of elections.

End corporate capture of regulatory agencies: Close the revolving door between government and lobbying, and crack down on companies submitting sham studies and information to government agencies.

Make mega-corporations pay their taxes: Eliminate tax subsidies and loopholes and make corporations pay taxes at the same rate as people.

Take on corporate welfare: Manage public resources for the public, by ending the giveaway of public resources at below-market rates and stopping new oil leases on federal land. License government inventions to create competition and require Big Pharma and other licensees to charge reasonable prices. Eliminate privatization scams, like Medicare Advantage, that cost taxpayers billions.

Promote competition and break up monopolies: Prohibit mergers among giant corporations. Empower consumers victimized by anti-competitive practices to sue monopolists. Impose special duties on giant online platform companies—the Big Tech corporations—not to discriminate in favor of their products and services over competitors. Give antitrust enforcers more power to break up established monopolies.

Restore the right to organize unions: Enact the Protecting the Right to Organize (PRO) Act, which would prevent employers from interfering in union elections, impose real penalties on employers who fire workers for organizing, and facilitate first contracts with newly formed unions. Then go beyond the PRO Act, including by recognizing unions whenever a majority of workers sign up for one ("card check").

Take urgent action to address the climate crisis: Expedite the transition to 100 percent clean energy, with major restructuring of transportation, manufacturing and buildings to advance efficiency and eliminate reliance on fossil fuels, with special attention paid to equity, within and among countries.

End data surveillance: Protect privacy and end Big Tech's data surveillance business model. Our most personal information must not be a corporate-controlled commodity.

Toughen corporate crime enforcement and penalties: End leniency deals for corporate wrongdoers and hold executives accountable for corporate crime. Boost the penalties for illegal corporate actions and prohibit law-breaking businesses from obtaining government contracts. Make it a crime for corporations to recklessly endanger their employees or the public.

Empower citizens to hold mega-corporations accountable: Ensure victims of corporate wrongdoing can seek justice in court, including by banning forced arbitration contracts and ensuring people can join together in class actions. Empower citizens to enforce the law against corporations that injure workers, rip off the public, pollute the environment or otherwise violate laws and regulations.

END NOTES

1   Ashley Kirzinger, Audrey Kearney, Mellisha Stokes, and Mollyann Brodie, "KFF Health Tracking Poll—May 2021: Prescription Drug Prices Top Public's Health Care Priorities," Kaiser Family Foundation, June 3, 2021, https://www.kff.org/health-costs/poll-finding/kff-health-tracking-poll-may-2021.

2   "The Public Broadly Supports the For the People Act," Navigator, June 17, 2021, https://navigatorresearch.org/the-public-broadly-supports-the-for-the-people-act/.

3   "Americans' Views on Money in Politics," New York Times / CBS News Poll, June 2, 2015, https://www.nytimes.com/interactive/2015/06/02/us/politics/money-in-politics-poll.html.

4   Jennifer Carman et al, "Exploring support for climate justice policies in the United States," Yale Program on Climate Change Communication, August 4, 2022, https://climatecommunication.yale.edu/publications/exploring-support-for-climate-justice-policies-in-the-united-states.

5   "New Poll: Voters Overwhelmingly Support Stricter Limits on Smog," American Lung Association, April 24, 2018, https://www.lung.org/media/press-releases/new-poll-smog.

6   Gallup Environment poll, https://news.gallup.com/poll/1615/environment.aspx.

7   "Public Opinion Surrounding Plastic Consumption and Waste Management of Consumer Packaging," Corona Insights report to the World Wildlife Fund, 2022, https://files.worldwildlife.org/wwfcmsprod/files/Publication/file/5k1qyg7hor_CI_Public_Opinion_Research_to_WWF_FINAL.pdf.

8   James Goodwin and Lew Blank, "A Blueprint for 'Regulatory Democracy' Empowering the Public in the Design and Implementation of New Safeguards," Data for Progress, June 2022, https://www.filesforprogress.org/datasets/2022/6/stop_corporate_capture_act_memo.pdf.

9   Aidan Smith, "Corporate Crackdown Project: Voters Want To Crack Down On Corporate Crime," Data for Progress and Revolving Door Project, December 2021, https://www.filesforprogress.org/memos/voters_want_crack_down_corporate_crime.pdf.

10 Ayelet Sheffey and Juliana Kaplan, "80% of Americans think the federal minimum wage is too low, new poll finds," Business Insider, March 16 2021, https://www.businessinsider.com/80-percent-americans-think-minimum-wage-is-too-low-2021-3.

11 "Americans Overwhelmingly Support Paid Family And Medical Leave," Navigator, September 23, 2022, https://navigatorresearch.org/americans-overwhelmingly-support-paid-family-and-medical-leave.

12 Brooke Auxier et al., "Americans and Privacy: Concerned, Confused and Feeling Lack of Control over Their Personal Information," Pew Research Center, November 15, 2019, https://www.pewresearch.org/internet/wp-content/uploads/sites/9/2019/11/Pew-Research-Center_PI_2019.11.15_Privacy_FINAL.pdf.

13 "Biden's Build Back Better Agenda," Americans for Tax Fairness, June 10, 2021, https://americansfortaxfairness.org/issue/new-poll-shows-overwhelming-support-bidens-plans-raise-taxes-wealthy-corporations.

14 Celinda Lake, Daniel Gotoff, and Eric Schoenfield, "Enforcement Working Group: Analysis of Findings from Focus Groups and a Nationwide Survey of Likely Voters," Lake Research, 2014, https://americansfortaxfairness.org/issue/new-poll-shows-overwhelming-support-bidens-plans-raise-taxes-wealthy-corporations.

15 Scott Neuman, "1 In 4 Americans Thinks The Sun Goes Around The Earth, Survey Says," NPR, February 14, 2014, https://www.npr.org/sections/thetwo-way/2014/02/14/277058739/1-in-4-americans-think-the-sun-goes-around-the-earth-survey-says.

16   Elisabeth Ponsot and Daniel Moritz-Rabson, "Americans Who Confronted 'Surprise' Medical Bills Share Their Stories," PBS Newshour, June 26, 2016, https://www.pbs.org/newshour/health/americans-who-confronted-surprise-medical-bills-share-their-stories.

17   Elisabeth Ponsot and Daniel Moritz-Rabson, "Americans Who Confronted 'Surprise' Medical Bills Share Their Stories," PBS Newshour, June 26, 2016, https://www.pbs.org/newshour/health/americans-who-confronted-surprise-medical-bills-share-their-stories.

18   Christopher Garmon and Benjamin Chartock, "One In Five Inpatient Emergency Department Cases May Lead To Surprise Bills," Health Affairs, January 2017, https://www.healthaffairs.org/doi/pdf/10.1377/hlthaff.2016.0970; Karen Pollitz, Matthew Rae, Gary Claxton, Cynthia Cox and Larry Levitt, "An Examination of Surprise Medical Bills and Proposals to Protect Consumers From Them," Peterson-KFF, February 10, 2020, https://www.healthsystemtracker.org/brief/an-examination-of-surprise-medical-bills-and-proposals-to-protect-consumers-from-them-3.

19   Leonard Berry and Paul Barach, "Hospital Outsourcing Often Prioritizes Profit Over Patients," The Conversation, August 20, 2021, https://theconversation.com/hospitals-often-outsource-important-services-to-companies-that-prioritize-profit-over-patients-165875.

20   Karen Pollitz, Matthew Rae, Gary Claxton, Cynthia Cox and Larry Levitt, "An Examination of Surprise Medical Bills and Proposals to Protect Consumers From Them," Peterson-KFF, February 10, 2020, https://www.healthsystemtracker.org/brief/an-examination-of-surprise-medical-bills-and-proposals-to-protect-consumers-from-them-3.

21   Margot Sanger-Katz, Julie Creswell and Reed Abelson, "Mystery Solved: Private-Equity-Backed Firms are Behind Ad Blitz on 'Surprise Billing,'" New York Times, September 13, 2019, https://www.nytimes.com/2019/09/13/upshot/surprise-billing-laws-ad-spending-doctor-patient-unity.html.

22   Mike Tanglis, "Private Equity's Investment," Public Citizen, March 11, 2020, https://www.citizen.org/article/private-equitys-investment.

23   Paul McLeod, "A Deal To End Surprise Medical Billing Was Tanked At The Last Minute," Buzzfeed News, December, 19, 2019, https://www.buzzfeednews.com/article/paulmcleod/surprise-billing-deal-richard-neal.

24   "Lobbying Data Summary," OpenSecrets, https://www.opensecrets.org/federal-lobbying/summary.

25   "Top Spenders," OpenSecrets, https://www.opensecrets.org/federal-lobbying/top-spenders.

26   "Business, Labor and Ideological Split in Lobbying Data," Open Secrets, https://www.opensecrets.org/federal-lobbying/business-labor-ideological.

27   "Revolving Door: Top Industries," Open Secrets, https://www.opensecrets.org/revolving/top.php?display=I.

28   Alan Zibel, "Revolving Congress: The Revolving Door Class of 2019 Flocks to K Street," Public Citizen, May 30, 2019, https://www.citizen.org/article/revolving-congress.

29   Eric Lipton and Ben Protess, "Banks' Lobbyists Help in Drafting Financial Bills," The New York Times, May 23, 2013, https://archive.nytimes.com/dealbook.nytimes.com/2013/05/23/banks-lobbyists-help-in-drafting-financial-bills.

30   Ibid.

31   Rob O'Dell and Nick Penzenstadler, "You Elected them to Write New Laws. They're Letting Corporations Do It Instead," USA Today, April 3, 2019, https://www.usatoday.com/in-depth/news/investigations/2019/04/03/abortion-gun-laws-stand-your-ground-model-bills-conservatives-liberal-corporate-influence-lobbyists/3162173002/.

32   Harvey Silvergate, "The Revolving Door at the Department of Justice," Forbes, June 22, 2011, https://www.forbes.com/sites/harveysilverglate/2011/06/22/revolving-door/?sh=3baf15415bf9.

33   Mandy Smithberger, "Brass Parachutes: Defense Contractors' Capture of Pentagon Officials Through the Revolving Door," Project on Government Oversight, November 5, 2018, https://s3.amazonaws.com/docs.pogo.org/report/2018/POGO_Brass_Parachutes_DoD_Revolving_Door_Report_2018-11-05.pdf.

34   Madison McVan, "In Washington, Agricultural Policymakers Circulate Among Farm Bureau, USDA and Industry," Minnesota Reformer, September 22, 2022, https://minnesotareformer.

com/2022/09/02/in-washington-agricultural-policymakers-circulate-among-farm-bureau-usda-and-industry/.

35 Rick Claypool, "The FTC's Big Tech Revolving Door Problem," Public Citizen, May 23, 2019, https://www.citizen.org/article/ftc-big-tech-revolving-door-problem-report/?eType=EmailBlastContent&eId=97f1bc62-2cbd-447d-8cc8-fbd40e030dbb.

36 Government Accountability Office, Defense Contracting: Post-Government Employment of Former DOD Officials Needs Greater Transparency, May 21, 2008, https://www.gao.gov/new.items/d08485.pdf.

37 Cited in Mandy Smithberger, "Brass Parachutes: Defense Contractors' Capture of Pentagon Officials Through the Revolving Door," Project on Government Oversight, November 5, 2018, https://s3.amazonaws.com/docs.pogo.org/report/2018/POGO_Brass_Parachutes_DoD_Revolving_Door_Report_2018-11-05.pdf.

38 Mandy Smithberger, "Brass Parachutes: Defense Contractors' Capture of Pentagon Officials Through the Revolving Door," Project on Government Oversight, November 5, 2018, https://s3.amazonaws.com/docs.pogo.org/report/2018/POGO_Brass_Parachutes_DoD_Revolving_Door_Report_2018-11-05.pdf.

39 Executive Order on Ethics Commitments by Executive Branch Personnel, January 20, 2021, https://www.whitehouse.gov/briefing-room/presidential-actions/2021/01/20/executive-order-ethics-commitments-by-executive-branch-personnel/.

40 Raymond Arke, "Oil and Mining Lobbyist David Bernhardt Nominated to be Secretary of Interior," Open Secrets, February 5, 2019, https://www.opensecrets.org/news/2019/02/oil-mining-lobbyist-david-bernhardt-nomed-to-be-secretary-of-interior/.

41 Juliet Eilperin, "Zinke's #2 Has So Many Conflicts of Interest He Has to Carry a List of Them All," Washington Post, November 19, 2019, https://www.washingtonpost.com/national/health-science/the-man-behind-the-curtain-interiors-no-2-helps-drive-trumps-agenda/2018/11/18/6403eb4c-e9ff-11e8-b8dc-66cca409c180_story.html.

42 Alan Zibel, "Bernhardt Buddies: Conflicts of Interest Abound at Trump's Interior Department," Public Citizen, January 15, 2020, https://www.citizen.org/article/bernhardt-buddies.

43 Ibid.

44 Jimmy Williams, "I Was a Lobbyist for More Than 6 years. I Quit. My Conscience Couldn't Take It Anymore." Vox, January 5, 2018, https://www.vox.com/first-person/2017/6/29/15886936/political-lobbying-lobbyist-big-money-politics.

45 Ibid.

46 Because of the way campaign finance works, most political spending comes from individuals, not directly from corporations. And most spending that corporations do is secret and untraceable. It is fair to say, however, that the vast majority of money spent to influence elections is spent by the corporate class. This chapter will be clear about whether spending being analyzed is done by individuals or corporations; but, at the end of the day, it all reflects the interest of the corporate class.

47 "Outside Spending," Open Secrets, https://www.opensecrets.org/outside-spending/.

48 Karl Evers-Hillstrom, "More Money, Less Transparency: A Decade Under Citizens United, Center for Responsive Politics," January 14, 2020, https://www.opensecrets.org/news/reports/a-decade-under-citizens-united.

49 Ibid. As startling as these figures are, they understate the importance of outside spending. Spending by parties and candidates themselves is far greater, but it is spread among all races nationwide. While candidates tend to raise and spend much more when their races are close, outside spenders focus like a laser on the close races where their funds will matter most. As a result, in an increasing number of cases, outside spending exceeds expenditures by candidates and parties. The Center for Responsive Politics documents outside spending surpassing candidate spending in 126 races in the decade after Citizens United was decided. Prior to Citizens United, such spending patterns were rare, occurring just 15 times in the prior decade.

50 The top 100 donors were responsible for 60 percent of all super PAC contributions. And the top five donors alone accounted for more than a quarter of all super PAC contributions. Alan Zibel,

"Oligarch Overload: How Ultra-Rich Donors Have Flooded American Politics With Cash Since Citizens United," January 15, 2020, Public Citizen, https://www.citizen.org/article/oligarch-overload.

51   See Alan Zibel, "Plutocrat Politics," May 15, 2019, Public Citizen, https://www.citizen.org/wp-content/uploads/outsidedonors.pdf.

52   See Adam Bonica and Jenny Shen, "The rich are dominating campaigns. Here's why that's about to get worse," The Washington Post, April 23, 2014, https://www.washingtonpost.com/news/monkey-cage/wp/2014/04/23/the-rich-are-dominating-campaigns-heres-why-thats-about-to-get-worse/ and https://www.opensecrets.org/overview/donordemographics.php.

53   Benjamin I. Page, Larry M. Bartels, and Jason Seawright, "Democracy and the Policy Preferences of Wealthy Americans" Perspectives on Politics, March 19, 2013, https://faculty.wcas.northwestern.edu/jnd260/cab/CAB2012%20-%20Page1.pdf.

54   Public Campaign, the Fannie Lou Hamer Project and the William C. Velasquez Institute, "The Color of Money: Campaign Contributions, Race, Ethnicity and Neighborhood, 2004 https://www.colorofmoney.org/majorfindings.html.

55   Alan Zibel, "Plutocrat Politics," Public Citizen, May 15, 2019, https://www.citizen.org/wp-content/uploads/outsidedonors.pdf.

56   Alan Zibel, "Oligarch Overload," Public Citizen, January 15, 2020, https://www.citizen.org/article/oligarch-overload.

57   Karl Evers-Hillstrom, "More Money, Less Transparency: A Decade Under Citizens United," Center for Responsive Politics, January 14, 2020, https://www.opensecrets.org/news/reports/a-decade-under-citizens-united.

58   Rick Claypool, "Corporations United," Public Citizen, January 15, 2020, https://www.citizen.org/article/corporations-united-citizens-united-10-years-report/.

59   John A. Henderson and Alexander Theodoridis, "Seeing Spots: An Experimental Examination of Voter Appetite for Partisan and Negative Campaign Ads," SSRN, July 14, 2015, https://papers.ssrn.com/sol3/papers.cfm?abstract_id=2629915.

60   Pénélope Daignault et. al., "The Perception of Political Advertising During an Election Campaign: A Measure of Cognitive and Emotional Effects," Canadian Journal of Communication, 2013, https://www.cjc-online.ca/index.php/journal/article/view/2566/2723 ("Negative televised election ads generate heightened attention levels and a higher level of physiological activation in individuals when compared with positive or mixed messages.").

61   Justin Ewers, "Hate Negative Political Ads All You Want. They Work.," Notre Dame News, October 23, 2006, https://news.nd.edu/news/hate-negative-political-ads-all-you-want-they-work; Stephen Craig and Paulina Rippere, "Political Cynicism and Negative Campaigns," APSA 2012 Annual Meeting Paper, July 15, 2012, https://papers.ssrn.com/sol3/papers.cfm?abstract_id=2108115 ("Our findings overall suggest that a relevant, hard-hitting negative ad can influence the choices of many voters regardless of their underlying feelings about government.").

62   Andrew Ricci, "The Dirty Secret About Negative Campaign Ads—They Work," The Hill, November 3, 2016, https://thehill.com/blogs/pundits-blog/presidential-campaign/304141-the-dirty-secret-about-negative-campaign-ads-they. "At the beginning of an election cycle, coming out early to define your opponent before they can define themselves can be instrumental in running their campaign off the rails before it has a chance to even begin," Ricci wrote. Early negative advertising "can substantially cut a rival campaign's legs out from underneath it." But negative ads also retain powerful impact in the later stages of an electoral contest, both dampening support for the opponent and energizing base supporters. "And even though most voters will remark on how tired they are of all the negative ads, the characterizations resonate with voters far more than positive pieces do."

63   Conor M. Dowling and Amber Wichowsky, "Attacks Without Consequence? Candidates, Parties, Groups, and the Changing Face of Negative Advertising," American Journal of Political Science 59, no. 1 (March 12, 2014), https://onlinelibrary.wiley.com/doi/abs/10.1111/ajps.12094. ("We find that candidates can benefit from having a party or group 'do their dirty work,' but particularly if a group does.") Studies have confirmed that voters are less likely to penalize candidates for attack ads issued by unknown groups. See Deborah Jordan

Brooks and Michael Murov, "Accessing Accountability in a Post-Citizens United Era," *American Politics Research* 40, no. 3 (April 2012), https://journals.sagepub.com/doi/abs/10.1177/1532673x11414791.

64   David Freedlander, "Super PACs Will be Back in 2016," *The Daily Beast*, July 14, 2017, https://www.thedailybeast.com/super-pacs-will-be-back-in-2016.

65   Quoted in Daniel Tokaji and Renata Strause, "The New Soft Money: Outside Spending in Congressional Elections," Election Law @ Moritz, Ohio State University Moritz College of Law, 2014, https://moritzlaw.osu.edu/thenewsoftmoney/wp-content/uploads/sites/57/2014/06/the-new-soft-money-WEB.pdf.

66   "Amazon Avoids More Than $5 Billion in Corporate Income Taxes, Reports 6 Percent Tax Rate on $35 Billion of US Income," Institute on Taxation and Economic Policy, last modified February 7, 2022, https://itep.org/amazon-avoids-more-than-5-billion-in-corporate-income-taxes-reports-6-percent-tax-rate-on-35-billion-of-us-income.

67   Galen Hendricks and Seth Hanlon, "The TCJA 2 Years Later: Corporations, Not Workers, Are the Big Winners," Center for American Progress, December 19, 2019, https://www.americanprogress.org/article/tcja-2-years-later-corporations-not-workers-big-winners.

68   "Corporate Tax Avoidance Under the Tax Cuts and Jobs Act," Institute on Taxation and Economic Policy, last modified July 29, 2021, https://itep.org/corporate-tax-avoidance-under-the-tax-cuts-and-jobs-act.

69   Ibid, p. 16.

70   Almost all the money allocated to TARP was paid back. In most cases, the government treated the bailout money as loans, which the banks and others had to pay back with interest. In the case of firms like the insurance giant AIG, the federal government took a major ownership stake and was eventually able to recover what it had invested.

71   "Troubled Assets Relief Program (TARP)," U.S. Department of the Treasury, https://home.treasury.gov/data/troubled-assets-relief-program.

72   Special Inspector General for the Troubled Assets Relief Program (SIGTARP), July 21, 2009, Quarterly Report to Congress. p. 129, https://www.sigtarp.gov/sites/sigtarp/files/Quarterly_Reports/July2009_Quarterly_Report_to_Congress.pdf.

73   Ryan Grim, "Dick Durbin: Banks 'Frankly Own The Place,'" HuffPost, May 30, 2009, https://www.huffpost.com/entry/dick-durbin-banks-frankly_n_193010.

74   Dean Baker, "Walking away from negative equity," *The Guardian*, February 1, 2010, https://www.theguardian.com/commentisfree/cifamerica/2010/feb/01/goldman-sachs-negative-equity.

75   House Hearing, U.S. Government Publishing Office: Too Big to Fail, October 22, 2009, https://www.govinfo.gov/content/pkg/CHRG-111hhrg52942/html/CHRG-111hhrg52942.htm.

76   David Cho, "Banks 'Too Big to Fail' Have Grown Even Bigger (The Big Get Bigger)," *Washington Post*, August 28, 2009, http://www.washingtonpost.com/wp-dyn/content/graphic/2009/08/28/GR2009082800426.html.

77   Yash M. Patel and Stuart Guterman, "The Evolution of Private Plans in Medicare," Commonwealth Fund, December 8, 2017, https://www.commonwealthfund.org/publications/issue-briefs/2017/dec/evolution-private-plans-medicare.

78   "Medicare Advantage Plans," https://www.medicare.gov/types-of-medicare-health-plans/medicare-advantage-plans.

79   Jeannie Fuglesten Biniek, Meredith Freed, Anthony Damico and Tricia Neuman, "Half of All Eligible Medicare Beneficiaries Are Now Enrolled in Private Medicare Advantage Plans," Kaiser Family Foundation, May 1, 2023, https://www.kff.org/policy-watch/half-of-all-eligible-medicare-beneficiaries-are-now-enrolled-in-private-medicare-advantage-plans; Meredith Freed, Jeannie Fuglesten Biniek, Anthony Damico, and Tricia Neuman, "Medicare Advantage in 2022: Enrollment Update and Key Trends," Kaiser Family Foundation, August 25, 2022, https://www.kff.org/medicare/issue-brief/medicare-advantage-in-2022-enrollment-update-and-key-trends/.

80   Ida Hellander, David U. Himmelstein, and Steffie Woolhandler, "Medicare Overpayments to Private Plans, 1985-2012: Shifting Seniors to Private Plans Has Already Cost Medicare US$282.6 Billion," *International Journal of Health Services* 43, no. 2 (April 2013): 305-319, https://journals.sagepub.com/doi/10.2190/HS.43.2.g.

81   Robert M. Kaplan and Paul Tang, "Upcoding: One Reason Medicare Advantage Companies Pay Clinicians to Make Home Health Checkups," Stat, January 19, 2013, https://www.statnews.com/2023/01/19/rein-in-upcoding-medicare-advantage-companies.

82   Added Bliss: "This finding raises three concerns: (1) payment integrity—if the diagnoses were inaccurate, then Medicare Advantage organizations received inappropriate payments; (2) quality of care—if the diagnoses were accurate, then beneficiaries may not have received appropriate care to treat these often-serious conditions; and (3) data integrity—if the diagnoses were accurate and beneficiaries received care, then Medicare Advantage organizations may not have reported all provided services in the encounter data as required." "Protecting America's Seniors," Testimony Before the United States House Committee on Energy and Commerce Subcommittee on Oversight and Investigations, June 28, 2022 (testimony of Erin Bliss, Assistant Inspector General for Evaluation and Inspections), https://energycommerce.house.gov/sites/democrats.energycommerce.house.gov/files/documents/Witness%20Testimony_Bliss_OI_2022.06.28_1.pdf.

83   Fred Schulte, "Researcher: Medicare Advantage Plans Costing Billions More Than They Should," Kaiser Health News, November 11, 2021, https://khn.org/news/article/medicare-advantage-overpayments-cost-taxpayers-billions-researcher-says.

84   Anna Wilde Mathews and Christopher Weaver, "Insurers Game Medicare System to Boost Federal Bonus Payments," Wall Street Journal, March 11, 2018, https://www.wsj.com/articles/insurers-game-medicare-system-to-boost-federal-bonus-payments-1520788658.

85   Ibid.

86   "Medicare Advantage: CMS Should Use Data on Disenrollment and Beneficiary Health Status to Strengthen Oversight," U.S. Government Accountability Office, April 2017, https://www.gao.gov/assets/690/684386.pdf. Other studies have reached very similar findings. One study found "that the switching rate from 2010 to 2011 away from Medicare Advantage and to traditional Medicare exceeded the switching rate in the opposite direction for participants who used long-term nursing home care (17 percent versus 3 percent), short-term nursing home care (9 percent versus 4 percent), and home health care (8 percent versus 3 percent). Momotazur Rahman, Laura Keohane, Amal N. Trivedi, Vincent Mor, "High-Cost Patients Had Substantial Rates Of Leaving Medicare Advantage And Joining Traditional Medicare," Health Affairs. 2015 Oct; 34(10): 1675-81, https://www.ncbi.nlm.nih.gov/pmc/articles/PMC4676406.

87   "Medicare Advantage: Beneficiary Disenrollments to Fee-for-Service in Last Year of Life Increase Medicare Spending," U.S. General Accountability Office, July 28, 2021, https://www.gao.gov/products/gao-21-482.

88   Reed Abelson and Margot Sanger-Katz, "'The Cash Monster Was Insatiable': How Insurers Exploited Medicare for Billions," New York Times, October 8, 2022, https://www.nytimes.com/2022/10/08/upshot/medicare-advantage-fraud-allegations.html.

89   Christi Grimm, "Some Medicare Advantage Organization Denials of Prior Authorization Requests Raise Concerns About Beneficiary Access to Medically Necessary Care," Office of the Inspector General, April 2022, https://oig.hhs.gov/oei/reports/OEI-09-18-00260.pdf.

90   There is no case that the crisis in Ukraine justifies more military spending. On the day Russia invaded Ukraine, the U.S. military budget was already more than 10 times greater than Russia's. Since then, Congress has appropriated more than $50 billion in supplemental funding for Ukraine, which includes both direct assistance and money to replenish U.S. weapons stockpiles. No evidence has emerged to indicate that more money in the underlying U.S. military budget will resolve the conflict. "Ukraine War Not a Reason to Increase Base Pentagon Budget," Women's Action for New Directions Education Fund, last modified June 2022, https://www.wand.org/_files/ugd/86749e_6b9692afce984aaabf923f651df74d04.pdf.

91   Jaspreet Gill, "As Republicans push Pentagon over inflation, Austin says FY23 budget is 'robust'" Breaking Defense, April 7, 2022, https://breakingdefense.com/2022/04/as-republican-push-pentagon-over-inflation-austin-says-fy23-budget-is-robust.

92   Some lawmakers have insisted that the defense budget must be raised to address inflation. But the president's budget increases already account for inflation; and, as Brown University's Costs of War Project notes, the Pentagon does not experience inflation in the ways measured by the Consumer Price Index. Even the comptroller for the U.S. Department of Defense pushed back on attempts to link the military budget to inflation at the April hearing.

93 Mike Stone, "U.S. Pentagon fails fourth audit but sees steady progress," Reuters, November 16, 2021, https://www.reuters.com/business/aerospace-defense/us-pentagon-fails-fourth-audit-sees-steady-progress-2021-11-16.

94 Craig Whitlock and Bob Woodward, "Pentagon buries evidence of $125 billion in bureaucratic waste," The Washington Post, December 5, 2016, https://www.washingtonpost.com/investigations/pentagon-buries-evidence-of-125-billion-in-bureaucratic-waste/2016/12/05/e0668c76-9af6-11e6-a0ed-ab0774c1eaa5_story.html.

95 William Hartung, "House military spending bill is a boon to the arms industry," Responsible Statecraft, July 15, 2022, https://responsiblestatecraft.org/2022/07/15/house-military-spending-bill-is-a-boon-to-the-arms-industry/, Elements included in the funding increase are listed here: https://republicans-armedservices.house.gov/sites/republicans.armedservices.house.gov/files/FY23%20NDAA%20Highlights%20.pdf.

96 "Corporate Power, Profiteering, And The 'Camo Economy,'" Costs of War, last modified September 2021, https://watson.brown.edu/costsofwar/costs/social/corporate.

97 Stacey Smith, "How A Law From The Civil War Fights Modern-Day Fraud," NPR, October 1, 2014, https://www.npr.org/sections/money/2014/10/01/352819369/how-a-law-from-the-civil-war-fights-modern-day-fraud.

98 "Corporate Power, Profiteering, And The 'Camo Economy,'" Costs of War, last modified September 2021, https://watson.brown.edu/costsofwar/costs/social/corporate.

99 Ibid.

100 "F-35 Joint Strike Fighter: Cost Growth and Schedule Delays Continue," U.S. Government Accountability Office, April 25, 2022, https://www.gao.gov/products/gao-22-105128. See also Dan Grazier, "F-35 Program Stagnated in 2021 but DOD Testing Office Hiding Full Extent of Problem," Project on Government Oversight, March 9, 2022, https://www.pogo.org/analysis/2022/03/f-35-program-stagnated-in-2021-but-dod-testing-office-hiding-full-extent-of-problem.

101 Melissa Nann Burke, "U.S. House debates future of littoral combat ships including the USS Detroit," Detroit News, July 14, 2022, https://www.detroitnews.com/story/news/politics/2022/07/14/house-debates-future-littoral-combat-ships-uss-detroit/10055378002.

102 Full Committee Hearing: "Fiscal Year 2023 Defense Budget Request from the Department of the Navy," May 11, 2022, https://armedservices.house.gov/hearings?ID=0CE42E6D-9589-41CB-AC90-FF8CE0E827FF.

103 Melissa Nann Burke, "U.S. House debates future of littoral combat ships including the USS Detroit," Detroit News, July 14, 2022, https://www.detroitnews.com/story/news/politics/2022/07/14/house-debates-future-littoral-combat-ships-uss-detroit/10055378002.

104 "1872 Mining Law," Earthworks, https://earthworks.org/issues/1872-mining-law.

105 Drew Kann and Kelly Yamanouchi, "Plant Vogtle reaches major milestone with one of its new reactors," Atlanta Journal-Constitution, August 3, 2022, https://www.ajc.com/news/plant-vogtle-reaches-major-milestone-with-one-of-its-new-reactors/VZ2JKMLRCRCL7ARRQHXCQ4257A.

106 "Vogtle To Receive $3.7 Billion Loan Guarantee—This Is A Mistake," Taxpayers for Common Sense, March 21, 2019, https://www.taxpayer.net/energy-natural-resources/perry-to-visit-vogtle-cue-great-taxpayer-cost.

107 "Biodiesel Subsidy Bonanza," Taxpayers for Common Sense, last modified August 2, 2022, https://www.taxpayer.net/agriculture/biodiesel-subsidy-bonanza-fact-sheet.

108 John DeCicco, "Biofuels turn out to be a climate mistake—here's why," The Conversation, October 5, 2016, https://theconversation.com/biofuels-turn-out-to-be-a-climate-mistake-heres-why-64463.

109 Andrea Cipriano, "Private Prisons Drive Up Cost of Incarceration: Study," The Crime Report, August 21, 2020, https://thecrimereport.org/2020/08/21/private-prisons-drive-up-cost-of-incarceration-study.

110 Kara Gotsch and Vinay Basti, "Capitalizing on Mass Incarceration: U.S. Growth in Private Prisons," The Sentencing Project, August 2, 2018, https://www.sentencingproject.org/publications/capitalizing-on-mass-incarceration-u-s-growth-in-private-prisons.

111 Milton R. Benjamin, "Nuclear Study Raises Estimates Of Accident Tolls," Washington Post, November 1, 1982, https://www.washingtonpost.com/archive/politics/1982/11/01/nuclear-study-raises-estimates-of-accident-tolls/6d97c5da-31c3-48da-bd82-d1308c367c3f.

112 "Price-Anderson Act: The Billion Dollar Bailout for Nuclear Power Mishaps," Public Citizen, last modified September 2004, https://www.citizen.org/wp-content/uploads/price_anderson_factsheet.pdf.

113 Jeffrey Dubin and Geoffrey Rothwell, "Subsidy to Nuclear Power Through Price-Anderson Liability Limit," Contemporary Economic Policy 8, no. 3 (July 1990): 73-79, https://onlinelibrary.wiley.com/doi/abs/10.1111/j.1465-7287.1990.tb00645.x.

114 Megan Brenan, "U.S. Business Sector Rating Average Worst Since 2008," Gallup, September 9, 2022, https://news.gallup.com/poll/400835/business-sector-average-rating-worst-2008.aspx.

115 Nicole Smith-Holt, "My son died from rationing insulin. Democrats' drug pricing plan still wouldn't help him," USA Today, December 10, 2019, https://www.usatoday.com/story/opinion/voices/2019/12/10/insulin-rationing-drug-prices-death-health-insurance-column/2629757001.

116 "Woman says her son couldn't afford his insulin—now he's dead," CBS News, January 4, 2019, https://www.cbsnews.com/news/mother-fights-for-lower-insulin-prices-after-sons-tragic-death.

117 "Governor Walz Signs Alec Smith Insulin Affordability Act," Office of Governor Tim Walz & Lt. Governor Peggy Flanagan, April 15, 2020, https://mn.gov/governor/news/?id=1055-428439.

118 "Drug Pricing Investigation," Committee on Oversight and Reform, U.S. House of Representatives, December 2021, https://oversight.house.gov/sites/democrats.oversight.house.gov/files/DRUG%20PRICING%20REPORT%20WITH%20APPENDIX%20v3.pdf.

119 Robert Langreth, "New Drug Prices Soar to $180,000 a Year on 20% Annual Inflation," Bloomberg, June 7, 2022, https://www.bloomberg.com/news/articles/2022-06-07/new-drug-prices-soar-to-180-000-a-year-on-20-annual-inflation.

120 Liz Hamel, Lunna Lopes, Ashley Kirzinger, et al., "Public Opinion on Prescription Drugs and Their Prices," Kaiser Family Foundation, April 5, 2022, https://www.kff.org/health-costs/poll-finding/public-opinion-on-prescription-drugs-and-their-prices.

121 Daniel Yetman, "What to Know About Human Insulin and How It Works," Healthline, October 21, 2021, https://www.healthline.com/health/diabetes/human-insulin#definition.

122 According to a 2020 study, the Big Three insulin manufacturers (Eli Lilly, Sanofi, and Novo Nordisk) all had patents on delivery devices. For example, while Novolog (insulin apart) is no longer covered by patents, the FlexPen typically used to deliver the insulin is covered by three patents. These device patents extend the effective monopoly on the drug. See Ryan Knox, "Insulin insulated: barriers to competition and affordability in the United States insulin market," Journal of Law and the Biosciences 7, no. 1, October 2020, https://academic.oup.com/jlb/article/7/1/lsaa061/5918811.

123 "Drug Pricing Investigation," Committee on Oversight and Reform, U.S. House of Representatives, December 2021, https://oversight.house.gov/sites/democrats.oversight.house.gov/files/DRUG%20PRICING%20REPORT%20WITH%20APPENDIX%20v3.pdf.

124 "Legislative Guide for Insulin for All," Public Citizen and T1 International, May 13, 2020, https://www.citizen.org/article/legislative-guide-for-insulin-for-all.

125 "T1International Publishes Survey on Type 1 Diabetes, COVID, and Insulin Rationing," T1International, October 18, 2021, https://www.t1international.com/blog/2021/10/18/t1international-survey-diabetes-covid-rationing.

126 Public Citizen, T1International, Legislative Guide for Insulin for All, 2020, https://www.citizen.org/article/legislative-guide-for-insulin-for-all/.

127 Doug Irving, "The Astronomical Price of Insulin Hurts American Families," Rand Review, January 6, 2021, https://www.rand.org/blog/rand-review/2021/01/the-astronomical-price-of-insulin-hurts-american-families.html.

128 "Drug Pricing Investigation," Committee on Oversight and Reform, U.S. House of Representatives, December 2021, https://oversightdemocrats.house.gov/sites/democrats.oversight.house.gov/files/DRUG%20PRICING%20REPORT%20WITH%20APPENDIX%20v3.pdf.

129 Juliette Cubanski, Sarah True, Anthony Damico, et al., "How Much Does Medicare Spend on Insulin?" KFF, April 1, 2019, https://www.kff.org/medicare/issue-brief/how-much-does-medicare-spend-on-insulin.

130 Baylee F. Bakkila, Sanjay Basu, and Kasia J. Lipska, "Catastrophic Spending On Insulin In The United States, 2017-18," Health Affairs 41, no. 7 (2022), https://www.healthaffairs.org/doi/10.1377/hlthaff.2021.01788.

131 Berkeley Lovelace, Jr., "Drugmaker Eli Lilly Caps the Cost of Insulin at $35 a Month, Bringing Relief for Millions," NBC News, March 1, 2023, https://www.nbcnews.com/health/health-news/eli-lilly-caps-cost-insulin-35-month-rcna72713.

132 Tami Luhby, "Sanofi Becomes Latest Drugmaker to Announce Insulin Price Cuts, Capping Cost at $35 for the Privately Insured," CNN, March 16, 2023, https://www.cnn.com/2023/03/16/health/sanofi-insulin-price-reduction/index.html.

133 Testimony of David J. Graham before the Senate Finance Committee, November 18, 2004, https://www.finance.senate.gov/imo/media/doc/111804dgtest.pdf.

134 Ibid.

135 Richard Horton, "Vioxx, the implosion of Merck, and aftershocks at the FDA," November 27, 2004, http://lists.healthnet.org/archive/html/e-drug/2004-11/msg00108.html.

136 Anna Wilde Mathews and Barbara Martinez, "E-Mails Suggest Merck Knew Vioxx's Dangers at Early Stage," Wall Street Journal, November 1, 2004, https://www.wsj.com/articles/SB109926864290160719.

137 Theresa Agovino, "Merck Knew Vioxx Dangers In 2000," CBS News, June 22, 2005, https://www.cbsnews.com/news/merck-knew-vioxx-dangers-in-2000.

138 David Brown, "Maker of Vioxx Is Accused of Deception," Washington Post, April 16, 2008, https://www.washingtonpost.com/wp-dyn/content/article/2008/04/15/AR2008041502086.html.

139 Snigdha Prakash, "Part 1: Documents Suggest Merck Tried to Censor Vioxx Critics," NPR, June 9, 2005, https://www.npr.org/2005/06/09/4696609/part-1-documents-suggest-merck-tried-to-censor-vioxx-critics.

140 Snigdha Prakash, "Part 2: Did Merck Try to Censor Vioxx Critics?," NPR, June 9, 2005, https://www.npr.org/templates/story/story.php?storyId=4696711.

141 Alex Berenson, "Merck Agrees to Settle Vioxx Suits for $4.85 Billion," New York Times, November 9, 2007, https://www.nytimes.com/2007/11/09/business/09merck.html.

142 "U.S. Pharmaceutical Company Merck Sharp & Dohme to Pay Nearly One Billion Dollars Over Promotion of Vioxx," U.S. Department of Justice, September 15, 2014, https://www.justice.gov/opa/pr/us-pharmaceutical-company-merck-sharp-dohme-pay-nearly-one-billion-dollars-over-promotion.

143 "FDA-Approved Prescription Drugs Later Pulled from the Market by the FDA," ProCon.org, December 1, 2021, https://prescriptiondrugs.procon.org/fda-approved-prescription-drugs-later-pulled-from-the-market.

144 "Opioid Data Analysis and Resources," Centers for Disease Control and Prevention, June 1, 2022, https://www.cdc.gov/opioids/data/analysis-resources.html.

145 "U.S. Overdose Deaths In 2021 Increased Half as Much as in 2020—But Are Still Up 15%," the Centers for Disease Control and Prevention, May 11, 2022, https://www.cdc.gov/nchs/pressroom/nchs_press_releases/2022/202205.htm.

146 Barry Meier, Pain Killer: An Empire of Deceit and the Origin of America's Opioid Epidemic (New York: Random House, 2018), p. 74.

147 Ibid. p. 78.

148 Ibid. p. 79-83.

149 Barry Meier, "Origins of an Epidemic: Purdue Pharma Knew Its Opioids Were Widely Abused," New York Times, May 29, 2018, https://www.nytimes.com/2018/05/29/health/purdue-opioids-oxycontin.html.

150 Barry Meier, "Sacklers Directed Efforts to Mislead Public About OxyContin, Court Filing Claims," New York Times, January 15, 2019, https://www.nytimes.com/2019/01/15/health/sacklers-purdue-oxycontin-opioids.html.

151 Eric Eyre, "Drug firms poured 780M painkillers into WV amid rise of overdoses," Charleston Gazette-Mail, December 17, 2016, https://www.wvgazettemail.com/news/legal_affairs/drug-firms-poured-m-painkillers-into-wv-amid-rise-of/article_99026dad-8ed5-5075-90fa-adb906a36214.html.

152 State of Tennessee v. Endo Health Solutions Inc. and Endo Pharmaceuticals Inc., Complaint filed in the Circuit Court of Knox County, Tennessee, Sixth Judicial District at Knoxville, May 14, 2019, https://www.tn.gov/content/dam/tn/attorneygeneral/documents/pr/2019/pr19-20-complaint.pdf.

153 Brendan Pierson, "Drugmaker Endo settles opioid claims by Tennessee counties, cities for $35 mln," Reuters, July 22, 2021, https://www.reuters.com/legal/litigation/drugmaker-endo-settles-opioid-claims-by-tennessee-counties-cities-35-mln-2021-07-22.

154 "Opioid Manufacturer Insys Therapeutics Agrees to Enter $225 Million Global Resolution of Criminal and Civil Investigations," U.S. Department of Justice, June 5, 2019, https://www.justice.gov/opa/pr/opioid-manufacturer-insys-therapeutics-agrees-enter-225-million-global-resolution-criminal.

155 Corporate Integrity Agreement and Conditional Exclusion Release Between the Office Of Inspector General and Insys Therapeutics, Inc., https://oig.hhs.gov/fraud/cia/agreements/Insys_Therapeutics_Inc_06052019.pdf.

156 Ibid.

157 U.S. Department of Justice, "Founder and Former Chairman of the Board of Insys Therapeutics Sentenced to 66 Months in Prison," January 23, 2020, https://www.justice.gov/usao-ma/pr/founder-and-former-chairman-board-insys-therapeutics-sentenced-66-months-prison.

158 Scott Higham and Sari Horwitz, "American Cartel: Inside the battle to bring down the opioid industry," Washington Post, July 7, 2022, https://www.washingtonpost.com/investigations/2022/07/07/american-cartel-book.

159 Ibid.

160 Ibid.

161 Scott Higham and Sari Horwitz, American Cartel: Inside the Battle to Bring Down the Opioid Industry (New York: Twelve, 2022).

162 Thomas R. Oliver, Philip R. Lee, and Helene L. Lipton, "A Political History of Medicare and Prescription Drug Coverage," Milbank Q. 82, no. 2 (June 2004): 283-354, https://www.ncbi.nlm.nih.gov/pmc/articles/PMC2690175.

163 Robert Pear and Richard A. Oppel Jr., "Results of Elections Give Pharmaceutical Industry New Influence in Congress," New York Times, November 21, 2002, https://www.nytimes.com/2002/11/21/us/results-of-elections-give-pharmaceutical-industry-new-influence-in-congress.html.

164 Thomas R. Oliver, Philip R. Lee, and Helene L. Lipton, "A Political History of Medicare and Prescription Drug Coverage," Milbank Q. 82, no. 2 (June 2004): 283-354, https://www.ncbi.nlm.nih.gov/pmc/articles/PMC2690175.

165 "The Part D Donut Hole," Medicare Interactive, https://www.medicareinteractive.org/get-answers/medicare-prescription-drug-coverage-part-d/medicare-part-d-costs/the-part-d-donut-hole.

166 Medicare Part D is the largest drug purchaser in the world, spending an estimated $145 billion in 2019 after rebates. See Tricia Neuman and Juliette Cubanski, "Relatively Few Drugs Account for a Large Share of Medicare Prescription Drug Spending," KFF, April 19, 2021, https://www.kff.org/medicare/issue-brief/relatively-few-drugs-account-for-a-large-share-of-medicare-prescription-drug-spending.

167 42 USC 1395w-111(i).

168 Mike Stuckey, "Tauzin Aided Drug Firms, Then They Hired Him," NBC News, March 22, 2006, http://www.nbcnews.com/id/11714763/t/tauzin-aided-drug-firms-then-they-hired-him/#.XA3OD-JOl9B.

169 Robert Pear, "House's Author of Drug Benefit Joins Lobbyists," New York Times, December 16, 2004, https://www.nytimes.com/2004/12/16/politics/houses-author-of-drug-benefit-joins-lobbyists.html.

170 "Roll Call 682 | Bill Number: H. R. 3," https://clerk.house.gov/Votes/2019682.

171 "Budgetary Effects of H.R. 3, the Elijah E. Cummings Lower Drug Costs Now Act," Congressional Budget Office, December 10, 2019, https://www.cbo.gov/system/ files?file=2019-12/hr3_complete.pdf.

172 Peter Sullivan, "House moderates signal concerns with Pelosi drug pricing bill," The Hill, May 12, 2021, https://thehill.com/homenews/house/553133-house-moderates-signal-concerns-with-pelosi-drug-pricing-bill.

173 "The Drug Development Process," U.S. Food and Drug Administration, January 4, 2018, https://www.fda.gov/patients/learn-about-drug-and-device-approvals/drug-development-process.

174 Katie Thomas, "The Story of Thalidomide in the U.S., Told Through Documents," New York Times, March 23, 2020, https://www.nytimes.com/2020/03/23/health/thalidomide-fda-documents.html.

175 "History of Food and Drug Regulation in the United States," https://eh.net/encyclopedia/ history-of-food-and-drug-regulation-in-the-united-states.

176 "Justification of Estimates for Appropriations Committees for Fiscal Year 2021," U.S. Department of Health and Human Services, https://www.fda.gov/media/135078/download (table on page 27).

177 Aaron Mitchell, Niti Trivedi, and Peter Bach, "The Prescription Drug User Fee Act: Much More Than User Fees," Medical Care 60, no. 4 (April 2022): 287-293, https://journals.lww.com/ lww-medicalcare/Abstract/2022/04000/The_Prescription_Drug_User_Fee_Act__Much_More_Than.4.aspx.

178 Peter Lurie and Sidney M. Wolfe, "FDA Medical Officers Report Lower Standards Permit Dangerous Drug Approvals," Public Citizen, December 2, 1998, https://www.citizen.org/article/ fda-medical-officers-report-lower-standards-permit-dangerous-drug-approvals.

179 Larry D. Sasich, Testimony Before the FDA's Public Meeting on the Prescription Drug User Fee Act (PDUFA), September 15, 2000, https://www.citizen.org/article/testimony-on-prescription-drug-user-fee-act-pdufa.

180 "With demise of Rezulin, FDA suggests alternatives," Relias Media, May 1, 2000, https://www. reliasmedia.com/articles/54582-with-demise-of-rezulin-fda-suggests-alternatives.

181 Final Summary Minutes of the Peripheral and Central Nervous System Drugs Advisory Committee Meeting, U.S. Food and Drug Administration, November 6, 2020, https://www.fda. gov/media/145690/download.

182 FDA Admin., Meeting Of The Peripheral And Central Nervous System Drugs Advisory Committee Webcast Recording, 2020, https://collaboration.fda.gov/p2uew93ez7dw [https:// perma.cc/KUK5-KW5S] (available at 02:12:36-02:12:43).

183 Patrizia Cavazzoni, "FDA's Decision to Approve New Treatment for Alzheimer's Disease," U.S. Food and Drug Administration, last modified June 7, 2021, https://www.fda.gov/drugs/news-events-human-drugs/fdas-decision-approve-new-treatment-alzheimers-disease.

184 Dave Muoio, "Aduhelm price cut, limited coverage leads CMS to lower Medicare premiums in 2023," Fierce Healthcare, May 27, 2022, https://www.fiercehealthcare.com/payers/aduhelm-price-cut-limited-coverage-leads-cms-lower-medicare-premiums-2023.

185 Tricia Neuman and Juliette Cubanski, "FDA's Approval of Biogen's New Alzheimer's Drug Has Huge Cost Implications for Medicare and Beneficiaries," KFF, June 10, 2021, https://www. kff.org/medicare/issue-brief/fdas-approval-of-biogens-new-alzheimers-drug-has-huge-cost-implications-for-medicare-and-beneficiaries.

186 "CMS Finalizes Medicare Coverage Policy for Monoclonal Antibodies Directed Against Amyloid for the Treatment of Alzheimer's Disease," Centers for Medicare & Medicaid Services, last modified April 7, 2022, https://www.cms.gov/newsroom/press-releases/cms-finalizes-medicare-coverage-policy-monoclonal-antibodies-directed-against-amyloid-treatment.

187 Ekaterina Galkina Cleary, Jennifer M. Beierlein, Navleen Surjit Khanuja, Laura M. McNamee, and Fred D. Ledley, "Contribution of NIH funding to new drug approvals 2010-2016," PNAS 115, no. 10 (February 2018): 2329-2334, https://www.pnas.org/doi/10.1073/pnas.1715368115.

188 Ibid.

189 Ibid.

190 "NIH News Release Rescinding Reasonable Pricing Clause," April 11, 1995, https://www.techtransfer.nih.gov/sites/default/files/documents/pdfs/NIH-Notice-Rescinding-Reasonable-Pricing-Clause.pdf.

191 "Investigation of Government Patent Practices and Policies: A Report of the Attorney General to the President," 1947, quoted in Background Materials on Government Patent Policy: The Ownership of Inventions Resulting in Federally Funded Research and Development. Volume II (Reports of Committees, Commissions and Major Studies, House Committee on Science and Technology, 1976), 22.

192 "The Bayh-Dole Act: Selected Issues in Patent Policy and the Commercialization of Technology," EveryCRSReport.com, June 10, 2005, https://www.everycrsreport.com/reports/RL32076.html#fn81.

193 See Peter S. Arno and Mickey Davis, "Why Don't We Enforce Existing Drug Price Controls? The Unrecognized and Unenforced Reasonable Pricing Requirements Imposed Upon Patents Deriving in Whole or in Part From Federally Funded Research," Tulane Law Review 75, no. 3 (2001): 631. See also David Halperin, "The Bayh-Dole Act and March-In Rights," March 2001, www.essentialinventions.org/legal/norvir/halperinmarchin2001.pdf. Here was how General Electric's general patent counsel described the role of march-in rights: "[I]f [a contractor] fails to supply the market adequately at a fair price, then there is reason for requiring it to license both the background patents and the patents stemming from the contract work." (Harry F. Manbeck, "Government Patent Policy: Hearings Before the Subcommittee on Science, Research and Technology of the House Committee on Science and Technology," 96th Congress (1979), 48.).

194 $88.54 per capsule, with four capsules required every day. See "Xtandi: 2021-2022 Request to US Department of Health and Human Services to Use the US Government's Rights in Patents," Knowledge Ecology Network, https://www.keionline.org/xtandi2021.

195 Rick Claypool and Zain Rizvi, "United We Spend," Public Citizen, September 30, 2021, https://www.citizen.org/article/united-we-spend-big-pharma-us-international-revenue-report.

196 Ed Silverman, "Small company offers Medicare cheap version of pricey cancer drug," STAT, April 27, 2016, https://www.statnews.com/pharmalot/2016/04/27/cancer-medicare-xtandi-biolyse-pharma.

197 Robert Mermell to Xavier Becerra, January 26, 2022, https://www.keionline.org/wp-content/uploads/Xtandi-Letter-Mermell-26Jan2022.pdf.

198 Ilkania Chowdhury-Paulino, Caroline Ericsson, Randy Vince Jr., R. et al., "Racial disparities in prostate cancer among black men: epidemiology and outcomes," Prostate Cancer Prostatic Diseases 25 (2022): 397-402, https://www.nature.com/articles/s41391-021-00451-z

199 Knowledge Ecology International to Francis Collins, Ashton Carter, and Sylvia Mary Mathews Burwell, January 14, 2016, https://www.keionline.org/wp-content/uploads/Xtandi-March-In-Request-Letter-14Jan2016.pdf.

200 Ibid.

201 See Francis Collins to Andrew Goldman, June 20, 2016, https://www.techtransfer.nih.gov/sites/default/files/documents/policy/pdfs/Final_Response_Goldman_6.20.2016.pdf and Alejandro Lopez-Duke to Andrew Goldman, https://www.keionline.org/wp-content/uploads/USArmy_Response_Xtandi_Request_5Aug2016.pdf.

202 Clare Love and David Reed to Mark Esper, February 4, 2019, https://www.keionline.org/wp-content/uploads/enzalutamide-march-in-royalty-free-Clare-Love-David-Reed-Army-4Feb2019.pdf.

203 "Drug Pricing Investigation Celgene and Bristol Myers Squibb—Revlimid," Staff Report, Committee on Oversight and Reform U.S. House of Representatives, September 2020, https://oversight.house.gov/sites/democrats.oversight.house.gov/files/Celgene%20BMS%20Staff%20Report%2009-30-2020.pdf.

204 Juliette Cubanski, Wyatt Koma, and Tricia Neuman, "The Out-of-Pocket Cost Burden for Specialty Drugs in Medicare Part D in 2019," KFF issue brief, February 2019, http://files.kff.org/attachment/Issue-Brief-the-Out-of-Pocket-Cost-Burden-for-Specialty-Drugs-in-Medicare-Part-D-in-2019.

205 "Drug Pricing Investigation Celgene and Bristol Myers Squibb—Revlimid," Staff Report, Committee on Oversight and Reform U.S. House of Representatives, September 2020, https://oversight.house.gov/sites/democrats.oversight.house.gov/files/Celgene%20BMS%20Staff%20Report%2009-30-2020.pdf, p. 24-30.

206 Thiru Balasubramaniam, "Background Information on Fourteen FDA Approved HIV/AIDS Drugs," last modified June 8, 2000, http://www.cptech.org/ip/health/aids/druginfo.html.

207 Donald G. McNeil Jr., "Indian Company Offers to Supply AIDS Drugs at Low Cost in Africa," New York Times, February 7, 2001, https://www.nytimes.com/2001/02/07/world/indian-company-offers-to-supply-aids-drugs-at-low-cost-in-africa.html.

208 Robert Weissman, "Big Pharma and AIDS: Act II Patents and the Price of Second-Line Treatment," Multinational Monitor, March/April 2007, https://www.multinationalmonitor.org/mm2007/032007/weissman.html.

209 "Global HIV & AIDS statistics—Fact sheet," UNAIDS, https://www.unaids.org/en/resources/fact-sheet.

210 DESCOVY cost information, https://www.gileadpriceinfo.com/descovy; Gilead Sciences, Inc "2021 Form 10-K Annual Report," https://investors.gilead.com/financials/sec-filings/sec-filings-details/default.aspx?FilingId=14745985.

211 "PrEP for HIV Prevention in the U.S.," Centers for Disease Control and Prevention, November 23, 2021, https://www.cdc.gov/nchhstp/newsroom/fact-sheets/hiv/PrEP-for-hiv-prevention-in-the-US-factsheet.html.

212 Jan Wolfe, "U.S. government sues Gilead over patent rights to HIV drugs," Reuters, November 7, 2019, https://www.reuters.com/article/ip-patent-gilead-idUSL2N27O00H.

213 Zain Rizvi, "Blind Spot: How the COVID-19 Outbreak Shows the Limits of Pharma's Monopoly Model," Public Citizen, February 19, 2020, https://www.citizen.org/article/blind-spot.

214 Zain Rizvi, "Leading COVID-19 Vaccine Candidates Depend on NIH Technology," Public Citizen, November 10, 2020, https://www.citizen.org/article/leading-covid-19-vaccines-depend-on-nih-technology.

215 Ryan Cross, "The tiny tweak behind COVID-19 vaccines," Chemical & Engineering News, September 29, 2020, https://tinyurl.com/yxoj472x.

216 Selam Gebrekidan and Matt Apuzzo, "Rich Countries Signed Away a Chance to Vaccinate the World," New York Times, March 21, 2021, https://www.nytimes.com/2021/03/21/world/vaccine-patents-us-eu.html.

217 Peter Maybarduk to Francis Collins, November 2, 2021, https://www.citizen.org/article/letter-urging-nih-to-reclaim-foundational-role-in-nih-moderna-vaccine.

218 Rebecca Robbins and Sheryl Gay Stolberg, "Moderna backs down in its vaccine patent fight with the N.I.H.," New York Times, December 17, 2021, https://www.nytimes.com/2021/12/17/us/moderna-patent-nih.html.

219 Zain Rizvi, "Sharing the NIH-Moderna Vaccine Recipe," Public Citizen, August 10, 2021, https://www.citizen.org/article/sharing-the-nih-moderna-vaccine-recipe.

220 Allie Clouse, "Fact check: Moderna vaccine funded by government spending, with notable private donation," USA Today, November 24, 2020, https://www.usatoday.com/story/news/factcheck/2020/11/24/fact-check-donations-research-grants-helped-fund-moderna-vaccine/6398486002.

221 Giacomo Tognini, "Surging Moderna Stock Mints The Vaccine Maker's Fifth Billionaire," Forbes, June 15, 2021, https://www.forbes.com/sites/giacomotognini/2021/06/15/surging-moderna-stock-mints-the-vaccine-makers-fifth-billionaire.

222 Chad Wells and Alison Galvani, "The global impact of disproportionate vaccination coverage on COVID-19 mortality," The Lancet, June 23, 2022, https://www.thelancet.com/journals/laninf/article/PIIS1473-3099(22)00417-0/fulltext.

223 "One Million and Counting: Estimates of Deaths in the United States from Ancestral SARS-CoV-2 and Variants," Public Citizen, June 1, 2022, https://www.citizen.org/article/one-million-and-counting-estimates-of-deaths-in-the-united-states-from-ancestral-sars-cov-2-and-variants.

224 Zoltan Kis and Zain Rizvi, "How to Make Enough Vaccine for the World in One Year," Public Citizen, May 26, 2021, https://www.citizen.org/article/how-to-make-enough-vaccine-for-the-world-in-one-year.

225 U.S. Energy Information Administration crude oil spot prices, WTI-Cushing, Oklahoma, https://www.eia.gov/dnav/pet/hist/RWTCD.htm.

226 Hanna Ziady, Big Oil Faces Scrutiny After Huge Jump in Profits, CNN, February 8, 2023, https://www.cnn.com/2023/02/08/energy/big-oil-profits/index.html.

227 "Whitehouse, Khanna, Colleagues Urge Speaker Pelosi and Leader Schumer to Bring Big Oil Windfall Profit Tax to the Floor," May 25, 2022, https://www.whitehouse.senate.gov/news/release/whitehouse-khanna-colleagues-urge-speaker-pelosi-and-leader-schumer-to-bring-big-oil-windfall-profit-tax-to-the-floor.

228 Geoff Garin, Jay Campbell and Corrie Hunt, "Memo Re: Connecting with Voters on Gas Prices," Hart Research Associates, March 15, 2022, https://www.lcv.org/article/poll-memo-connecting-with-voters-on-gas-prices.

229 "Largest Oil Spills Affecting U.S. Waters Since 1969," National Oceanic and Atmospheric Administration Office of Response and Restoration, April 5, 2017, https://response.restoration.noaa.gov/oil-and-chemical-spills/oil-spills/largest-oil-spills-affecting-us-waters-1969.html.

230 Hana Vizcarra, "Deepwater Horizon Ten Years Later: Reviewing agency and regulatory reforms," Harvard Environmental & Energy Law Program, May 4, 2020, https://eelp.law.harvard.edu/2020/05/deepwater-horizon-ten-years-later-reviewing-agency-and-regulatory-reforms.

231 U.S. Department of Justice, "BP Exploration and Production Inc. Agrees to Plead Guilty to Felony Manslaughter, Environmental Crimes and Obstruction of Congress Surrounding Deepwater Horizon Incident," November 15, 2012, https://www.justice.gov/opa/pr/bp-exploration-and-production-inc-agrees-plead-guilty-felony-manslaughter-environmental.

232 Lauren C. Peres et al., "The Deepwater Horizon Oil Spill and Physical Health among Adult Women in Southern Louisiana: The Women and Their Children's Health (WaTCH) Study," Environmental Health Perspective, January 22, 2016, https://www.ncbi.nlm.nih.gov/pmc/articles/PMC4977051.

233 Shanna Devine, "Testimony Before the U.S. House of Representatives Committee on Energy and Commerce on 'Mismanaging Chemical Risks: EPA's Failure to Protect Workers,'" March 13, 2019, https://www.citizen.org/wp-content/uploads/migration/shanna_devine_written_house_energy_and_commerce_testimony_march.pdf.

234 Mark A. D'Andrea and G. Kesava Reddy, "The Development of Long-Term Adverse Health Effects in Oil Spill Cleanup Workers of the Deepwater Horizon Offshore Drilling Rig Disaster," Frontiers in Public Health, April 26, 2018, https://www.ncbi.nlm.nih.gov/pmc/articles/PMC5932154, Rocky Kistner, "Remember the BP Oil Spill? These Cleanup Workers Are Still Suffering After 9 Years," Mother Jones, June 10, 2019, https://www.motherjones.com/environment/2019/06/remember-the-bp-oil-spill-these-cleanup-workers-are-still-suffering-after-9-years and Paul A. Sandifer et al., "Human Health and Socioeconomic Effects of the Deepwater Horizon Oil Spill in the Gulf of Mexico," Oceanography, June 3, 2021, https://tos.org/oceanography/article/human-health-and-socioeconomic-effects-of-the-deepwater-horizon-oil-spill-in-the-gulf-of-mexico-1.

235 Paul A. Sandifer et al., "Human Health and Socioeconomic Effects of the Deepwater Horizon Oil Spill in the Gulf of Mexico," Oceanography, June 3, 2021, https://tos.org/oceanography/article/human-health-and-socioeconomic-effects-of-the-deepwater-horizon-oil-spill-in-the-gulf-of-mexico-1.

236 Ibid.

237 "A Deadly Toll: The Devastating Wildlife Effects of Deepwater Horizon—and the Next Catastrophic Oil Spill," Center for Biological Diversity, https://www.biologicaldiversity.org/programs/public_lands/energy/dirty_energy_development/oil_and_gas/gulf_oil_spill/a_deadly_toll.html.

238 Ibid.

239 "BP CEO apologizes for 'thoughtless' oil spill comment," Reuters, June 2, 2010, https://www.reuters.com/article/us-oil-spill-bp-apology/bp-ceo-apologizes-for-thoughtless-oil-spill-comment-idUSTRE6515NQ20100602.

240 U.S. Department of Justice, "BP Exploration and Production Inc. Agrees to Plead Guilty to Felony Manslaughter, Environmental Crimes and Obstruction of Congress Surrounding Deepwater Horizon Incident," November 15, 2012, https://www.justice.gov/opa/pr/bp-exploration-and-production-inc-agrees-plead-guilty-felony-manslaughter-environmental.

241 National Commission on the BP Deepwater Horizon Oil Spill and Offshore Drilling, Deep Water, The Gulf Oil Disaster and the Future of Offshore Drilling, Report to the President, January 2011, https://www.govinfo.gov/content/pkg/GPO-OILCOMMISSION/pdf/GPO-OILCOMMISSION.pdf.

242 This is true even though pipelines are safer than trucking and other means of transport.

243 Chiara Belvederesi, Megan S. Thompson and Petr E. Komers, "Statistical analysis of environmental consequences of hazardous liquid pipeline accidents," Heliyon, November 7, 2008, https://www.ncbi.nlm.nih.gov/pmc/articles/PMC6226826

244 "TransCanada's Keystone XL Southern Segment: Construction Problems Raise Questions About the Integrity of the Pipeline," Public Citizen, November 2013, https://www.citizen.org/wp-content/uploads/migration/keystone_report_november_2013.pdf.

245 Chiara Belvederesi, Megan S. Thompson and Petr E. Komers, "Statistical analysis of environmental consequences of hazardous liquid pipeline accidents," Heliyon, November 7, 2008, https://www.ncbi.nlm.nih.gov/pmc/articles/PMC6226826.

246 The Pipeline Fighters Hub, Bold Education Fund, https://pipelinefighters.org/pipelinefights.

247 Kathleen Finn et. al., "Responsible Resource Development and Prevention of Sex Trafficking: Safeguarding Native Women and Children on the Fort Berthold Reservation," Harvard Journal of Law & Gender, 2017, https://scholar.law.colorado.edu/cgi/viewcontent.cgi?article=1671&context=faculty-articles.

248 Jihan Dahanayaka, "Enbridge's Line 3 Pipeline: Mixing Oil and Sexual Violence," The McGill International Review, November 1, 2021, https://www.mironline.ca/enbridges-line-3-pipeline-mixing-oil-and-sexual-violence.

249 United Nations, "USA: Environmental racism in "Cancer Alley" must end—experts," March 2, 2021, https://www.ohchr.org/en/press-releases/2021/03/usa-environmental-racism-cancer-alley-must-end-experts?LangID=E&NewsID=26824.

250 Ben Kunstman et. al., "Environmental Justice and Refinery Pollution: Benzene Monitoring Around Oil Refineries Showed More Communities at Risk in 2020," Environmental Integrity Project, April 29, 2021, https://environmentalintegrity.org/wp-content/uploads/2021/04/Benzene-Report-embargoed-for-4.29.21-1.pdf.

251 Christopher W. Tessum et al., "PM2.5 polluters disproportionately and systemically affect people of color in the United States," Science Advances, April 28, 2021, https://www.science.org/doi/10.1126/sciadv.abf4491.

252 Aidan Farrow, Kathryn A Miller and Lauri Myllyvirta, "Toxic Air: The Price of Fossil Fuels," Greenpeace Southeast Asia, February 2020, https://storage.googleapis.com/planet4-southeastasia-stateless/2020/02/21b480fa-toxic-air-report-110220.pdf.

253 Ibid.

254 The term is also applied to certain kinds of mineral wealth.

255 "Doe v. Unocal: The First Case of its Kind: Holding a U.S. Company Responsible for Rape, Murder, and Forced Labor in Myanmar," EarthRights International, 2005, https://earthrights.org/case/doe-v-unocal.

256 Matthew F. Smith, Naing Htoo and Paul Donowitz, "Total Impact 2.0: A Response to the French Oil Company Total Regarding Its Yadana Natural Gas Pipeline in Military-Ruled Burma (Myanmar)," EarthRights International, December 15, 2009, https://earthrights.org/wp-content/uploads/publications/total-impact-2-0.pdf.

257 "Myanmar: Chevron, Total Suspend Some Payments to Junta," Human Rights Watch, May 28, 2021, https://www.hrw.org/news/2021/05/28/myanmar-chevron-total-suspend-some-payments-junta.

258 Amnesty International, "Nigeria: Shell complicit in the arbitrary executions of Ogoni Nine as writ served in Dutch court," June 29, 2017, https://www.amnesty.org/en/latest/press-release/2017/06/shell-complicit-arbitrary-executions-ogoni-nine-writ-dutch-court.

259 "Shell lawsuit (re oil pollution in Nigeria)," Business & Human Rights Resource Centre, February 4, 2021, https://www.business-humanrights.org/en/latest-news/shell-lawsuit-re-oil-pollution-in-nigeria.

260 Nimi Princewill and Krystina Shveda, "Shell escaped liability for oil spills in Nigeria for years. Then four farmers took them to court—and won," CNN, May 26, 2022, https://www.cnn.com/2022/05/25/africa/shell-oil-spills-nigeria-intl-cmd/index.html.

261 Chris Jochnick, "Amazon Oil Offensive," Multinational Monitor, January 1995, https://www.multinationalmonitor.org/hyper/issues/1995/01/mm0195_07.html.

262 Ibid.

263 Sara Randazzo, "Litigation Without End: Chevron Battles On in 28-Year-old Ecuador Lawsuit," The Wall Street Journal, May 2, 2021, https://www.wsj.com/articles/litigation-without-end-chevron-battles-on-in-28-year-old-ecuador-lawsuit-11619975500.

264 United Nations, "What Is Climate Change?," https://www.un.org/en/climatechange/what-is-climate-change.

265 Christopher Flavelle, "Climate Change Could Cut World Economy by $23 Trillion in 2050, Insurance Giant Warns," The New York Times, April 22, 2021, https://www.nytimes.com/2021/04/22/climate/climate-change-economy.html.

266 David Suzuki and Ian Hanington, "The woman who discovered global warming—in 1856!," David Suzuki Foundation, March 5, 2020, https://davidsuzuki.org/story/the-woman-who-discovered-global-warming-in-1856.

267 Neela Banerjee, Lisa Song and David Hasemyer, "Exxon: The Road Not Taken," Inside Climate News, September 16, 2015, https://insideclimatenews.org/news/16092015/exxons-own-research-confirmed-fossil-fuels-role-in-global-warming.

268 Ibid.

269 Ibid.

270 Benjamin Franta, "Shell and Exxon's secret 1980s climate change warnings," The Guardian, September 19, 2018, https://www.theguardian.com/environment/climate-consensus-97-per-cent/2018/sep/19/shell-and-exxons-secret-1980s-climate-change-warnings.

271 "The Case for Climate Action: Building a Clean Economy for the American People," Dark Money chapter, Senate Democrats' Special Committee on the Climate Crisis, August 26, 2020, https://www.whitehouse.senate.gov/imo/media/doc/Dark%20Money%20Chpt%20SCCC%20Climate%20Crisis%20Report.pdf.

272 Robert Weissman, "Summit Games: Bush Busts UNCED," Multinational Monitor, July 1992, https://multinationalmonitor.org/hyper/issues/1992/07/mm0792_06.html.

273 Robert Brulle, "Advocating inaction: a historical analysis of the Global Climate Coalition," Environmental Politics, April 11, 2022, https://www.climatefiles.com/bp/brulle-paper-references-advocating-inaction-environmental-politics-april-2022

274 Ross Gelbspan, The Heat is On: The High Stakes Battle Over the Earth's Climate, Reading, MA: Addison-Wesley Publishing, 1997, p. 9.

275 Ibid.

276 Charlie Cray, "Exposing the PR Experts," Multinational Monitor, April 2001, https://www.multinationalmonitor.org/mm2001/01april/book.html.

277 "Reinventing Energy: Making the Right Choices," American Petroleum Institute, 1996, https://www.climatefiles.com/trade-group/american-petroleum-institute/1996-reinventing-energy.

278 "Denial and Deception: A Chronicle of ExxonMobil's Efforts to Corrupt the Debate on Global Warming," Greenpeace International, 1998, https://web.archive.org/web/20160309000929/http://www.greenpeace.org/usa/wp-content/uploads/legacy/Global/usa/planet3/PDFs/leaked-api-comms-plan-1998.pdf.

279 John H. Cushman Jr., "Industrial Group Plans to Battle Climate Treaty," The New York Times, April 26, 1998, https://www.nytimes.com/1998/04/26/us/industrial-group-plans-to-battle-climate-treaty.html.

280 Kate Yoder, "They derailed climate action for a decade. And bragged about it.," Grist, April 15, 2022, https://grist.org/accountability/how-the-global-climate-coalition-derailed-climate-action.

281 Mark J. Palmer, "Oil and the Bush Administration," Earth Island Journal, 2002, https://www.earthisland.org/journal/index.php/magazine/entry/oil_and_the_bush_administration.

282 "The Case for Climate Action: Building a Clean Economy for the American People," Dark Money chapter, Senate Democrats' Special Committee on the Climate Crisis, August 26, 2020, https://www.whitehouse.senate.gov/imo/media/doc/Dark%20Money%20Chpt%20SCCC%20Climate%20Crisis%20Report.pdf.

283 Ibid.

284 Testimony of Dylan Tanner, Executive Director of InfluenceMap, before Senate Democrats' Special Committee on the Climate Crisis, October 29, 2019, https://www.democrats.senate.gov/imo/media/doc/Dylan_Tanner_Testimony.pdf.

285 "The Case for Climate Action: Building a Clean Economy for the American People," Dark Money chapter, Senate Democrats' Special Committee on the Climate Crisis, August 26, 2020, https://www.whitehouse.senate.gov/imo/media/doc/Dark%20Money%20Chpt%20SCCC%20Climate%20Crisis%20Report.pdf.

286 James Rainey, "Bob Inglis, a Republican believer in climate change, is out to convert his party," NBC News, September 30, 2018, https://www.nbcnews.com/news/us-news/bob-inglis-republican-believer-climate-change-out-convert-his-party-n912066.

287 Rick Claypool, "Corporate Oil and Auto Insiders Fuel Trump Policies," Public Citizen, May 23, 2018, https://www.citizen.org/wp-content/uploads/migration/auto-and-oil-corporations-swamp-trump-may-2018-report.pdf

288 "Memorandum Re: Investigation of Fossil Fuel Industry Disinformation from Chairwoman Carolyn B. Maloney and Chairman Ro Khanna," Committee on Oversight and Reform, U.S. House of Representatives, September 14, 2022, https://oversight.house.gov/sites/democrats.oversight.house.gov/files/2022.09.14%20FINAL%20COR%20Supplemental%20Memo.pdf.

289 Ibid.

290 Matt Egan, "Big Oil is going all-out to fight climate rules in Build Back Better," CNN Business, October 3, 2021, https://www.cnn.com/2021/10/03/business/climate-biden-oil-reconciliation/index.html.

291 Daniel Quiggin, Kris De Meyer, Lucy Hubble-Rose and Antony Froggatt, Climate change risk assessment 2021. Summary of research findings. Chatham House, September 2021, https://www.chathamhouse.org/sites/default/files/2021-09/2021-09-14-climate-change-risk-assessmentsummary-quiggin-et-al_0.pdf.

292 Aidan Farrow, Kathryn A Miller and Lauri Myllyvirta, "Toxic Air: The Price of Fossil Fuels," Greenpeace Southeast Asia, February 2020, https://storage.googleapis.com/planet4-southeastasia-stateless/2020/02/21b480fa-toxic-air-report-110220.pdf.

293 Candace Vahlsing and Danny Yagan, "Quantifying Risks to the Federal Budget from Climate Change," White House Office of Management and Budget, April 4, 2022, https://www.whitehouse.gov/omb/briefing-room/2022/04/04/quantifying-risks-to-the-federal-budget-from-climate-change See also: "The economics of climate change," Swiss Re Institute, April 22, 2021, https://www.swissre.com/institute/research/topics-and-risk-dialogues/climate-and-natural-catastrophe-risk/expertise-publication-economics-of-climate-change.html.

294 Douglas Koplow and Aaron Martin, Fueling Global Warming: Federal Subsidies to Oil in the United States, Chapter 4, Earthtrack: June 1998, https://www.earthtrack.net/document/fueling-global-warming-federal-subsidies-oil-united-states.

295 Watson Institute for International and Public Affairs, "Costs of War: Economic Costs," Brown University, September 2021, https://watson.brown.edu/costsofwar/costs/economic.

296 "Royally Losing II: Below market royalty rates cost taxpayers billions of dollars in new revenue as oil and gas companies cash in on high prices," Taxpayers for Common Sense, May 2022, https://www.taxpayer.net/energy-natural-resources/royally-losing-ii.

297 Ibid.

298 Alan Zibel, "Royal Ripoff: 20 Oil Companies Exploiting Public Lands Allowed to Shortchange American Taxpayers by Up To $5.8 Billion Since 2013" Public Citizen, June 21 2022, https://www.citizen.org/wp-content/uploads/royalripoff-final.pdf.

299 Jesse Prentice-Dunn, "The dismal legacy of Trump's 'Energy Dominance' agenda," Westwise, January 25, 2021, https://medium.com/westwise/the-dismal-legacy-of-trumps-energy-dominance-agenda-872eea6a2560.

300 U.S. Department of the Interior, "Fact Sheet: President Biden to Take Action to Uphold Commitment to Restore Balance on Public Lands and Waters, Invest in Clean Energy Future," January 27, 2021, https://www.doi.gov/pressreleases/fact-sheet-president-biden-take-action-uphold-commitment-restore-balance-public-lands.

301 Adam Aton, "Fossil Fuel Extraction on Public Lands Produces One Quarter of U.S. Emissions," Scientific American, November 27, 2018, https://www.scientificamerican.com/article/fossil-fuel-extraction-on-public-lands-produces-one-quarter-of-u-s-emissions.

302 Democratic Presidential Primary Debate, CNN Transcript, March 15, 2020, https://transcripts.cnn.com/show/se/date/2020-03-15/segment/03.

303 Josh Lederman, "Federal judge blocks Biden's ban on leases for drilling on public lands," NBC News, June 15, 2021, https://www.nbcnews.com/politics/politics-news/federal-judge-blocks-biden-s-ban-leases-drilling-public-lands-n1270972.

304 U.S. Department of the Interior, "Share Interior Department Report Finds Significant Shortcomings in Oil and Gas Leasing Programs," November 26, 2021, https://www.doi.gov/pressreleases/interior-department-report-finds-significant-shortcomings-oil-and-gas-leasing-programs.

305 Jim Noe, Elizabeth Leoty Craddock and Kayla Gebeck Carroll, "Inflation Reduction Act Advances Stalled Offshore Oil and Gas Lease Sales," Holland & Knight, August 8, 2022, https://www.hklaw.com/en/insights/publications/2022/08/inflation-reduction-act-advances-stalled-offshore-oil-and-gas.

306 See "Fossil Fuel Subsidies: A Closer Look at Tax Breaks and Societal Costs," Environmental and Energy Study Institute, July 29, 2019, https://www.eesi.org/papers/view/fact-sheet-fossil-fuel-subsidies-a-closer-look-at-tax-breaks-and-societal-costs and Janet Redman et al, "Dirty Energy Dominance: Dependent on Denial," Oil Change International, October 2017, https://priceofoil.org/content/uploads/2017/10/OCI_US-Fossil-Fuel-Subs-2015-16_Final_Oct2017.pdf.

307 OECD Companion to the Inventory of Support Measures for Fossil Fuels, March 2021, https://www.oecd-ilibrary.org/environment/oecd-companion-to-the-inventory-of-support-measures-for-fossil-fuels-2021_e670c620-en.

308 "The Tax Break-Down: Intangible Drilling Costs," Committee for a Responsible Federal Budget, October 17, 2013, https://www.crfb.org/blogs/tax-break-down-intangible-drilling-costs.

309 Estimated Budget Effects Of The Revenue Provisions Contained In The President's Fiscal Year 2023 Budget Proposals, JCX-17-22 (July 25, 2022), https://www.jct.gov/publications/2022/jcx-17-22.

310 Ibid.

311 Matthew Gardner and Steve Wamhoff, "IRS Clock Runs Out, Saving 14 Large Companies $1.3 Billion," Institute on Taxation and Economic Policy, May 18, 2021, https://itep.org/irs-clock-runs-out-saving-14-large-companies-1-3-billion.

312 Ibid.

313 John Harris, "Tim Berners-Lee: "'We Need Social Networks Where Bad Things Happen Less,'" The Guardian, March 15, 2021, https://www.theguardian.com/lifeandstyle/2021/mar/15/tim-berners-lee-we-need-social-networks-where-bad-things-happen-less.

314 Brian A. Primack, Ariel Shensa, Jaime E. Sidani, Erin O. Whaite, Liu yi Lin, Daniel Rosen, Jason B. Colditz, Ana M. Radovic and Elizabeth Miller, "Social Media Use and Perceived Social Isolation Among Young Adults in the U.S, Am J Prev Med. 2017 Jul; 53(1): 1-8, https://www.ncbi.nlm.nih.gov/pmc/articles/PMC5722463/.

315 Holly B Shakya and Nicholas A Christakis, "Association of Facebook Use With Compromised Well-Being: A Longitudinal Study," Am J Epidemiol 2017 Feb 1;185(3):203-211, https://pubmed.ncbi.nlm.nih.gov/28093386/.

316 Barbara Jiotsa, Benjamin Naccache, Mélanie Duval, Bruno Rocher and Marie Grall-Bronnec, "Social Media Use and Body Image Disorders: Association between Frequency of Comparing One's Own Physical Appearance to That of People Being Followed on Social Media and Body

Dissatisfaction and Drive for Thinness," Int J Environ Res Public Health. 2021 Mar; 18(6): 2880, https://www.mdpi.com/1660-4601/18/6/2880.

317 Jean Twenge, "Is Screen Time Bad for Teens?" Psychology Today, April 6, 2022, https://www.psychologytoday.com/gb/blog/our-changing-culture/202204/is-screen-time-bad-teens.

318 Georgia Wells, Jeff Horwitz, Deepa Seetharaman, "Facebook Knows Instagram is Toxic for Teen Girls, Company Documents Show," Wall Street Journal, September 14, 2021, https://www.wsj.com/articles/facebook-knows-instagram-is-toxic-for-teen-girls-company-documents-show-11631620739?mod=article_inline.

319 Matt Burgess, "All the Data Google's Apps Collect About You and How to Stop It," Wired, May 4, 2021, https://www.wired.co.uk/article/google-app-gmail-chrome-data.

320 Douglas Schmidt, "Google Data Collection," August 15, 2018, https://digitalcontentnext.org/wp-content/uploads/2018/08/DCN-Google-Data-Collection-Paper.pdf.

321 Ryan Nakashima, "Google Tracks Your Movements, Like it or Not," Associated Press, August 13, 2018, https://www.apnews.com/828aefab64d4411bac257a07c1af0ecb.

322 Ibid.

323 Dylan Curran, "Are You Ready? Here is All the Data Facebook and Google Have On You," The Guardian, March 28, 2018, https://www.theguardian.com/commentisfree/2018/mar/28/all-the-data-facebook-google-has-on-you-privacy.

324 Jon Knight, "Here's What Google Maps Does With Your Data," GadgetHacks, April 4, 2018, https://smartphones.gadgethacks.com/how-to/heres-what-google-maps-does-with-your-data-0183930/.

325 Ben Tinker, "How Facebook 'Likes' Predict Race, Religion and Sexual Orientation," CNN.com, April 11, 2018, https://www.cnn.com/2018/04/10/health/facebook-likes-psychographics.

326 Natasha Singer, "What You Don't Know About How Facebook Uses Your Data," New York Times, April 11, 2018, https://www.nytimes.com/2018/04/11/technology/facebook-privacy-hearings.html.

327 David Nield, All the Ways Facebook Tracks You—and How to Limit It," Wired, January 12, 2020, https://www.wired.com/story/ways-facebook-tracks-you-limit-it.

328 "How Apps on Android Share Data with Facebook," Privacy International, December 29, 2018, https://privacyinternational.org/report/2647/how-apps-android-share-data-facebook-report.

329 Dan Milmo, "Facebook and Instagram Gathering Browsing Data from Under-18s, Study Says," The Guardian, November 16, 2021, https://www.theguardian.com/technology/2021/nov/16/facebook-and-instagram-gathering-browsing-data-from-under-18s-study-says.

330 "About Meta Pixel," Meta Business Help Center, https://www.facebook.com/business/help/742478679120153?id=1205376682832142.

331 Dylan Curran, "Are You Ready? Here is All the Data Facebook and Google Have On You," The Guardian, March 28, 2018, https://www.theguardian.com/commentisfree/2018/mar/28/all-the-data-facebook-google-has-on-you-privacy.

332 Aleksandra Korolova, "Facebook's Illusion of Control Over Location-Related Ad Targeting," Medium, December 18, 2018, https://medium.com/@korolova/facebooks-illusion-of-control-over-location-related-ad-targeting-de7f865aee78. See also: https://twitter.com/birnbaum_e/status/1207000504129245184/photo/3.

333 https://twitter.com/birnbaum_e/status/1207000504129245184/photo/2.

334 Yuntao Wang, Zhou Su, Ning Zhang, Rui Xing, Dongxiao Liu, Tom H. Luan, and Xuemin Shen, "A Survey on Metaverse: Fundamentals, Security, and Privacy," September 9, 2022, https://arxiv.org/pdf/2203.02662.pdf.

335 Matthew Keys, "A Brief History of Facebook's Ever-Changing Privacy Settings," Medium, March 21, 2018, https://medium.com/@matthewkeys/a-brief-history-of-facebooks-ever-changing-privacy-settings-8167dadd3bd0.

336 Federal Trade Commission, "Facebook Settles FTC Charges That It Deceived Consumers By Failing To Keep Privacy Promises," November 29, 2011, https://www.ftc.gov/news-events/press-releases/2011/11/facebook-settles-ftc-charges-it-deceived-consumers-failing-keep.

337 Ibid.

338 "Privacy and Security Enforcement, Federal Trade Commission,https://www.ftc.gov/news-events/topics/protecting-consumer-privacy-security/privacy-security-enforcement.

339 "About Audience Targeting," Google Ads Help, https://support.google.com/google-ads/answer/2497941?hl=en

340 Dan Shewan, "9 Mind-Bending Ways to Use Psychographics in Your Marketing," May 20, 2022, https://www.wordstream.com/blog/ws/2017/08/16/psychographics-in-marketing.

341 "About Facebook Travel Ads," Meta Business Help Center, https://www.facebook.com/business/help/1690794621187911?id=221593351918232.

342 "Use Location Targeting," Meta Business Help Center, https://www.facebook.com/business/help/365561350785642?id=176276233019487.

343 "Google Ads Help: About Advanced Location Options," Google, https://support.google.com/google-ads/answer/1722038.

344 "About Audience Targeting," Google Ads Help, https://support.google.com/google-ads/answer/2497941?hl.

345 "About Meta Pixel," Meta Business Help Center, https://www.facebook.com/business/help/742478679120153?id=1205376682832142.

346 Tim Wu, The Attention Merchants: The Epic Scramble To Get Inside Our Heads, New York: Knopf, 2016.

347 Cristiano Lima, "A Whistleblower's Power: Key Takeaways from the Facebook Papers," The Washington Post, October 26, 2021, https://www.washingtonpost.com/technology/2021/10/25/what-are-the-facebook-papers/.

348 Jeremey B. Merrill and Will Oremus, "Five points for anger, one point for a 'like,'" The Washington Post, October 26, 2021, https://www.washingtonpost.com/technology/2021/10/26/facebook-angry-emoji-algorithm/.

349 Jack Nicas, "How YouTube Drives People to the Internet's Darkest Corners," Wall Street Journal, February 7, 2018, https://www.wsj.com/articles/how-youtube-drives-viewers-to-the-internets-darkest-corners-1518020478.

350 Jeff Chester, Kathryn Montgomery, Katharina Kopp, "Big Food, Big Tech and the Global Childhood Obesity Pandemic, Center for Digital Democracy, May 2021, https://www.democraticmedia.org/article/big-food-big-tech-and-global-childhood-obesity-pandemic.

351 Zeke Faux, "How Facebook Helps Shady Advertisers Pollute the Internet," Bloomberg Businessweek, March 27, 2018, https://www.bloomberg.com/news/features/2018-03-27/ad-scammers-need-suckers-and-facebook-helps-find-them#xj4y7vzkg.

352 "Financial Products and Services," Google, https://support.google.com/adspolicy/answer/2464998?hl=en#zippy=%2Cunited-states; https://www.tiktok.com/legal/bc-policy?lang=en ; "Prohibited Financial Products and Services," Meta, https://www.facebook.com/policies_center/ads/prohibited_content/short_term_loans.

353 Kevin Wack, "Payday Lenders Are Finding Ways Around Google's Ad Ban," American Banker, October 11, 2017, https://www.americanbanker.com/news/payday-lenders-are-finding-ways-around-googles-ad-ban; Sergio Flores and Nicholas Kjeldgaard, "Payday Loan Ads On Social Media Targeting New, Young Audience," NBC7, June 15, 2022, https://www.nbcsandiego.com/news/investigations/nbc-7-responds/payday-loan-ads-on-social-media-targeting-new-young-audience/2972920/.

354 "BBB Tip: What You Should Know About Payday Loan Ads on Social Media," Better Business Bureau, June 7, 2022, https://www.bbb.org/article/news-releases/27118-bbb-tip-what-you-should-know-about-payday-loans-on-social-media.

355 For a more detailed description of these categories of algorithmic discrimination, see: Jane Chung, "Racism In, Racism Out: A Primer on Algorithmic Racism," Public Citizen, August 17, 2021, https://www.citizen.org/article/algorithmic-racism/.

356 Maddy Varner, Aaron Sankin, Andrew Cohen and Dina Haner, "How We Analyzed Allstate's Car Insurance Algorithm," The Markup, February 25, 2020, https://themarkup.org/allstates-algorithm/2020/02/25/show-your-work-car-insurance-suckers-list.

357 Aaron Klein, "Reducing Bias in AI-Based Financial Services," Brookings, July 10, 2020, https://www.brookings.edu/research/reducing-bias-in-ai-based-financial-services/.

358　Lisa Rice and Deidre Swesnik, "Discriminatory Effects of Credit Scoring on Communities of Color," Suffolk University Law Review, Vol. XLVI:935 (2013), https://cpb-us-e1.wpmucdn.com/sites.suffolk.edu/dist/3/1172/files/2014/01/Rice-Swesnik_Lead.pdf.

359　Ziad Obermeyer, Brian Powers, Christine Vogeli and Sendhil Mullainathan, "Dissecting Racial Bias in an Algorithm Used to Manage the Health of Populations," Science, October 25, 2019, https://www.science.org/doi/10.1126/science.aax2342.

360　Jeff Larson, Surya Mattu, Lauren Kirchner and Julia Angwin, "How We Analyzed the Recidivism Algorithm," ProPublica, May 23, 2016, https://www.propublica.org/article/how-we-analyzed-the-compas-recidivism-algorithm.

361　Kristian Lum and William Isaac, "To Predict and Serve?" Significance, October 7, 2016, https://rss.onlinelibrary.wiley.com/doi/epdf/10.1111/j.1740-9713.2016.00960.x.

362　"Investigation of Competition in Digital Markets," Majority Staff Report and Recommendations, 2020, https://judiciary.house.gov/uploadedfiles/competition_in_digital_markets.pdf?utm_campaign=4493-519, p. 12-15.

363　Ibid. p. 258.

364　Ibid. p. 144-147.

365　Ibid. p. 193.

366　Ibid. p. 193-194.

367　Ibid. p. 217.

368　Shoshana Zuboff, The Age of Surveillance Capitalism: The Fight for a Human Feature at the New Frontier of Power, New York: Public Affairs, 2019, p. 498.

369　Ibid. p. 506.

370　Ibid. p.513.

371　"Investigation of Competition in Digital Markets," Majority Staff Report and Recommendations, 2020, https://judiciary.house.gov/uploadedfiles/competition_in_digital_markets.pdf?utm_campaign=4493-519.

372　Calculation based on data from OpenSecrets, https://www.opensecrets.org/federal-lobbying/top-spenders.

373　Emily Birnbaum, "Amazon's Jassy blitzes Congress over antitrust bill," Politico, June 17, 2022, politico.com/news/2022/06/17/amazon-jassy-antitrust-bill-00040461.

374　Anna Massoglia and Julia Forrest, "Dark money groups battle bipartisan efforts to limit big-tech," Open Secrets, June 22, 2021, https://www.opensecrets.org/news/2021/06/dark-money-groups-battle-efforts-to-limit-big-tech.

375　David Moore, "Big Tech Lobbyists Butter Up the Dems," Sludge, July 21, 2022, https://readsludge.com/2022/07/21/big-tech-lobbyists-butter-up-the-dems.

376　"Introducing the Chamber of Progress: A New Industry Coalition Promoting Technology's Progressive Future," Chamber of Progress, March 29, 2021, https://www.prnewswire.com/news-releases/introducing-the-chamber-of-progress-a-new-industry-coalition-promoting-technologys-progressive-future-301257114.html.

377　Ben Brody, "These firms helped elect Democrats. Now they work for Big Tech.," Protocol, June 23, 2022, https://www.protocol.com/policy/tech-lobbying-democratic-firms.

378　Karl Evers-Hillstrom and Chris Mills Rodrigo, "Battle over Big Tech bills goes down to the wire," The Hill, July 5, 2022, https://thehill.com/business-a-lobbying/business-lobbying/3544374-battle-over-big-tech-bills-goes-down-to-the-wire.

379　National security letter on antitrust to Nancy Pelosi and Kevin McCarthy, September 15, 2021, https://www.documentcloud.org/documents/21062393-national-security-letter-on-antitrust.

380　Emily Birnbaum, "12 former security officials who warned against antitrust crackdown have tech ties," Politico, September 22, 2021, https://www.politico.com/news/2021/09/22/former-security-officials-antitrust-tech-ties-513657.

381　John McKinnon, Ryan Tracy, and Chad Day, "Big Tech Has Spent $36 Million on Ads to Torpedo Antitrust Bill," \], June 9, 2022, https://www.wsj.com/articles/big-tech-has-spent-36-million-on-ads-to-torpedo-antitrust-bill-11654767000.

382 Emily Birnbaum, "Google, Apple Rivals to Launch Ad Campaign for Bill Against Big Tech," Bloomberg, November 9, 2022, https://bit.ly/3HyU51g.

383 "Don't Break What Works," Meta Ad Library, https://www.facebook.com/ads/library/?active_status=all&ad_type=political_and_issue_ads&country=US&view_all_page_id=102558898865449&search_type=page&media_type=all.

384 Unless otherwise specified, data in this section come from Public Citizen analysis of data from OpenSecrets.Org, including from two reports, Jane Chung, "Big Tech, Big Cash: Washington's New Power Players," March 24, 2021, https://www.citizen.org/article/big-tech-lobbying-update and Mike Tanglis, "New Economy Titans, Old School Tactics," July 31, 2019, https://www.citizen.org/article/new-economy-titans-old-school-tactics.

385 Anna Edgerton, Leah Nylen, and Emily Birnbaum, "Amazon Hires Senior Senate Aide, Boosting Efforts to Stymie New Tech Antitrust Bill," Bloomberg, August 1, 2022, https://www.bloomberg.com/news/articles/2022-08-01/amazon-hires-senior-senate-aide-as-antitrust-lobbying-rages.

386 Josh Sisco, "Amazon hires key Senate Judiciary staffer working on tech antitrust bills," Politico, August 1, 2022, https://www.politico.com/news/2022/08/01/amazon-hires-senate-judiciary-staffer-00048805.

387 Anna Edgerton, Leah Nylen, and Emily Birnbaum, "Amazon Hires Senior Senate Aide, Boosting Efforts to Stymie New Tech Antitrust Bill," Bloomberg, August 1, 2022, https://www.bloomberg.com/news/articles/2022-08-01/amazon-hires-senior-senate-aide-as-antitrust-lobbying-rages.

388 Paul Farhi, "David Brooks of New York Times criticized for undisclosed financial ties to project he praised," Washington Post, March 4, 2021, https://www.washingtonpost.com/lifestyle/media/david-brooks-facebook-weave-aspen/2021/03/04/2493b798-7d06-11eb-a976-c028a4215c78_story.html.

389 "Find Out Which Groups Get Big Tech Funding," Tech Transparency Project, May 30, 2022, https://www.techtransparencyproject.org/articles/find-out-which-groups-get-big-tech-funding.

390 David Mikkelson, "Did Al Gore Say 'I Invented the Internet'?," Snopes, May 5, 2005, https://www.snopes.com/fact-check/internet-of-lies/. It also turns out that people who did help invent the internet say that Gore deserves as much credit as any politician for supporting the programs that stood up for the internet.

391 Ben Tarnoff, "How the internet was invented," The Guardian, July 15, 2016, https://www.theguardian.com/technology/2016/jul/15/how-the-internet-was-invented-1976-arpa-kahn-cerf.

392 Abby Monteil, "50 inventions you might not know were funded by the US government," Stacker, December 9, 2020, https://stacker.com/stories/5483/50-inventions-you-might-not-know-were-funded-us-government.

393 Karla Walter, "Advancing Ownership in Cutting-Edge Industries," Center for American Progress, April 19, 2018, https://www.americanprogress.org/article/advancing-ownership-cutting-edge-industries.

394 Tobias Burns, "Republicans, Hungarians team up to fight Biden on global tax deal," The Hill, July 20, 2022, https://thehill.com/policy/international/3568044-republicans-hungarians-team-up-to-fight-biden-on-global-tax-deal.

395 "U.S. companies have repatriated $1 trillion since tax overhaul," Los Angeles Times, December 19, 2019, https://www.latimes.com/business/story/2019-12-19/companies-repatriate-1-trillion-since-tax-overhaul.

396 "Multinational Corporations Would Receive $413 Billion in Tax Breaks from Congressional Repatriation Proposal," ITEP, last modified December 16, 2017, https://itep.org/multinational-corporations-would-receive-over-half-a-trillion-in-tax-breaks-from-the-house-repatriation-proposal.

397 "Apple, Microsoft Poised to Reap Nearly $75 Billion From a Single Provision of Trump's Tax Plan," Public Citizen, November 14, 2017, https://www.citizen.org/news/apple-microsoft-poised-to-reap-nearly-75-billion-from-a-single-provision-of-trumps-tax-plan.

398 "Wall Street Titans Poised to Reap $28 Billion From a Single Provision of Senate Tax Bill," Public Citizen, November 28, 2017, https://www.citizen.org/news/wall-street-titans-poised-to-reap-28-billion-from-a-single-provision-of-senate-tax-bill.

399 "Big Pharma a Big Winner in Trump's Proposed Tax Plan," Public Citizen, November 20, 2017, https://www.citizen.org/article/big-pharma-a-big-winner-in-trumps-proposed-tax-plan.

400 For further details on Apple's offshore holdings, see Simon Bowers, "Leaked Documents Expose Secret Tale Of Apple's Offshore Island Hop," The International Consortium of Investigative Journalists, November 6, 2017, https://www.icij.org/investigations/paradise-papers/apples-secret-offshore-island-hop-revealed-by-paradise-papers-leak-icij.

401 Matthew Gardner, "Amazon Avoids More Than $5 Billion in Corporate Income Taxes, Reports 6 Percent Tax Rate on $35 Billion of US Income," ITEP, February 7, 2022, https://itep.org/amazon-avoids-more-than-5-billion-in-corporate-income-taxes-reports-6-percent-tax-rate-on-35-billion-of-us-income.

402 Ibid.

403 "Amazon Opens Search for Amazon HQ2—A Second Headquarters City in North America," Business Wire, September 7, 2017, https://www.businesswire.com/news/home/20170907005717/en/Amazon-Opens-Search-for-Amazon-HQ2-%E2%80%93-A-Second-Headquarters-City-in-North-America.

404 Ibid.

405 Leticia Miranda, Nicole Nguyen, and Ryan Mac, "Here Are The Most Outrageous Incentives Cities Offered Amazon In Their HQ2 Bids," BuzzFeed News, November 14, 2018, https://www.buzzfeednews.com/article/leticiamiranda/amazon-hq2-finalist-cities-incentives-airport-lounge.

406 David Dayen and Rachel Cohen, "Amazon HQ2 Will Cost Taxpayers At Least $4.6 Billion, More Than Twice What The Company Claimed, New Study Shows," The Intercept, November 15, 2018, https://theintercept.com/2018/11/15/amazon-hq2-long-island-city-virginia-subsidies.

407 Jim Dallke, "Philadelphia was at one point a top 3 choice for Amazon's HQ2. A new book details what happened next," Philadelphia Business Journal, May 17, 2021, https://www.bizjournals.com/philadelphia/news/2021/05/17/giants-fan-sinks-philadelphia-chance-at-amazon-hq2.html.

408 J. David Goodman, "Amazon Pulls Out of Planned New York City Headquarters," New York Times, February 14, 2019, https://www.nytimes.com/2019/02/14/nyregion/amazon-hq2-queens.html.

409 Amazon tracker, https://www.goodjobsfirst.org/amazon-tracker.

410 John Lippert and Natalie Moore, "Amazon's Massive Chicago-Area Expansion Was Fueled By $741 Million From Taxpayers" WBEZ, October 26, 2020, https://www.wbez.org/stories/amazons-massive-chicago-area-expansion-was-fueled-by-741-million-from-taxpayers/300fa829-1b71-4d9e-a2f4-1776e88d4cb3.

411 "Watchdog Urges Niagara County IDA To Give No Subsidies To Amazon Warehouse," Reinvent Albany, August 8, 2022, https://reinventalbany.org/2022/08/watchdog-urges-niagara-county-ida-to-give-no-subsidies-to-amazon-warehouse/.

412 Robert Creenan, "Niagara County IDA approves Amazon tax incentives," Niagara Gazette, August 10, 2022, https://www.niagara-gazette.com/news/niagara-county-ida-approves-amazon-tax-incentives/article_2b8759f8-18cb-11ed-b27a-bfd628bd0886.html.

413 Gregory Scruggs, "Amazon's $1.5 million political gambit backfires in Seattle City Council election," Reuters, November 10, 2019, https://www.reuters.com/article/us-usa-election-seattle/amazons-15-million-political-gambit-backfires-in-seattle-city-council-election-idUSKBN1XL09B.

414 Alana Semuels, "How Amazon Helped Kill a Seattle Tax on Business," Atlantic, June 13, 2018, https://www.theatlantic.com/technology/archive/2018/06/how-amazon-helped-kill-a-seattle-tax-on-business/562736/.

415 Ibid.

416 Mike Baker, "Amazon Tests 'Soul of Seattle' With Deluge of Election Cash," New York Times, October 30, 2019, https://www.nytimes.com/2019/10/30/us/seattle-council-amazon-democracy-vouchers.html.

417 Alana Semuels, "How Amazon Helped Kill a Seattle Tax on Business," Atlantic, June 13, 2018, https://www.theatlantic.com/technology/archive/2018/06/how-amazon-helped-kill-a-seattle-tax-on-business/562736.

418 Ibid.

419 Ibid.

420 Daniel Beekman and Paul Roberts, "'This is a change election': Amazon-backed Seattle Chamber endorses City Council candidates," Seattle Times, June 19, 2019, https://www.seattletimes.com/seattle-news/politics/this-is-a-change-election-amazon-backed-seattle-chamber-endorses-city-council-candidates.

421 Mike Baker, "Amazon Tests 'Soul of Seattle' With Deluge of Election Cash," New York Times, October 30, 2019, https://www.nytimes.com/2019/10/30/us/seattle-council-amazon-democracy-vouchers.html.

422 Seattle Democracy Voucher Program, https://www.seattle.gov/democracyvoucher.

423 Mike Baker, "Amazon Tests 'Soul of Seattle' With Deluge of Election Cash," New York Times, October 30, 2019, https://www.nytimes.com/2019/10/30/us/seattle-council-amazon-democracy-vouchers.html.

424 "NFFC Applauds Proposed Reforms for Contract Farmers," National Family Farm Coalition, May 26, 2022, https://nffc.net/nffc-applauses-proposed-reforms-for-contract-farmers/.

425 Heidi Shierholz, Margaret Poydock, John Schmitt and Celine McNicholas, "Latest Data Release on Unionization is a Wake-Up Call to Lawmakers," Economic Policy Institute, January 20, 2022, https://www.epi.org/publication/latest-data-release-on-unionization-is-a-wake-up-call-to-lawmakers.

426 "Bronfenbrenner Outlines Employer Anti-Union Efforts to Congress," September 19, 2022, ILR News, https://www.ilr.cornell.edu/news/research/bronfenbrenner-outlines-employer-anti-union-efforts-congress.

427 For examples of comprehensive plans, see "The Six Sector Solution to the Climate Crisis," UN Environment Program, 2020, https://www.unep.org/interactive/six-sector-solution-climate-change/; Vision for Equitable Climate Action, U.S. Climate Action Network, May 2020, https://equitableclimateaction.org/wp-content/uploads/2020/05/Vision-for-Equitable-Climate-Action-May-2020-final-1.pdf; "What is the Green New Deal?" Sunrise Movement, https://www.sunrisemovement.org/green-new-deal.

428 Bill Aull, Dymfke Kuijpers and Daniel Laubli, The State of the Grocery Retail Around the World," McKinsey, October 6, 2022, https://www.mckinsey.com/industries/retail/our-insights/the-state-of-grocery-retail-around-the-world.

429 Jonathon Ramsey, "Ford might mine profits selling its data on you—of which it has a lot," November 19, 2018, Autoblog, https://www.autoblog.com/2018/11/19/ford-reorganization-customer-data-mining/?ncid=edlinkusauto00000015.

430 Khari Johnson, "The iRobot Deal Would Give Amazon Maps Inside Millions of Homes," Wired, August 5, 2022, https://www.wired.com/story/amazon-irobot-roomba-acquisition-data-privacy/.

431 Kim S. Nash, "Casinos hit the Jackpot with Customer Data," Computerworld, July 2, 2001, https://www.computerworld.com/article/2582546/casinos-hit-jackpot-with-customer-data.html.

432 "Data Protection in the EU," https://ec.europa.eu/info/law/law-topic/data-protection/data-protection-eu_en.

433 "Privacy and Digital Rights for All," https://www.citizen.org/about/coalitions/digitalrights4all.

434 "2019 Crime in the United States," Federal Bureau of Investigation, https://ucr.fbi.gov/crime-in-the-u.s/2019/crime-in-the-u.s.-2019/topic-pages/property-crime.

435 Marianne Levine, "Behind the minimum wage fight, a sweeping failure to enforce the law," Politico, February 18, 2018, https://www.politico.com/story/2018/02/18/minimum-wage-not-enforced-investigation-409644.

436 Katherine Drabiak and Jay Wolfson, "What Should Health Care Organizations Do to Reduce Billing Fraud and Abuse?" AMA Journal of Ethics, March 2020, https://journalofethics.ama-assn.org/article/what-should-health-care-organizations-do-reduce-billing-fraud-and-abuse/2020-03.

437 Nathan Bomey, "BP's Deepwater Horizon Costs Total $62B," USA Today, July 14, 2016, https://www.usatoday.com/story/money/2016/07/14/bp-deepwater-horizon-costs/87087056/.

438 "Financial Regulatory Reform: Financial Crisis Losses and Potential Impacts of the Dodd-Frank Act, Government Accountability Office, January 16, 2013, https://www.gao.gov/products/gao-13-180.

439 Rick Claypool, "Enforcement Abyss," Public Citizen, April 25, 2022, https://www.citizen.org/article/enforcement-abyss/.

440 Rick Claypool, "The Usual Corporate Suspects," Public Citizen, November 12, 2021, https://www.citizen.org/article/usual-corporate-suspects-report/.

441 Laura Antonini and Harvey Rosenfield, "Reboot Required: The Civil Justice System Has Crashed," Consumer Education Foundation, February 2022, https://www.representconsumers.org/wp-content/uploads/2022/02/2022.02.15_Reboot-Required.pdf..

442 Transunion v. Ramirez, 94 U. S. _ (2021), https://www.supremecourt.gov/opinions/20pdf/20-297_4g25.pdf.

443 There are important exceptions to the child labor prohibition; significant enforcement failures regarding the minimum wage, child labor and length of work week (before time and a half compensation is mandated). But the quality of improvement in American lives has nonetheless been dramatic. James Lardner, "Good Rules: 10 Stories of Successful Regulation," Demos, 2011, http://www.demos.org/sites/default/files/publications/goodrules_1_11.pdf.

444 Yannet Lathrop, T. William Lester and Matt Wilson, "Quantifying the Impact of the Fight for $15," National Employment Law Center, July 27, 2021, https://www.nelp.org/publication/quantifying-the-impact-of-the-fight-for-15-150-billion-in-raises-for-26-million-workers-with-76-billion-going-to-workers-of-color/.

445 Clean Air Act rules saved 164,300 adult lives in 2010. In February 2011, EPA estimated that by 2020 they would save 237,000 lives annually. EPA air pollution controls saved 13 million days of lost work and 3.2 million days of lost school in 2010, and EPA estimated that they would save 17 million work-loss days and 5.4 million school-loss days annually by 2020. See "The Benefits and Costs of the Clean Air and Radiation Act from 1990 to 2020," U.S. Environmental Protection Agency, Office of Air and Radiation, April 2021,, https://www.epa.gov/clean-air-act-overview/benefits-and-costs-clean-air-act-1990-2020-second-prospective-study.

446 "Safer Vehicles and Highways: 4.2 Million Lives Saved," Center for Study of Responsive Law, January 2021, https://csrl.org/2021/02/05/safer-vehicles-and-highways-4-2-million-u-s-lives-spared-since-1966/.

447 "The Impact of the Americans with Disabilities Act," National Council on Disability, 2007, http://www.ncd.gov/publications/2007/07262007.

448 Through regulations facilitating effective implementation of the Drug Price Competition and Patent Term Restoration Act of 1984 ("Hatch-Waxman"), including by limiting the ability of brand-name pharmaceutical companies to extend and maintain government-granted monopolies. Dan Troy, Drug Price Competition and Patent Term Restoration Act of 1984 (Hatch-Waxman Amendments), Statement before the Senate Committee on the Judiciary, June 17, 2003, https://www.judiciary.senate.gov/imo/media/doc/Troy%20Testimony%20061703.pdf.

449 See Joseph E. Stiglitz, Freefall: America, free markets, and the sinking of the world economy: WW Norton & Co., 2010; Robert Kuttner, The Squandering of America: how the failure of our politics undermines our prosperity: Vintage, 2008.

450 Michael Greenwood, "8 million lives saved since surgeon general's tobacco warning 50 years ago," Yale News, January 7, 2014, https://news.yale.edu/2014/01/07/8-million-lives-saved-surgeon-general-s-tobacco-warning-50-years-ago.

451 Alton Hornsby, Jr., "Looking Back on the Fight for Equal Access to Public Accommodations," Economic Policy Institute, July 2, 2014, https://www.epi.org/publication/fight-equal-access-public-accommodations/; https://www.ncbi.nlm.nih.gov/pmc/articles/PMC4808815/; Josh Silver, "The purpose and design of the Community Reinvestment Act (CRA): An examination of the 1977 hearings and passage of the CRA," National Community Reinvestment Coalition, June 14, 2019, https://ncrc.org/the-purpose-and-design-of-the-community-reinvestment-act-cra-an-examination-of-the-1977-hearings-and-passage-of-the-cra/.

452 Ashley Kirzinger and Lunna Lopes, "KFF Health Tracking Poll—May 2021," Kaiser Family Foundation, May 27, 2021, https://www.kff.org/health-costs/poll-finding/kff-health-tracking-poll-may-2021/.

453 Elena Rosenthal, "The Public Broadly Supports the For the People Act," Navigator Research, March 16, 2021, https://navigatorresearch.org/the-public-broadly-supports-the-for-the-people-act/.

454 Thomas B. Edsall, "Poll Reveals How Much Americans Really Know About Money in Politics," The New York Times, June 2, 2015, https://www.nytimes.com/interactive/2015/06/02/us/politics/money-in-politics-poll.html

455 American Lung Association, "New Poll: Majority of Americans Want Smog Standards Strengthened to Protect Their Health," American Lung Association, March 25, 2015, https://www.lung.org/media/press-releases/new-poll-smog

456 Frank Newport, "Environment," Gallup, March 25, 2021, https://news.gallup.com/poll/1615/environment.aspx.

457 Files for Progress, "New Memo: Majority of Voters Support Stop Corporate Capture Act," Files for Progress, June 21, 2022, https://www.filesforprogress.org/datasets/2022/6/stop_corporate_capture_act_memo.pdf.

458 Files for Progress, "New Poll: Voters Want Crack Down on Corporate Crime," Files for Progress, May 17, 2022, https://www.filesforprogress.org/memos/voters_want_crack_down_corporate_crime.pdf.

459 Sonam Sheth, "80% of Americans Think the Minimum Wage Is Too Low," Business Insider, March 29, 2021, https://www.businessinsider.com/80-percent-americans-think-minimum-wage-is-too-low-2021-3.

460 Lee Rainie and Monica Anderson, "Americans Overwhelmingly Support Paid Family and Medical Leave," Navigator Research, May 12, 2021, https://navigatorresearch.org/americans-overwhelmingly-support-paid-family-and-medical-leave/.

461 Aaron Smith, Monica Anderson, and Andrew Perrin, "Americans and Privacy: Concerned, Confused and Feeling Lack of Control Over Their Personal Information," Pew Research Center, November 15, 2019, https://www.pewresearch.org/internet/wp-content/uploads/sites/9/2019/11/Pew-Research-Center_PI_2019.11.15_Privacy_FINAL.pdf.

462 OpenSecrets, "Outside Spending." Accessed April 22, 2023. https://www.opensecrets.org/outside-spending/.

463 Alan Zibel, "Oligarch Overload: How Billionaire-Backed Members of Congress Are Using Their Fortunes to Influence Politics." Public Citizen. September 22, 2020. https://www.citizen.org/article/oligarch-overload/.

464 Ibid.

465 Rick Claypool, "Corporations United: A Decade After Citizens United, A Majority of Americans Believe Corporations Have Too Much Power in Elections," Public Citizen, January 14, 2020. https://www.citizen.org/article/corporations-united-citizens-united-10-years-report/.

466 Alex Rowell and Seth Hanlon, "Two Years Later, Corporations—Not Workers—Are the Big Winners from TCJA," Center for American Progress, December 20, 2019, https://www.americanprogress.org/article/tcja-2-years-later-corporations-not-workers-big-winners.

467 Congressional Budget Office, "H.R. 3, Lower Drug Costs Now Act of 2019," December 10, 2019, https://www.cbo.gov/system/files?file=2019-12/hr3_complete.pdf.

468 Phil Galewitz, "Medicare Advantage Overpayments Cost Taxpayers Billions, Researcher Says," Kaiser Health News, June 29, 2021, https://kffhealthnews.org/news/article/medicare-advantage-overpayments-cost-taxpayers-billions-researcher-says/.

469 People Over Pentagon, "A Guide to Cuts," https://peopleoverpentagon.org/guidetocuts.

470 Craig Whitlock, "Pentagon Buries Evidence of $125 Billion in Bureaucratic Waste," The Washington Post, December 5, 2016, https://www.washingtonpost.com/investigations/pentagon-buries-evidence-of-125-billion-in-bureaucratic-waste/2016/12/05/e0668c76-9af6-11e6-a0ed-ab0774c1eaa5_story.html.

471 Liz Hamel, Lunna Lopes, Ashley Kirzinger, et al., "Public Opinion on Prescription Drugs and Their Prices," Kaiser Family Foundation, April 5, 2022, https://www.kff.org/health-costs/poll-finding/public-opinion-on-prescription-drugs-and-their-prices.

472 Ken Alltucker, "More than 1.3M Americans Ration Life-saving Insulin Due to Cost. That's 'Very Worrisome to Doctors," USA Today, October 17, 2022, https://www.usatoday.com/story/news/health/2022/10/17/high-cost-insulin-prompts-1-3-million-americans-ration-drug/10498626002/.

473 Andrew W. Mulcahy, et. al., "U.S. Prescription Drug Prices Are 2.5 Times Those in Other OECD Countries," Rand, 2021m https://www.rand.org/pubs/research_briefs/RBA1296-1.html.

474 Testimony of David J. Graham, November 18, 2004, https://www.finance.senate.gov/imo/media/doc/111804dgtest.pdf.

475 "Percentage of overdose deaths involving methadone declined between January 2019 and August 2021," National Institute on Drug Abuse, July 13, 2022, https://nida.nih.gov/news-events/news-releases/2022/07/percentage-of-overdose-deaths-involving-methadone-declined-between-january-2019-august-2021.

476 "Lobbying: Industries," Open Secrets, https://www.opensecrets.org/federal-lobbying/industries?cycle=a.

477 "Budgetary Effects of H.R. 3, the Elijah E. Cummings Lower Drug Costs Now Act," Congressional Budget Office, December 10, 2019, https://www.cbo.gov/system/files?file=2019-12/hr3_complete.pdf.

478 Ekaterina Galkina Cleary, Jennifer M. Beierlein, Navleen Surjit Khanuja, Laura M. McNamee, and Fred D. Ledley, "Contribution of NIH funding to new drug approvals 2010-2016," PNAS 115, no. 10 (February 2018): 2329-2334, https://www.pnas.org/doi/10.1073/pnas.1715368115.

479 Allie Clouse, "Fact check: Moderna vaccine funded by government spending, with notable private donation," USA Today, November 24, 2020, https://www.usatoday.com/story/news/factcheck/2020/11/24/fact-check-donations-research-grants-helped-fund-moderna-vaccine/6398486002.

480 Ellen Francis, "Moderna Founders Made Forbes List of America's Richest During Pandemic," The Washington Post, October 6, 2021, https://www.washingtonpost.com/business/2021/10/06/moderna-vaccine-forbes-400-richest-list.

481 Aleks Phillips, "Pfizer and Moderna Quadrupling Price of Covid Vaccine Raises Concerns," Newsweek, January 21, 2023, https://www.newsweek.com/pfizer-moderna-covid19-vaccine-price-rises-concerns-lawmakers-1777774.

482 Hanna Ziady, "Big Oil Faces Scrutiny After Huge Jump in Profits," CNN, February 8, 2023, https://www.cnn.com/2023/02/08/energy/big-oil-profits/index.html.

483 U.S. Department of Justice, "BP Exploration and Production Inc. Agrees to Plead Guilty to Felony Manslaughter, Environmental Crimes and Obstruction of Congress Surrounding Deepwater Horizon Incident," November 15, 2012, https://www.justice.gov/opa/pr/bp-exploration-and-production-inc-agrees-plead-guilty-felony-manslaughter-environmental.

484 See "Fossil Fuel Subsidies: A Closer Look at Tax Breaks and Societal Costs," Environmental and Energy Study Institute, July 29, 2019, https://www.eesi.org/papers/view/fact-sheet-fossil-fuel-subsidies-a-closer-look-at-tax-breaks-and-societal-costs and Janet Redman et al, "Dirty Energy Dominance: Dependent on Denial," Oil Change International, October 2017, https://priceofoil.org/content/uploads/2017/10/OCI_US-Fossil-Fuel-Subs-2015-16_Final_Oct2017.pdf.

485 Georgia Wells, Jeff Horwitz, Deepa Seetharaman, "Facebook Knows Instagram is Toxic for Teen Girls, Company Documents Show," Wall Street Journal, September 14, 2021, https://www.wsj.com/articles/facebook-knows-instagram-is-toxic-for-teen-girls-company-documents-show-11631620739?mod=article_inline.

486 Jeremey B. Merrill and Will Oremus, "Five points for anger, one point for a 'like,'" The Washington Post, October 26, 2021, https://www.washingtonpost.com/technology/2021/10/26/facebook-angry-emoji-algorithm/.

487 Jeff Chester, Kathryn Montgomery, Katharina Kopp, "Big Food, Big Tech and the Global Childhood Obesity Pandemic, Center for Digital Democracy, May 2021, https://www.democraticmedia.org/article/big-food-big-tech-and-global-childhood-obesity-pandemic; Zeke Faux, "How Facebook Helps Shady Advertisers Pollute the Internet," Bloomberg Businessweek, March 27, 2018, https://www.bloomberg.com/news/features/2018-03-27/ad-scammers-need-suckers-and-facebook-helps-find-them#xj4y7vzkg; Kevin Wack, "Payday Lenders Are

Finding Ways Around Google's Ad Ban," American Banker, October 11, 2017, https://www.americanbanker.com/news/payday-lenders-are-finding-ways-around-googles-ad-ban.

488 Jane Chung, "Racism In, Racism Out: A Primer on Algorithmic Racism," Public Citizen, August 17, 2021, https://www.citizen.org/article/algorithmic-racism/.

489 "Apple, Microsoft Poised to Reap Nearly $75 Billion From a Single Provision of Trump's Tax Plan," Public Citizen, November 14, 2017, https://www.citizen.org/news/apple-microsoft-poised-to-reap-nearly-75-billion-from-a-single-provision-of-trumps-tax-plan.

490 Amazon tracker, https://www.goodjobsfirst.org/amazon-tracker.

491 "Crime in the United States: 2019," Federal Bureau of Investigation, https://ucr.fbi.gov/crime-in-the-u.s/2019/crime-in-the-u.s.-2019/topic-pages/property-crime.

492 Mariane Levine, "Beyond the Minimum Wage Fight, a Sweeping Failure to Enforce the Law," Politico, February 18, 2018, https://www.politico.com/story/2018/02/18/minimum-wage-not-enforced-investigation-409644.

493 "Financial Regulatory Reform: Financial Crisis Losses and Potential Impacts of the Dodd-Frank Act, Government Accountability Office, January 16, 2013, https://www.gao.gov/products/gao-13-180.

494 Jesse Eisinger, "Why Only One Top Banker Went to Jail for the Financial Crisis," New York Times, April 30, 2014, https://www.nytimes.com/2014/05/04/magazine/only-one-top-banker-jail-financial-crisis.html.

495 "Death on the Job: The Toll of Neglect," AFL-CIO, April 26, 2022, https://aflcio.org/reports/death-job-toll-neglect-2022.

496 Cedric Michel, "Violent Street Crime Versus Harmful White-Collar Crime," Critical Criminology, August 21, 2015, https://www.researchgate.net/publication/283885030_Violent_Street_Crime_Versus_Harmful_White-Collar_Crime_A_Comparison_of_Perceived_Seriousness_and_Punitiveness#pf10.

497 Russell Mokhiber, "Study Finds Major Corporations Engage in Wrongdoing Twice a Week," Corporate Crime Reporter, September 8, 2021, https://www.corporatecrimereporter.com/news/200/study-finds-major-corporations-engage-in-wrongdoing-twice-a-week.

498 Rick Claypool, "Enforcement Abyss," Public Citizen, April 25, 2022, https://www.citizen.org/article/enforcement-abyss.

ACKNOWLEDGEMENTS

It's almost a truism that all books are collective projects, but this one was more collective than most. We drew very heavily on the work of amazing colleagues at Public Citizen and we relied on vital investigative and analytic work of allied organizations, including the Institute on Taxation and Economic Policy, Knowledge Ecology International and Open Secrets, among many others.

Lots and lots of people helped us pull this project together, not all of whom know we relied on their work and assistance.

Huge thanks to: Elizabeth Beavers, Omar Baddar, Michael Carome, Jane Chung, Rick Claypool, Jamie Douglas, Stephanie Donne, Rhoda Feng, Amanda Fleming, Lisa Gilbert, Eagan Kemp, Steve Knievel, Paul Levy, Taylor Lincoln, Peter Maybarduk, Ralph Nader, Patrice O'Malley, Joanne Omang, Darcey Rakestraw, John Richard, Zain Rizvi, David Rosen, Michael Tanglis, Chris Shaw, Aileen Walsh, Steve Wamhoff, Sidney Wolfe, Savannah Wooten and Alan Zibel. We so much appreciate all of your help and we are honored to be friends and colleagues with all of you.

AUTHOR BIOGRAPHIES

Robert Weissman is president of Public Citizen and an expert on corporate and government accountability. At Public Citizen, he has helped lead the charge for a constitutional amendment to overturn the Supreme Court's *Citizens United* decision, lower the price of prescription drugs and advance corporate accountability. He worked as director of the corporate accountability organization Essential Action from 1995 to 2009. From 1989 to 2009, he was editor of the *Multinational Monitor,* a magazine that tracked multinational corporations. He previously worked as a public interest attorney at the Center for Study of Responsive Law. With Russell Mokhiber, Weissman is co-author of *Corporate Predators: The Hunt for Mega-Profits and the Attack on Democracy and On the Rampage: Corporations Plundering the Global Village* (both Common Courage Press). He is a graduate of Harvard College and Harvard Law School.

Joan Claybrook was president of Public Citizen from 1982 until she retired in 2009. During that time she played a key role in many successful advocacy campaigns, including enactment of the McCain-Feingold law that placed federal limits on money in political campaigns, preventing enactment of a federal law that would have limited consumer rights to sue multinational companies for sale of defective products, securing congressional enactment of a mandate for airbags in all consumer vehicles which have saved over 60,000 lives in the U.S., and laws to prevent vehicle rollover and to require rear cameras in all vehicles. She was appointed by President Jimmy Carter in 1977-1981 to head the National Highway Traffic Safety Administration, where she issued the airbag rule, the first ever federal fuel economy standards, tire safety rules and initiated the New Car Assessment Program requiring motor vehicle manufacturers to label their new cars with safety data to inform consumers before purchase. This consumer information program has been copied across the world. Before serving as NHTSA Administrator she worked with Ralph Nader to create Congress Watch, Public Citizen's lobby arm. She is a graduate of Goucher College in Baltimore, Maryland, and Georgetown University Law Center and received honorary degrees from both.

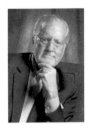

Joseph W. Cotchett has a legendary reputation for his courtroom accomplishments. The legal press has called him one of the 100 Most Influential Lawyers in America. He is the senior partner at Cotchett, Pitre & McCarthy, and has tried over 100 cases to verdict. He has successfully taken on the FBI, the U.S. Navy, Charles Keating, Bernie Madoff, the National Football League, Wall Street and other corporate giants, along with their accountants, lawyers, and executives on behalf of consumers, public entities and everyday citizens without the means to do so. He has authored numerous books on law, ethics, corporate practices and civil rights. He has an engineering degree from California Polytech University and a J.D. from the University of California, San Francisco Law. In 2011 he was inducted into the American Trial Lawyer Hall of Fame. He is a former Colonel in the U.S. Army, receiving the Legion of Merit for his services in the Airborne Special Forces and JAG Corp.

Public Citizen is among the nation's leading consumer advocacy and progressive policy organizations. Founded by Ralph Nader, the organization has helped pass countless laws, won dozens of cases at the U.S. Supreme Court and forced the removal of dangerous drugs from the market. Altogether, these efforts have helped save millions of lives, saved consumers and taxpayers billions of dollars, and made our nation more fair and just. Public Citizen has published numerous books and hundreds of reports on corporate, consumer and advocacy issues since it was founded over 50 years ago.

INDEX